NORDIC WAYS

András Simonyi, *Project Director*

Debra L. Cagan, *Editor*

CENTER FOR TRANSATLANTIC RELATIONS

András Simonyi, Project Director and Debra L. Cagan, Editor, Nordic Ways
Washington, DC: Center for Transatlantic Relations, 2016
© Center for Transatlantic Relations, 2016

Center for Transatlantic Relations
The Paul H. Nitze School of Advanced International Studies
The Johns Hopkins University
1717 Massachusetts Avenue, NW, Suite 867
Washington, DC 20036
Tel: (202) 663-5880
Email: transatlantic@jhu.edu
http://transatlanticrelations.org

ISBN 13: 978-0-9907721-1-8

Cover Photograph by Agnete Schlichtkrull.
Thank you to the Danish Design Center for lending the photograph for the cover.

Table of Contents

1. The Nordic Countries as a Political-Sociological Concept and as a Distinct Entity

2. 21ˢᵗ Century Challenges–Sustaining the Nordic Model in a Globalized Political and Economic World

3. The Nordic Social-Economic Way to Ensure Childhood Development, Quality Education and Healthcare

4. The Nordic Creative Process—Central to Innovation in the Arts, Technology and Business

5. Management and Economics–Embracing an Integrated Economic Model for Partnership Between Management and Labor

6. Energy and Environment as an Existential Concept— The Responsibility of Being Arctic Nations

Foreword

The year it has taken to publish this book, 2016, has not been the best for liberal-democratic societies. Our way of life is being threatened from the outside and from within. Terrorism, backsliding of democracy, the disenchantment of losers of unchecked globalization, migrations, the unintended consequences of the tech revolution, rising disruptive powers, our international institutions cracking at the seams—all have been on the rise. Some in our midst are trying to turn back the clock of history, revert to solutions alien to our democratic, modern and increasingly tolerant societies.

Yet there is group of countries which have done remarkably well in the face of these challenges to our modern, democratic societies. Their search for ideas does not cease. Denmark, Finland, Iceland, Norway and Sweden are an endless source of inspiration. They might just hold the clues to solving the security, social, political, environmental and technological threats and challenges of the 21st Century. These seemingly small countries have been pouring out ideas as well as practical solutions for the last fifty years. Their no nonsense, down to earth, self-critical and pragmatic approaches can be traced back to their culture, their past struggles, their fight with the elements and the understanding that democracy, tolerance, diversity and acceptance combined with healthy competition and care for the most vulnerable is the right mix. They have also realized that together they are a force to be reckoned with regionally and globally.

It is not always that their solutions are the most intriguing, but their mindset which leads them down a path at the end of which they score as top performers in so many fields; facing head on their threats and challenges. It is this mindset we attempted to capture through this collection of essays.

The book you are about to read is the result of hard work by outstanding authors and equally great personalities, from all walks of life, leaders in their field of experience. I am most grateful to them for having devoted time and effort to write their pieces. It has been an honor and a pleasure to work with them all.

I want to thank Dagfinn Høybråten, Secretary General of the Nordic Council of Ministers for his support. We owe gratitude to Nauja Bianco from the Council for her early encouragement and considerable help.

I also wish to express my sincere appreciation to the members of our working group, Senior Visiting Scholar Ulla Rønberg and Senior Visiting Fellow Madeleine Lyrvall, who have worked tirelessly to ensure that this project is compelling, insightful and rich with great authors and tremendous subject matter.

Thank you to our stars of the future, Visiting Fellows Mariette Hägglund, Robert Eklund and Senior Adviser Alix Lawson, and to our publisher manager, Peggy Irvine. And thank you to Heidi Obermeyer, our Program Coordinator.

Finally, I owe a great deal of thanks for the incredible personal friendship and collegiality of Debra Cagan, and her American perspective, who is our Project Editor, Senior United States State Department Fellow at the Center for Transatlantic Relations (CTR) at the Paul H. Nitze School of Advanced International Studies, without whom this book would never have been accomplished.

Without their devotion, this project would not have succeeded. They have all opened my eyes to subtleties of Nordic life, which I as a life-long student of the region have not noticed before.

I hope you enjoy reading "Nordic Ways."

András Simonyi, Project Director
Washington D.C., September 2016

Ambassador András Simonyi is the Managing Director of the Center for Transatlantic Relations at the Paul H. Nitze School of Advanced International Studies (SAIS), Johns Hopkins University.

We Want to Express

Our Appreciation

to Our Partners

norden

The Nordic Council of Ministers (NCM) is the official forum for Nordic Intergovernmental cooperation and is the key contributor to the Nordic Ways project. Addressing an American audience provides the Nordic Council of Ministers with an opportunity to both strengthen its presence and its efforts to advance Nordic interests internationally while ensuring a more accurate understanding of the Nordic model in a North American setting. The NCM along with our key partner, Johns Hopkins University, School for Advanced International Studies, Center for Transatlantic Relations in the Nordic Ways Project is central in profiling the Nordic societies, intergovernmental cooperation, and the Nordic way of life, while setting the tone for prosperous cooperation opportunities.

The NCM was created in 1971 and consists of 11 Council of Ministers: 10 individual ministerial policy councils in addition to the Council of Ministers for Nordic cooperation. The Ministers for Nordic cooperation act on behalf of their respective Prime Ministers and assume responsibility for the coordination of intergovernmental cooperation. The guidelines for cooperation prioritize areas such as maritime issues, trade and economic development, the environment, climate and energy, research, innovation, education and training, culture and health.

Nordic cooperation, one of the most extensive forms of regional cooperation anywhere in the world, involves Denmark, Finland, Iceland, Norway and Sweden as well as the Faroe Islands, Greenland and the Åland Islands. Notably, cooperation between the NCM and neighboring countries has increased substantially. Nordic cooperation promotes Nordic and regional interests and values in a globalized world and shared Nordic values make the region one of the most innovative and competitive. The Nordic countries have a long tradition of trust-based cooperation stemming from a common historical, cultural and geographical heritage. "Together we are stronger" therefore accurately defines the vision of Nordic cooperation.

**Nordic Council of Ministers
Finnish Presidency 2016**

www.norden2016.fi

We are grateful for the unstinting support and generous contribution from the Finnish Presidency of the Nordic Council of Ministers that has helped make this project possible.

EMBASSY OF SWEDEN

Washington

We want to express our gratitude to the Swedish Government, especially to the Ministry of Foreign Affairs for their generous contribution and support for the Nordic Ways project.

ROYAL NORWEGIAN EMBASSY

The Royal Norwegian Embassy in Washington D.C. is working to expand and further deepen the strong connections between Norway and the United States.

**Embassy
of Iceland**

ÍSLANDSSTOFA
PROMOTE ICELAND

This remarkable book about "Nordic Ways" has come about thanks to the efforts of CTR Managing Director András Simonyi, a friend and tireless champion of the Nordic countries, as well as with the shepherding of Project Editor Debra Cagan and a number of others, not least the distinguished Nordic authors that have contributed their time and thought to this project and the kind support of Promote Iceland. There is no magic Nordic formula or silver bullet, but rather the success of the Nordic countries is a testament to the solid shared foundations of this family of nations. The unshakable respect for human rights, determination to advance the cause of gender equality, trust in democratic principles and shared focus on addressing threats to the environment underpin the success of the Nordic countries. In addition to that bedrock we attempt to be good custodians of our individual and shared culture, both past and as it evolves in the present. Most of all the "Nordic model" such as it is, is an iterative process of improvement, a continuous effort to get better.

EMBASSY OF DENMARK

We want to express our gratitude for the ongoing support and assistance from the Embassy of Denmark.

**EMBASSY OF FINLAND
WASHINGTON D.C.**

We are thankful for the support and considerable assistance from the Embassy of Finland.

Nordic Ways are Not Just for Nordic Companies

As an enterprise foundation, the first priority of the Ramboll Foundation is to be an active and engaged owner of the Ramboll Group, a leading engineering, design and consultancy company with a strong Nordic heritage. The ferris wheel in Tivoli, Copenhagen, was one of Ramboll's very first projects. Does it get any more Nordic than that?

Since 1945 Ramboll has grown together with the Nordic societies it has served. Building enduring structures, increasing mobility and improving livability in Denmark, Norway, Sweden and Finland have been keys to success. Along the way, the self-perception at Ramboll has been that things were done in a distinctively Nordic way, and we have told our clients much the same. This "Nordic flavor" was readily understood. After all, most clients and employees were Nordic themselves. The no-nonsense honesty, the appreciation of the better argument over the formal hierarchy, the firm belief in the value of equality and the decency, trust and integrity that are so deeply rooted in the Nordic countries and in Ramboll's culture were intuitively appreciated.

Even our ownership structure, with an enterprise foundation as the majority owner insistent on creating long-term value rather than quarterly profits, is less exotic in a region where successful companies like Maersk, Novo Nordisk and Carlsberg are also foundation-owned.

But things have changed. Today, Ramboll has 300 offices in 35 countries. In the company's early days, key employees engaged in open discussion while sitting around a table, valued the discussion itself, and reached understandings. This is no longer possible with 13,000 employees spread across the world. The attributes of being Nordic are not necessarily intuitively understood within all the countries in which Ramboll operates. More importantly, what we once thought was unique to Nordic companies and societies may well be universal values or principles elsewhere in the world.

One attribute that I'm not afraid to identify as Nordic is the willingness to question everything and to challenge our core beliefs. In the Nordic countries very few things are sacred and even fewer cannot be discussed. Therefore I was delighted to learn that John Hopkins, SAIS, Center for Transatlantic Relations wanted to examine what it really means to be Nordic.

I genuinely believe that there is something extremely valuable in the Nordic heritage—something that can help us define and realize a prosperous and sustainable future for all. It is of the utmost importance to the Ramboll Foundation that these Nordic roots continue to influence the company. But I also believe that our Nordic heritage is something which we have to discuss and challenge. We have to discuss it to fully understand and communicate what it entails, and we have to challenge it and get inspired by what other regions of the World have to offer to evolve and fully leverage our potential.

This is why the Ramboll Foundation is supporting this initiative. I value our collaboration with the Center for Transatlantic Relations, and I hope that these essays will inspire decision makers, organizations and employees around the world.

Flemming Bligaard Pedersen,
Chairman of the Board of Trustees
Ramboll Foundation

VAISALA

Leadership Comes from Curiosity

As a niche company in a country like Finland, Vaisala has had to reach out globally from the very beginning. The Vaisala way has always been to connect with scientists and experts around the world. That has created a network, which helps Vaisala in its mission: building a better world through observations.

Vaisala's roots are in the weather, an area of expertise which comes naturally to Finns, with the harsh Nordic climate.

Reliable weather observations are needed in weather forecasting, which can tell us whether to don a raincoat, but also warn of weather that can pose a risk to businesses or lives. Weather information helps ensure smooth and safe traffic flow on the roads, rails and in the skies, and it is key in the development of sustainable energy of tomorrow, with the sun and wind as sources.

Many industrial processes also require strictly controlled conditions that are monitored using Vaisala technology. In addition to product quality and safety, monitoring makes it possible to regulate indoor conditions accurately, improving air quality and saving energy.

Every day, millions of live around the world are touched by Vaisala, a world leader in developing and producing products and services that provide the means of influencing and better understanding the environment.

From its beginnings 80 years ago, Vaisala has been dedicated to developing the best measurement solutions, to make our lives safer, more productive and more comfortable. To keep its position at the top, Vaisala invests heavily in R&D: in 2015 over 11% of its turnover.

Even today, Vaisala is driven by curiosity—the desire to understand the unknown. In a world of shifting global economies and environments, this is more important than ever.

Kemira

Kemira's history dates back nearly 100 years and is firmly rooted in the Nordic values of trust, creativity and expertise. Our heritage is in Finland, one of the world's most innovative countries (Global Innovation Index 2016). We are a global chemicals company serving customers in water-intensive industries. Our focus is on pulp & paper, oil & gas, mining and water treatment, where we provide expertise, application know-how and chemicals that improve our customers' product quality as well as process and resource efficiency. In 2015, Kemira had annual revenue of EUR 2.4 billion and around 4,700 employees. Kemira shares are listed on the Nasdaq Helsinki Ltd.

VOLVO

We want to thank Volvo for their generous contribution and support.

KONGSBERG

KONGSBERG is an international, knowledge-based group that delivers high-technology systems and solutions to customers in defense and aerospace, the energy sector and the merchant marine. KONGSBERG is Norway's premier defense company and a world leader of remote controlled weapon systems, tactical communication, air defense systems and 5th gen strike missiles.

The Nammo Group is a technology-driven defense and aerospace group, specializing in high-performance solutions. Its broad portfolio includes shoulder-launched munitions systems, military and sports ammunition, rocket motors for military and space applications, and demilitarization services. Nammo's global and diverse workforce spans across the United States, Canada, Europe, Australia and UAE.

Innovation Norway

Innovation Norway is the Norwegian Government's most important tool for innovation and development of Norwegian enterprises and industry, supporting companies in developing their competitive advantage and to enhance innovation.

Introduction

András
Simonyi

Ulla
Rønberg

The challenges facing the Nordics are being met with a positive, creative, innovative belief that they can persevere, that they have the resilience and staying power to succeed.

In the last few years there has been a healthy buzz and curiosity surrounding the countries of the North, the Nordics as they are commonly known. And this interest has not subsided suggesting there is a lasting attraction for the countries in the United States and Asia.

But who are they really? While Danes, Finns, Icelanders, Norwegians and Swedes seem at a distance very much alike, just try to peep into a pub in Copenhagen, a sauna in Helsinki, a boat in the Norwegian fjords, the Blue Lagoon in Iceland or a ski slope in Sweden and you will discover they have their distinctive traits, culture, style and sense of humor. Their sameness and indeed their differences are their strengths. What binds them together is their shared history and values, and perhaps most importantly, their shared vision of the future, their destiny to succeed together.

The notion of Nordic coolness, efficiency and resilience has swept through the U.S. in the arts and design world and in political debates; it has become a staple in discussions about societal, environmental and gender issues. International statistics again and again show Nordic countries occupying top spots when it comes to quality of life, beautiful and livable cities, close to zero corruption. The Nordic people have fundamental trust in their institutions, elected officials, and in each other. They have respect for individual rights, equality and freedom of expression. As U.S. President Obama has said, "sometimes it could be tempting to put these five nations in charge and let them rule the world."

The admiration is at times fraught with misunderstandings and misperceptions. Isn't it politically naive and unrealistic to suggest that these five, small European nations can offer viable practical solutions to some of the outstanding and burning problems with which larger countries, like the United States have to deal? Or are their solutions confined to small, mostly homogeneous and peaceful nations, with extensive social welfare, with no real inner tensions and manageable levels of threats?

On the contrary, Nordic countries are not some "utopian" universe isolated from the challenges that face the rest of the world. While surrounded mostly by water, they do share borders with Russia and Germany, the two dominant European powers. They are the Northern anchor to Europe and the West's entry to the East. This places them in a unique, strategic position, by no means insignificant, with substantial security challenges. Three of the Nordics, Denmark, Iceland and Norway are members of NATO and three, Denmark, Finland and Sweden are members of the European Union. All have strong transatlantic ties, and are devoted to a robust relationship with the United States.

All is not well and beautiful though, even in the "Norden." In a world where open market economies and disruptive technologies thrive in parallel, permanent adaptation and innovation is demanded. Unless these challenges are taken head on, they could threaten the traditional Nordic social-democratic welfare model. The ongoing migration of people from the Middle East and Africa, many of whom seek the security and benefits of Nordic welfare societies, pose new and unforeseen challenges to the Nordic societal norms and integrity, until recently thought to be irreversible. Our strong belief is that these countries are capable and willing to make the necessary changes to their policies.

Moreover the Nordics are not immune to the problems of Europe and the transatlantic community. Populist and isolationist ideologies could undermine the highly praised Nordic view of humanity that is inclusive and embracing and threaten the cohesiveness of their societies.

And so with all of these challenges, why are these countries still so successful? The combined economies of the Nordic countries hold 12th place among the world's largest economies, and according to Forbes Magazine are ranked first among "Best Countries for Business." At the same time they prioritize welfare for the many, not the few, and offer equal access to what are considered necessities in "serious" democracies: education, legal systems, healthcare, care of children, elderly and other people in need. The deal is that: you pay high taxes, you get a lot back and you have a big say in how your money is spent. Perhaps they have found, like very few others, the right balance between market forces and strong support for the vulnerable: Competition, but on a level playing field.

This book does not claim to have all of the answers and is certainly not attempting to paint an idealistic, faultless model. But it is not "snake-oil" either. The book is promoting a mindset, the Nordic mindset. It is demonstrating why the Nordic countries are not just a "socialist utopia" but rather a reality-based "Capitalism With a Heart."

The 45 essays, written by highly esteemed authors each of them leaders in their fields, shed light on a wide range of topics that show The Nordic Way of doing things. And, they aim to underpin the fact that the Nordics have a good thing going! They can help show the way in areas that are relevant to the future and have the capacity to inspire political leaders and decision makers in the world to think differently. Perhaps most important they have the ambition to make a difference.

The essays are as carefully crafted like a Finn Juhl armchair or an Alvar Aalto vase. What manifests itself in the end is a picture of dynamic countries rooted in a set of shared values that constitute the firm pillars of their societies, constantly questioning the validity of their "product." "Keep what's right, change what is necessary" could be their slogan. With values like openness, democracy, trust, equality, freedom and individual rights, combined with a strong sense of creativity and design, their market economies will continue to work for the benefit of most.

How is this relevant to an American audience? The historic ties between the Nordic countries and the United States, that strong transatlantic bond, are important underpinnings to their achievements. But then, as it is often stated: There is no country big enough to face the global challenges alone, and there are no countries too small not to be able to make a difference. In a totally interconnected world inspiration can and should come from everywhere and anywhere. This is what makes the Nordic countries relevant in the context of the road ahead for the United States. That is The Nordic Way.

1. The Nordic Countries as a Political-Sociological Concept and as a Distinct Entity

The relevance of "Norden" in the age of challenges to the liberal-democratic model. These values and freedoms, cooperation and consensus-based politics, the vital importance of transparency, accountability, and a lack of corruption, are what it means to be "Norden."

Prosperous Countries Have Prosperous Neighbors

Urban Ahlin

"We have gone from war and competition to cooperation and competitiveness."

It is easy for me as a Swede to be proud of my nation. It is well-organized, peaceful, prosperous, democratic and equitably gender equal. But I also believe that Sweden owes a great deal of its fortune to its neighboring countries. In fact, in Sweden we even sing about the Nordic region in our national anthem, and I think this is a good point to be made.

The five Nordic countries all have their own national characteristics, but we also have more features in common than ones that separate us. Nordic cooperation is among the oldest and most extensive forms of regional cooperation in existence. It is based upon common values and it has made us all stronger. Together, we perform better than we would on our own. Prosperous countries have prosperous neighbors—this is the core of Nordic cooperation as I see it. The Nordic countries are all interdependent. No matter how globalized the economic system might be. When it comes to exports we still trade mostly with our neighbors. Of all Swedish exports, 24 percent goes to Nordic countries. While our exports to Brazil, Russia, India, China and South Africa (BRICS countries) amounted to 7.2 percent in 2015, exports to Norway alone totaled 10.3 percent. In short, our exports to the Nordic countries were approximately three times larger than our exports to BRICS.

As is often the case with neighboring countries, the Nordic countries share a complex history. We have waged war upon each other. Certain regions have belonged to different countries over the course of time, and we have made peace and cooperated. After World War II, steps were taken towards the formalized and political cooperation that we know today.

This cooperation is not only based on common values, but also on a common will to enhance the region's competitiveness. Nordic cooperation exists on many levels and concerns many different fields. What is often referred to as "the Nordic Model"—that is, societies characterized by a high level of welfare, equality and economic development—has been seen as a role model by many. At the same time, it has been questioned. How can a system with high taxes and an extensive welfare sector survive the changes brought by the times in which we live?

Another challenge to the Nordic way of life has arisen with the migration crisis. For centuries, the citizens of our Nordic countries have been able to cross Nordic borders without passports or visas. This has made it easier for our citizens to work, visit and study in the other countries. The region of Öresund is the most densely populated part of the Nordic region and has, for a long time, been seen as a hub for business and as a common labor market.

However, this no longer functions as smoothly as it used to. The migration crisis has led to the adoption of various measures. Swedish authorities now perform ID checks at the border with Denmark. Critics say that cross-border commuting times have increased as a result of this.

I do believe that continued cooperation is as important as ever. We are relatively small and scarcely populated countries, peripheral to the European continent, but with strong and open economies. We also tend to embrace new ideas and technology such as the internet and the gaming industry, which is also important for our connectivity to the world and our economies. The Nordic countries contribute to developments around the world, but also with a focus on developments at home. We should continue to broaden our cooperation. We need to cooperate on environmental issues just as extensively as we do when it comes to business, trade and the labor market.

We must also make use of our strength and competitiveness in other critical areas. For example, cooperation in the field of security policy has gained substantial interest and attention. Sweden and Finland have taken several steps in their bilateral cooperation, but Nordic cooperation in this field is also increasing in importance. The Nordic countries have made different choices along the way. Some are EU members (European Union), some are NATO members (North Atlantic Treaty Organization) and some are both. This has not been an obstacle to practical cooperation in certain areas between our countries, nor has it been an obstacle to us contributing to the same NATO or EU operations.

The Nordic model and Nordic cooperation are gaining increasing interest in the U.S. In May 2016, President Obama met with Nordic prime ministers and presidents in the White House and referred to the Nordic countries as role models. The President is reported to have said that the Nordics, "punch above their weight," and I believe the President is right.

We have achieved this status thanks to our pragmatic search for common solutions to common challenges. I believe the Nordic experience can serve as a good example of practical work that benefits all. We have gone from war and competition to cooperation and competitiveness. This is a model that holds promise for the U.S. and other parts of the world.

The Nordic Model: Why and How?

Bertel Haarder

"There is nothing utopian about the Nordic societies."

In most situations, it is beneficial to appear bigger and stronger than you are. This is true of people, and it is true of states. But the Nordic countries have a peculiar tendency to make themselves smaller than they are. We dwellers of the North cling to the small-state mentality that was forced upon us during the Napoleonic Wars, the World Wars and the Cold War. But we will have to live with the fact that we're both bigger and stronger than we think.

This was clear during the Nordic-American summit held in Washington, in May 2016. President Obama invited government leaders from all five Nordic countries to discuss global challenges and suggest Nordic solutions. The message was clear. If the Nordic countries are considered as a whole, the Nordic region is among the most important in the world. To the rest of the world, we are not the nation-states of Norway, Iceland, Sweden, Finland, and Denmark. We are the Nordic region, and we have something to offer.

If you consider the Nordic countries as an economic region, it is among the twelve strongest economies in the world, and an obvious candidate for the G20. The Nordic countries generally do well in international comparisons. For example, the Nordic countries are at the top of the Human Development Index and are among the easiest countries in the world in which to do business. There is record low corruption, and people have confidence in each other and their institutions.

We live in the most stable region in the world with no bilateral conflicts. Despite a past of intense rivalry and internal wars in Scandinavia, the last 200 years have offered peace and greater cooperation between countries.

Our cultural products are well renowned. Nordic books generate great interest internationally, particularly in the German market. More than 200 Icelandic titles were translated for the Frankfurt Book Fair a couple of years ago. By comparison, China only had 100 titles translated for the same event. Germans look lovingly north while we ourselves gaze to the Anglo-Saxon world, which has until recently ignored us, that is until the TV series *Borgen* (*The Castle*) opened the floodgates in the United Kingdom, and the social model of the Nordic countries became a U.S. election theme. Nordic films and TV series are selling like hotcakes all over the world, making our democracy, life-style and commitment to gender equality famous around the globe.

International observers have pointed out that there is a particular sense of quality in the Nordic countries both with respect to our consumer habits and production – and particularly, our aesthetic production. The Nordic countries have enjoyed broad international recognition for everything from music to furniture design, from architecture to film and literature. Designers such as Alvar Aalto and Arne Jacobsen are world-renowned, as are Stieg Larsson's, Karl Ove Knausgaard's and Jussi Adler Olsen's books, not to mention the music of Björk and MØ. Our common potential was clear during the joint Nordic cultural event "Nordic Cool" at the Kennedy Center in Washington, D.C. in 2013, which was not simply a Nordic-funded campaign. It was primarily American money that financed the presentation of 700 Nordic artists. And it is a certain sign of quality that others are willing to pay for it.

This positive attention naturally goes together with the success of the Nordic social model, stable economies, corruption-free democracies, and the Nordic welfare system. This creates respect and garners attention. But in order to understand the Nordic social model, you must first and foremost understand the fundamental values on which the model and Nordic social solutions have been created.

The Basis of the Nordic Model: Community, Liberty, Equal Opportunities, and Trust

When, in the 1800s, the Nordic kingdoms began to develop into modern democratic states, their societies were homogeneous. Immigration was limited, and the religious sphere was dominated by a particularly Nordic form of Protestantism. Over the course of the nineteenth century a series of popular movements helped create a strong national identity with a focus on both equality and liberty. In Denmark, the most important figure was the pastor, poet, and author N. F. S. Grundtvig, whose vision of an enlightened people shaped a new form of societal paradigm.

Unlike the rest of Europe, the Nordic countries were not particularly engaged in imperial projects. Certainly, both Denmark and Sweden had minor possessions abroad, but they were not large enough to make an imprint on their domestic self-image. The cultural horizon of the broader population did not stretch beyond the country's boundaries. However, these homogenous social structures did not imply that people were equal. To the contrary. Society was divided by economic class affiliations. The upper class consisted of a small group of landowners and government officials. The middle class consisted of small farmers and tradesmen, and the lower class consisted of a large group of industrial and agricultural workers. There was no overlap between population groups, and social mobility was low.

On the other hand, there were very strong class affiliations and professional sense of belonging. Industrial and agricultural workers created professional organizations through labor unions and powerful social-democratic movements. Small farmers banded together in so-called cooperative movements through which they pooled their resources and achieved economies of scale and political influence while the landowners and government officials tried to cling to power and the status quo. Large, broad popular associations formed the basis for modern Nordic democracy in which there is only a short distance between the people and the decision makers. Public participation is paramount. The Nordic countries are certainly very community-oriented, but they are particularly focused on voluntary associations, which ensure dynamism and participation. While community and equality are cherished values, so is individual freedom of both thought and life-style.

In particular, working class and farmers' associations had great influence in the development of the social model that is today known as the Nordic model. Through the struggles to produce an equal and more efficient society, the labor unions, the social democratic parties and the cooperative movement gave rise to the Nordic social and cooperative model. The Nordic societies gradually became more receptive of the desires of citizens, and by the start of the twentieth century the Nordic welfare states began to take shape. The social movements and professional organizations became an integral part of the so-called Nordic cooperative model in which the state establishes important policies in collaboration with representative organizations of affected population groups.

In the Nordic cooperative model, civil society organizations and labor unions participate directly in the political system. For example, there is a tradition for labor market policies in the Nordic countries to be implemented through so-called tripartite negotiations between the state, employers' associations, and labor unions. In this manner, decisions gain legitimacy because all relevant parties are responsible for them. As opposed to most other countries in the West, the Nordic countries do not have politically-fixed minimum wages in the labor market. Instead, labor unions negotiate directly with employer interest organizations and the state for a so-called collective bargaining agreement that sets wages.

The interplay between state and citizens through the cooperative model has created the social welfare institutions that are today praised as a part of the Nordic model: free and equal access to healthcare; publicly-financed schools and higher education; a fine-meshed social safety net; publicly-financed care for children and the elderly; and liberal maternity leave to name but a few. These universal institutions and systems create, at least in theory, equal opportunities for all citizens regardless of social background.

Because of the Nordic social model the Nordic countries are often portrayed as socialist Utopias. This is clearly a misunderstanding. There is nothing utopian about the Nordic societies. We experience the exact same challenges as the rest of the liberal western world. At the same time the Nordic model is not socialist. The Nordic model represents a set of values based on a mixture of the social consciousness of socialism and the marked oriented view on competitiveness stemming from liberalism. Thus, the Nordic societies can at best be described as social liberal.

This strange mix of socialism and liberalism goes back to the postwar era when the Nordic social democratic governments chose not to nationalize the large private enterprises as other European countries, as for example the UK did. In Denmark and the rest of the Nordic region there was a forth sightedness among the social democratic governments who understood that the state never will be good at running companies. On the contrary, they realized that there was a need for competitive companies that could drive the economy, thereby generating tax revenues which in turn could fund the establishment of the social welfare state.

The combination of a liberal market economy and a socially inclined state demands continuous social and economic reforms. Shifting governments since the 1970s have therefore gradually transformed the welfare system to fit the economic reality and balance the social vision with the demands for economic competitiveness. Thus, despite being depicted as socialist, the Nordic countries are among the most open and competitive economies in the world.

The sound social contract in the Nordic societies is based on a high degree of trust. Trust in the state and in each other. The high degree of trust has made possible a political culture characterized by the notion of the common best and the idea that everyone has a common responsibility to move society forward. Among other things, this has created what is commonly known in the Nordic countries as pragmatic rationalism, an unwritten rule that regardless of the government in power it will enter into compromises across the political spectrum. Thus a broad political ownership is ensured.

Another characteristic of Nordic society is liberty and tolerance. When it comes to the question of voting rights for women, equal rights, and personal freedom, the Nordic countries have been ahead of the rest of the world. Nordic society is based on the idea that everyone has the right to have an opinion and shape their own lives as long as they hurt no one else. Liberty, community, trust, and equal opportunity are the glue that keeps Nordic societies together and functioning.

The Nordic social model has created Nordic solutions we can be proud to share with the world. But it is important to understand that this does not come without hard work and great cost. The welfare state is extremely expensive and the Nordic model is only possible because of our high taxes. A high tax rate requires a huge amount of trust in society, a sense of community and social responsibility. However, there have been times throughout history when there is pressure on solidarity and economic sustainability. That is the case now with huge numbers of immigrants fleeing the Middle East. This Nordic model is not a self-service buffet of social solutions that can be incorporated either socially or cost-free into other countries. And Nordic societies are not the utopias that are often suggested by international observers. It all comes at a price.

Nordic Cooperation

The Nordic countries enjoy a multi-branched collaboration through the Nordic Council of Ministers, which is a multilateral organization that has existed since 1971 much in the same way as the EU. The organization consists of a number of councils that deal with various policy areas in which Nordic government ministers meet and discuss everything from freedom of movement to cultural collaboration. Unlike other multilateral organizations, the collaboration here is connected to a common set of cultural values and a relationship between peoples, which provides the collaboration with popular legitimacy and support.

The high level of trust that exists in the Nordic countries stretches beyond national boundaries. Being Nordic is a part of a common identity. We understand each other both linguistically and culturally. Therefore, the collaboration is not alien or distant for our people in the same way that collaboration within the EU or the UN can be. There is a belief that we actually want the best for each other and that a solution that works in Norway will likely also work in Finland and Denmark.

The Nordic countries are like a family. We help each other by exchanging experiences and advice on how we can develop our national societies. When it makes sense, we also participate in international exchange initiatives in order to get inspiration from other countries and regions, as well as to share our experiences.

In a time in which Western liberal democracies are under pressure, the Nordic countries must not only help each other, but also look outward for inspiration. And in turn Nordic countries can provide inspiration and provide a good example of how people can cooperate to handle some of the social challenges we all face today. We must uphold our democratic traditions and demonstrate that our free society can handle the challenges of globalization only if we stand together and help each other across national boundaries.

Even though critics have called Nordic collaboration a "coffee club," it must be one of the most successful ever! In our common parliament, the Nordic Council, national parliamentarians meet to discuss common Nordic initiatives, proposals and resolutions. At the annual week-long assembly Nordic Prime Ministers and Presidents and other ministers meet with each other and with parliamentarians who can hold them responsible for their acts or omissions. This form of transnational trust is unique. And it can only be done because we have the same set of cultural values and a uniform social model.

What will bind Nordic cooperation together in the future is what has always bound it together. As the well-known Norwegian author Bjørnstjerne Bjørnson wrote "I Will Defend My Country of the three-foiled North/that shall be gathered again/and become itself." These countries found their way to themselves by finding what is common among them. This is the recipe for the Nordic cooperation of today.

The Nordic Countries—
The Five Swans

Vigdís Finnbogadóttir

"Today, no political party would dream of proposing a list of candidates for election which was not comprised of a roughly equal number of men and women, alternating in their ranking."

The Nordic countries—Iceland, Denmark, Norway, Sweden and Finland and the autonomous territories of the Faroe Islands, Greenland and Åland, plus the Saami regions—have long been seen as leaders in democracy, social equality and environmental responsibility. These common characteristics contribute to lifestyles and attitudes in our countries which are so similar that we citizens of the Nordic region feel quite at home when we visit our neighbors or dwell there awhile, studying or enjoying life in different surroundings and experiencing their language and culture. It is this special sense of belonging and shared heritage that binds Nordic nations together with intangible bonds like the wondrous fetter that bound the wolf Fenrir of ancient Norse mythology, the system of beliefs which prevailed until the Nordic countries accepted the Christian religion in the early Middle Ages. In myth, the wolf's magical bond was spun from the *sinews* of a *bear,* the *roots* of a *mountain,* the *sound* of a *cat's* footfall, the *beard* of a *woman,* the *breath* of a *fish* and the *spittle* of a *bird.* Those are indeed ties that bind.

In the years before World War II, the Danish poet Hans Hartvig Seedorff likened the Nordic countries to five white swans flying together – never forgetting where they have come from or where they are going. The symbol of the five swans has since become the emblem of Nordic cooperation.

The Nordic countries are, however, very different in many ways; in their geography, for instance. The windswept volcanic island in the north Atlantic that is Iceland contrasts sharply with the verdant lowlands of Denmark, or the lofty mountains and deep fjords of Norway—that long, narrow country with abundant offshore oil resources—and the boreal expanses and rolling countryside of Sweden, rich in minerals such as copper and iron in the earth's depths. The Faroes—literally "sheep isles"—are a cluster of green islands rising out of the blue sea. Greenland, the farthest west, is dominated by its glacial ice cap, while the easternmost of the Nordic countries is Finland, with dense forests and innumerable lakes. The Baltic islands of Åland are literally a transport link between Sweden and Finland. But despite their diversity Nordic nations are linked by numerous bonds, one of the strongest of which is language.

Most of the modern Nordic languages have evolved from Old Norse, which closely resembles the language still spoken in Iceland today, and which are to a varying extent mutually intelligible. The Finnish language, on the other hand, is a Finno-Ugric tongue related to Estonian and, more distantly, Hungarian. A sizeable number of Finns have Swedish as their mother tongue. Greenland Inuit and Saami also stem from different language families. The Nordic countries have made it their policy to enable as many Nordic citizens as possible to communicate in a Nordic language.

Nordic countries are bound, of course, by their shared history. During the latter half of the 13th century, the Old Icelandic Commonwealth which had existed from about 900 AD became part of the Norwegian kingdom, which also included Greenland and the Faroes. In the late 14th century, Norway, together with its Atlantic dependencies, then became part of the Danish kingdom, which was merged with Sweden in the short-lived Kalmar union in 1397. After its dissolution, Denmark retained its Atlantic possessions Iceland, the Faroes and Greenland, as well as Norway. After 1814, Norway was in a personal union with Sweden until it regained full independence in 1905, and in 1944 Icelanders founded the modern Republic of Iceland on 17 June, which since then has been our National Day.

The Norwegian settlers who originally settled Iceland in the 9th century spoke the lingua franca of the Norse region. This is the language in which unique literary works were preserved on vellum in Iceland during the Middle

Ages—including stories of feud and conflict, of mythological heroes, explorations and courtly romance. And in the early 13th century the Icelandic medieval historian Snorri Sturluson wrote, among other things, his Edda, the single most invaluable source for ancient Norse myths, as well as his monumental history of the kings of Norway, Heimskringla—the Orb of the World. This literature has been of major significance for the sense of identity of Nordic nations.

Languages in the Nordic countries are a vital factor in our identity and preserve a rich literary heritage. Iceland's medieval literature, especially the Sagas of Icelanders—written in vernacular prose about everyday people and events at a time when other European nations used Latin as their literary language and royalty or religion as their subject—have survived in vellum manuscripts that are renowned around the world. As an indication of the creative energy of the Nordic languages, authors from every one of the five countries have won the Nobel Prize for literature. In a globalized world, language is a key factor in national identity. Its historical significance for Icelandic independence is part of the motivation for prompting this small language community to establish at the University of Iceland a center focusing on the languages of the world: the Vigdís International Centre for Multilingualism and Intercultural Understanding, under the auspices of UNESCO.

Ever since the early twentieth century, before our Danish poet likened the Nordic nations to five white swans flying together, friendship among all the Nordic peoples has been nurtured by non-political associations which strengthened relations between individual communities and regions. In the post-war years, after Denmark and Norway were liberated from German occupation, the Nordic countries joined together to form a political Nordic Council, a platform for collaboration among parliamentarians of the different countries. The Council, established in 1952 with headquarters in Copenhagen, consists of representatives from all the Nordic countries, as well as the self-governing regions. The delegates address the mutual interests of all our countries which are bound together by age-old ties. The Nordic Council's remit also includes culture and the arts in the member countries; it awards the Nordic literature, music, children's literature, film and environment prizes each year.

The ambiance of all Nordic societies has so much in common that their citizens, venturing to travel outside the region to the south, east or west, often feel they have arrived home once more upon entering the first Nordic city on the route homeward—even though quite a long journey may remain to reach the final destination. Through the centuries, Copenhagen in particular has been a gateway from the Nordic countries to mainland Europe, where we northerners have always headed in search of knowledge and inspiration.

We Icelanders have long valued this close collaboration and the solidarity among Nordic peoples. We are always aware of where we belong. Today, Icelanders now number about 330,000, more than double the population when the Republic was established in 1944. Like our Nordic neighbours, in recent years we have earned a reputation for gender equality, although we ourselves think that we still have a long way to go; there is a persistent gender pay gap which seems to be hard to overcome.

We have, however, reached the point where 43 percent of our members of parliament and 50 percent of the government are women. The demand for equality was spotlighted in 1975, when Iceland made headlines around the world on United Nations Day, October 24. The women of Iceland walked out of their workplaces for one afternoon to gather in the thousands in the center of the capital, Reykjavík and in communities around the country. The world press reported: "Women Strike in Iceland." On the Women's Day-off, the Icelandic economy ground to a halt—pointing out clearly the essential contribution of women in every field of national life. They are actually the pillars of society, no less than men. For years, women had traditionally been placed on political parties' lists of parliamentary candidates to boost men into office, but times have changed since the Women's Day-off. Today, no political party would dream of proposing a list of candidates for election which was not comprised of a roughly equal number of men and women, alternating in their ranking.

Five years after the Women's Day-off, the Icelandic people voted for the world's first democratically-elected female head of state. Another three years after that women established a political party, the Women's Alliance, which changed the face of Icelandic politics. Women had proven their right to and assumed a vital role in society.

In few aspects of society, however, is the role of women more significant than in passing on a nation's heritage to its children. No small part of that is language, which is why we refer appropriately enough to native languages as "mother" tongues.

The Nordic Model: Pragmatic and Value Based Politics for the Future

Jonas Gahr Støre

"Frankly speaking, I would have been surprised if someone would have predicted a small generation ago that Nordic experiences would make it to somewhere high up on the U.S. political agenda."

The Nordic Model

At the time of writing this essay, there has been much focus on the Nordic countries in the United States. It has recently been a point of reference in debates between presidential candidates, and was highlighted through the U.S.–Nordic Summit in Washington in May.

Frankly speaking, I would have been surprised if someone would have predicted a small generation ago that Nordic experiences would make it to somewhere high up on the U.S. political agenda. I have always been cautious about believing that one political and social model can be exported to another cultural setting. But indeed, models, and lessons from models, if they exist, can be a source of either inspiration or rejection. What we have seen in recent years is that some key experiences common in the Nordic countries are attracting interest from far outside our region.

The Nordic countries have been much praised for enjoying a high standard of living, and for being ranked highest in measures of employment, gender equality, productivity and adaptability. Especially now after the financial crises, small, open and social market economies, perform relatively well compared with many other industrialized nations.

Let us recall, however, that this attraction has not always been the case. I recall meetings at the World Economic Forum in Davos in the early 1990s when leaders from the financial world would warn against pursuing a Nordic route in the emerging age of globalization. The state was too big, the unions too strong, the taxes too high, and the elites too few. However, as the Nordic countries passed the financial crises with lower unemployment, sounder public finances, and higher productivity levels than most other OECD-countries, this criticism subsided. In 2011, the World Economic Forum allocated an entire session to the "Nordic Model."

What is the reality? In short, I believe the key is that the Nordic countries have managed to combine economic efficiency and equity. While the gap between rich and poor is now at its highest level in 30 years in most OECD-countries, a key factor in the success of the Nordic countries has been our pursuit of policies that promote fairness and equity. Today, the very same quarters are referring to the Nordic countries as a success-story and at the same time warning about increasing inequality in many countries as an impediment to growth.

At the heart of it, implicitly or explicitly, is a notion of a common Nordic model.

Recently, the organization of Nordic Social-Democratic parties and Labor Confederations (SAMAK) commissioned a broad based study termed NORMOD, which focused on determining common factors defining the "Nordic Model."

It found that while there obviously are clear differences between the Nordic countries, they share some characteristics that distinguish them from other countries. The Nordic model is characterized by the interplay between the following:

- A policy of sound macroeconomic management with strong emphasis on securing full employment;

- A regulated labor market with strong partners on both the employer and the employee side, with coordinated wage formation; and

- Comprehensive, tax-financed welfare systems focusing on redistribution of income and wealth.

Ideological Utopianism?

Before I elaborate further on this model, let me dwell a bit on a few nuances that I consider important.

The term "model" carries different undercurrents of meaning. In the United States or in other parts of the world, the Nordic model is at times clothed in ideological terms, often as a socialist utopia. A stronger commitment to the tools, rather than the results, is implied.

I believe that values, rather than ideology, should be the navigating light in the territory of politics. Pragmatism rather than orthodoxy is the best guide in choosing the policy tools, asking the simple question; what works? And to me, this is a hallmark of Nordic social democracy; value based pragmatism.

A pragmatic approach opens up a large toolbox. The public sector is a potent tool for reaching common goals, effectively and cost-effectively. This includes providing education for all—at schools where we all meet and interact, providing a safe environment where the focus in fighting crime is also on rehabilitation rather than solely on punishment, providing good health care for all where the focus is also on prevention and promoting healthy lifestyles.

In providing equal opportunities one can harness a great productive capacity. It enables a larger segment of the population to pursue their talents and realize their potential. In the Nordic countries it is important to point to the immense economic importance of women's participation in work life, largely a result of providing affordable public child care for all, and gradually extending parental leave to help families combine care for the new born with high participation in the workforce.

We have to create value in order to share it. Economic growth is key for sustaining the Nordic model. The market economy is a great tool for achieving economic growth and for distributing benefits. However the market is a good servant, but not a good master. Rules and regulations can level the playing field, where the "laissez fair" approach fails. Tax incentives can nudge the market in a desired direction, such as green growth. Providing affordable high quality kindergartens is good for the children and their parents, and it is good for the economy by allowing parents complete their education and engage in the productive economy. In pursuing a competitive economy, the focus must be broader than solely on wage and tax levels. Education, trust, transparency and security are key to understanding how to be competitive in an increasingly knowledge-based global economy.

The political tool box in the Nordic countries involves using the capacity and potential of both the public and private sector. This pragmatic approach entails a keen interest in results that should guide policy choices.

The Elements of the Nordic Model

Let me elaborate further on what I see as key elements in the Nordic model:

Everyday democracy: Policies are important, but how they are developed is equally important. A key feature of the Nordic countries is the interplay between the partners of work life and civil society on the one hand, and the political sphere (government, parliament, political parties) on the other. This interaction can be termed "everyday democracy," a broad web of exchange of information, negotiations, debate and day-to-day influence. This stream of engagement invigorates democracy and provides input to better policies.

Income: In many countries around the world, labor unions are weak and split and wages are often determined locally. In Norway, a high number of workers are organized with the majority also represented in the Norwegian Labor Confederation. This enables a system where wages are negotiated centrally, rather than in each company. It lifts the wages and work conditions for groups of employees that otherwise, because of weak bargaining power, would fall behind and could end up as the "working poor." This system of wage setting also has the effect of rewarding the most productive companies in that they would pay the same wages as less productive ones, providing a premium to reinvest in the business. As a guiding principle, the first round of a negotiation would be conducted by the industries exposed to international competition. Their outcome sets the standards for the other sectors, more shielded from competition, such as the public sector.

Taxation: The Nordic countries have a relatively high level of taxation. This is necessary to finance broad based and high quality public services within such areas as health, education and elder-care. In many other countries, such services are often covered by the individual. Experience shows that this has a tendency to create private bureaucracies which are often less effective than a uniform public one. More importantly it increases inequality, where many of those who do not have the means are left behind. An active use of tax policies can check inequalities and social injustice, provide incentives to boost employment and pursue common goals such as green, climate friendly growth.

Security: A common denominator of the Nordic countries is the presence of a social security net that enables people to take more risks. If you know that the alternative is unemployment and poverty, you cling to your present job. The Nordic Model has developed a social security net that enables workers to retrain if jobs are lost, and provides payed sick leave, among other benefits. Safe and free workers are willing to take more risk, and dare voice their concern and disagreements when there is something that needs improving. In such an environment, workers are a source of innovation and increased productivity.

Conflict Partnership: We have strong and representative organizations in the labor force representing workers as well as employers. Much of the fundamentals of the so called Nordic Model are to be found in the aligned balance of power between employers and employees through their representative organizations. This "conflict partnership" has the advantage of providing predictability and "rules of the game" for solving problems and conflicts as they occur. Management and employees can use more of their time and energy to focus on improving productivity and developing the business together.

Tripartite Cooperation: A key feature of the Nordic model is the cooperation between the employers and employee organizations on the one hand, and the government on the other, in an organic system of cooperation. This tri-partite system gives potency to economic policy, securing high employment and flexibility through shifting economic cycles. Public policies can be shaped in tune with their partners in the work force. For example, in the past during times of international economic downturn and pressure on employment, wage demands are lower, while a higher wage premium is reaped in times of economic upturn and higher profits.

Adapting the Nordic Model for the Future

The future of the Nordic model hinges upon maintaining the fine balance between its three components: government macro-economic policy; an organized work life; and a comprehensive welfare state. High employment distributes wealth through wages, a necessary base for taxation that again is fundamental for a sustainable welfare state. Changes affecting any one of these components will also have systemic effects.

And changes are coming. One major change is from new technology. 3-D printing, robotization and digitalization will transform many jobs beyond the factory floor. This will present us with new challenges. There will be a push towards a higher proportion of workers in low skill service jobs. We can expect an increase in many of the segments of the work force that have not traditionally had a high level of organization/unionization. These challenges have to be met. However, new jobs will also be created. A high quality educational system with broad coverage will be key and equally so will be a highly trained work force.

In Norway, we see industry that left in the 70s, returning from low cost zones in Asia, such as a modern ship-building industry. The complex requirements of modern production put the emphasis elsewhere than on low labor costs. In this setting, a low-wage strategy is not the right answer. The focus should be on inclusive policies that maintain and build trust, which is essential for cooperation, flexibility and growth.

Immigration marks another strand of change. The conflicts ravaging the Middle East are also impacting the Nordic countries through a large flow of refugees seeking asylum. This will affect the demographic make-up and labor markets of the Nordic countries for years to come. Immigration must not forge increasing division in the labor market. In doing our share and showing solidarity, significant effort will be required to make the path to employment as short as possible. Work, income and taxation are critical for both integration and the Nordic model.

From some corners we see an attempt to stir up fear relating to immigration, invariably playing into the hands of populists. Fear is not really about change itself, it is about uncertainty. Do our elected representatives understand the changes? Do they know how to deal with them? Do our politicians have a plan?

Politics matters. In the end, good governance in the Nordic countries, as in democracies elsewhere, hinges on political leaders showing that they are worthy of people's trust by providing realistic policies to match the problems and opportunities they face.

One final point. International cooperation and the multilateral system is in a state of flux. Globally, women's rights, decent work and a host of other rights and standards are being put into the box of "western values." Cooperation in Europe is under pressure, pulling in the direction of fragmentation, when instead common action and leadership is needed. The combined economies of the Nordic countries ranks us as the 12th largest in the world. I believe stronger Nordic cooperation is needed. Together we have an audible voice. Let's get to work.

Is There Such a Thing as a Nordic Model?

Carl Bildt

"The fact that the Nordic world consists of relatively small societies that throughout their histories have hardly known civil wars or significant social strife, has also contributed to their successful evolution over the decades."

Let's be clear. I have always been reluctant to speak about any Nordic Model, let alone some Super Nordic Model that by being adopted by everyone would instantly transform our world into a far better place.

There are two reasons for this. The first is that I simply don't believe in models of this sort. Every nation or society, shaped by forces unique to itself, will have to find its own way. Wholesale import of models is unlikely to work. The second is that the differences between the Nordic countries themselves are not insignificant. In Sweden you can certainly deliver speeches praising the alleged Swedish model, but talks about a Danish model would likely be received with more than a fair dose of skepticism.

With these caveats it is obvious that the five Nordic nations have been able to develop societies considered to be among the more successful around the world. Thus the question whether there are any lessons to be learned from others is a relevant one.

All the Nordic countries were late-comers in terms of development. Sweden went from being one of the poorest countries in Europe in 1870 to becoming one of the richest in the world by 1970. Its growth and economic performance over the course of a century was matched only by Japan. And

Norway and Sweden were, after Ireland, the countries that lost the largest share of its population through emigration to America.

Sweden was fortunate in not being drawn into the large wars that dominated the European continent during the first half of the 20th century, and while both Denmark and Norway were occupied by Nazi Germany they did not suffer the destruction that affected most of the central and eastern parts of Europe.

Indeed during the wartime years, Sweden could strengthen its industry through a rearmament program, thus being well suited to deliver many of the investment goods that Western Europe needed during the decades when it rose from the ruins.

These were in many respects the "golden decades" of Sweden. There was strong economic growth and a political stability furthered by an election system that greatly favored the large Social Democratic party. In the watershed 1948 election this party had been forced to abandon it's more radical policies, and could then rule in a climate much more conducive to broad political compromise.

Finland's fate was different. While initially less developed, it also lost substantial territory in World War II, had to care for a large displaced population, as well as pay substantial war reparations to the Soviet Union. During the immediate postwar decades large numbers of Finns immigrated to Sweden to seek work there.

By the late 1960s strain was beginning to show in the economic model of Sweden. West Germany's successful rebuilding had taken the country from primarily a market for Swedish industry to a fierce competitor. And a Britain with which Scandinavia always had strong economic links, struggled with the loss of Empire and had to knock on the door of the European Economic Communities.

If the previous decades had seen a slow but steady growth of what came to be called the welfare state, the rise of public expenditure had always been roughly in line with the rise of GDP (Gross Domestic Product). But now the relationship changed, and we saw a period where rapidly rising public expenditure went hand in hand with slower growth and a deteriorating Swedish position on the global markets. Politics also became more polarized.

The economic crisis of the early 1990s, and the policy shifts that occurred in this period, including entering the EU in 1995, was the unavoidable consequence. The policy shifts included a certain trimming of parts of the welfare state as well as extensive liberalization of different parts of the economy. These shifts, which coincided with a period of rapid global growth and accelerating integration, led Sweden to a new period of strong economic growth and an improved position on the global markets. After decades of current account deficits, Sweden now entered a prolonged period of substantial surplus.

The so called Swedish model was allegedly "back in business."

Over the decades, the development of Sweden had also been profoundly influenced by demographic factors. It was the demand for a larger labor force in the early 1970s that led to changes in taxation making it difficult for a family to sustain itself on only one wage. This in turn paved the way for a gradual increase in female participation in the workforce. Prior to that, waves of immigrants from Southern Europe had met the demands for labor from a then rapidly expanding economy.

With a stronger presence in the economy, women also pressed for a larger role in society as a whole. While Norway was certainly first with a women-dominated cabinet under Prime Minister Brundtland, Sweden and the other Nordic countries soon prided themselves on the important role of women in political life.

Although similar in important respects, there are also significant differences between the Nordic countries. In the key area of labor market regulation, Sweden has gone further than Denmark with regulations, while the latter has been successful with its so called, "flex security model" of more liberal labor markets and more extensive social security provisions. And while all countries invest heavily in education, Finland with a sometimes more traditional approach has achieved substantially better grades for its results in the Program for International Student Assessment (PISA) evaluations.

Looking ahead, all countries face significant challenges in integrating the refugees and migrants that have come to their countries during the last few years. Sweden has, per capita, taken a larger share of refugees than any other Western country. But the combination of a relatively regulated labor market and aspects of the tax system, has led to higher levels of unemployment among refugees, this after years of having much lower unemployment than in other EU countries. This will have to be addressed.

The success of this different model of the Nordic world cannot be seen independently of the economic trajectory of these countries. Impressive periods of economic growth, a result of strong domestic policies in a global economy, has made the gradual expansion of social programs possible. The fact that the Nordic world consists of relatively small societies that throughout their histories have hardly known civil wars or significant social strife, has also contributed to their successful evolution over the decades.

This might not be a model, but there are certainly lessons to be learned.

Portrait of the North

Per Stig Møller

"The significance the Nordic peoples had for the rest of Europe lay in being different."

The Nordic countries stretch from the Polar Sea in the north to Germany in the south. From Russia in the east to the United Kingdom in the west. They have different time zones and different climates. Yet, they are inhabited by people who have been tightly linked for over 1000 years. They have warred with each other for centuries. They have entered into unions and dissolved them. Norway and Denmark were a united kingdom for 400 years until 1814 when the Congress of Vienna awarded Norway to Sweden as compensation for the loss of Finland to Russia—from which Finland broke free after the First World War. During the Second World War, Iceland broke loose from Denmark, which today exists in a Commonwealth with the Faeroe Islands and Greenland, which in turn received Home Rule in 2009.

Despite all this strife, all the gripes and grudges that have existed between the Nordic realms, they have grown together and created societies and social systems that resemble each other. Once an eternally turbulent region, they have become a terrain of calm, concordance and cooperation. The Nordic peoples have established kindred democratic welfare societies based on the same values: respect for the individual, gender equality and equality before the law. The Nordic countries have the least corruption, the least inequality and some of the greatest welfare and wealth in the world. All this in spite of the fact that Northerners had not been favored by the hand of nature before Norway discovered huge quantities of oil beneath the sea. Until then, only fish had been pulled up from the ocean.

Most of the year it is cold and blanketed by dark or twilight. Northerners have had to protect themselves against frost and dank and used a lot of energy to build houses that sheltered them from rain, damp and cold. They shared their roof with animals to keep warm. They toiled to cultivate the parsimonious earth and lived in small, scattered communities. Throughout most of their history, they lived short, arthritis-ridden lives in poverty and pulled together because they knew this was a prerequisite for getting through and surviving the next winter. This is why Northerners are less individualists and more collectivists and have greater faith in authority than so many other revolutionary peoples.

This is also why Northerners are skeptical of anything new and anyone who comes from the outside with new ideas and ways of living. They move only hesitantly toward change. The centuries-long struggle to scrape out a living has not afforded the leisure and refuge to sit and ruminate over other possibilities or to develop great systems and utopias. Northerners are hard-nosed realists. The greatest Nordic philosopher, Søren Kierkegaard, took aim precisely at the dialectical castles in the clouds that the German philosopher Hegel had constructed to the great enthusiasm of the rest of Europe. But not in the North, where Kierkegaard turned Hegel upside down and created existential philosophy, the center of which is not the system but "the single individual" who must learn to live in doubt and despair. That is why Kierkegaard was against democracy, which he dismissed as "nonsense" because in a democracy the majority, "the majesty of numbers," decided over everyone: "The compact majority," the Norwegian dramatist Henrik Ibsen called it.

The individual must not disappear into the mass, because for Kierkegaard and Ibsen individuals must take responsibility for their choices and stand by their actions and opinions—whatever the cost, thundered Henrik Ibsen solemnly, allowing Nora to leave the "doll's house" of marriage in which she had been trapped. "He is strongest who stands alone," he wrote—to which the Danish humorist Storm P. added: "Providing he's sober!"

Against all the great, incomprehensible philosophers, the Swedish poet J.H. Kellgren wrote at the end of the 18th century, "You are not a genius just because you are crazy." No, you have to keep your feet planted firmly on the ground and not let all of these strange, foreign speculations go to your head.

The Norwegian-Danish comic playwright Ludvig Holberg tutored his audience in the 1720s when he had one of his most famous characters rebuke an attorney for his learned, lawyerly, Latin phrases with the words: "Speak Danish, you black dog! Then we can hold our own." A hundred years later, Swedish poet Esaias Tegnér expressed it a bit more kindly, when he wrote: "What's said obscurely is what's thought obscurely." Speech must be straightforward and understandable, so anyone can follow along and respond—however wonderful or fantastic the tales may be as in Isak Dinesen (Denmark), William Heinesen (Faeroe Islands), Halldor Laxness (Iceland), or Pär Lagerkvist (Sweden).

In the small Nordic villages and settlements, everybody knew everything about everybody. In a community where everyone knows everyone's business, there is—beyond helpfulness—also pettiness and envy. You should not put on airs with your learning or brag about your wealth. "You're not to think you're anything special," as it was put in the Law of Jante, which the 20th century Danish-Norwegian author Aksel Sandemose drew up in irritation and anger at Nordic pettiness. In these tiny societies, no one is worth more than anyone else simply because they may have a higher rank or a larger fortune than others.

But precisely because of this special Nordic spirit, which demands simplicity, clarity, and clean lines, it has become the hallmark for what is particularly Nordic in architecture and design from Finland's Alvar Aalto to Sweden's Ikea. There are no contortions or curlicues here, no gilding or ornamentation. Here, material and form are treated honestly. Towns and dwellings are to be lived in. The spare Nordic light must be let in; essential and expensive heat must not be let out. Therefore, the North is in the forefront of developing low-energy housing and energy-saving technology. In Nordic metropolises, the bicycle trumps expensive, energy-guzzling cars.

Northerners have not done much to inspire the rest of Europe. To the contrary, they viewed themselves as the antithesis of the decadent Roman Empire, which they invaded in the transition from Late Antiquity. The Vikings then wreaked havoc on European coasts, subjugated large parts of England, Normandy, southern Italy and Sicily, colonized Greenland, reached Newfoundland and perhaps other places on the North American continent.

Only later did inspiration come from the South to the North. Christianity arrived around the year 1000 and in the 16th century, Luther's Reformation. With this came absolutism, the Enlightenment, and in the wake of the 1848 democratic revolutions in France and Germany, democracy.

The significance the Nordic peoples had for the rest of Europe lay in "being different." Barbarians, they were called. The Roman Tacitus presented them as courageous and violent with very different manly ideals than the womanly Romans.

In Montesquieu's *Spirit of the Laws*, the difference of the Nordic peoples is explained by climate, which has imparted to them a different physiognomy and sensibility than Europeans in the temperate zones. While the heat has made those in the warm countries pusillanimous, the cold has made the peoples of frosty climes courageous; and, as a result, they have maintained their freedom. Moreover, the cold has made Northerners resistant to pain but also less inclined to seek "pleasures" and "physical love;" whereas "in warmer climates love is liked for its own sake, it is the only cause of happiness, it is life itself." Perhaps, this is why Søren Kierkegaard feared physical love and never found happiness?

Having explained how very different Northerners are thanks to their climatic conditions, Montesquieu summarizes in this way: "In northern countries, we meet with a people who have few vices, many virtues, a great share of frankness and sincerity." This, he concludes, is what separates Northerners radically from peoples farther south in Europe: you get a feeling you are moving ever farther away from morality itself the farther you move from the North. But the price Northerners pay for these virtues is the loss of happiness. We find recurring in much of Nordic literature and art people who are cheerless, dutiful, oppressed by the collective and spiritually lonely. At the beginning of the 20th century, the Swedish author Hjalmar Söderberg wrote about "the incurable isolation of the soul," and the Norwegian Edvard Munch painted "The Scream." The scream of a forsaken human being in despair unto death. The scream that received its philosophical shape in Søren Kierkegaard and its dramatic presentation in August Strindberg, who had the daughter of the god Indra sigh: "Men are to be pitied."

Despite his success and European acclaim, the Danish fairytale writer Hans Christian Andersen was deeply unhappy. In his fairy tales, anyone who sticks out, who is different, is given what for. He longs incurably for a happy love with a woman "who is life," but he never experienced it. The feeling of being cheated by life comes out in melancholy and gloom in the great Nordic filmmakers, Carl Th. Dreyer, Ingmar Bergman, and Lars von Trier. Northerners, plagued by cold and dark, yearn for warmth and sun. This longing comes out in the Nordic music of the Norwegian Edvard Grieg, the Finn Jean Sibelius, and the Dane Carl Nielsen, who express a love for the Nordic spring, the awakening of nature and white nights.

The Northerner yearns, longs for, pines away, and seeks happiness anywhere but in the spare, miserly North, as thousands of Nordic emigrants demonstrated in the 19th century when they swarmed to God's chosen land, the United States. At that time, there was not enough work for everyone in the Nordic countries; the stingy earth did not provide bread for all. The Swedish author Vilhelm Moberg depicted the harsh conditions of these wanderers in his great series of novels *The Emigrants*.

More than a million Northerners only travel abroad every year as a holiday destination because now they are rich. In the nineteenth century, farmers joined together in cooperatives. Folk high schools were created, so not a single young person was left behind in ignorance because, as their creator the Danish psalmist N.F.S. Grundtvig asked: "Is light just for the learned?" To which, he answered, "No!" The workers formed labor unions; and, after a long strike in 1899, a special labor market system was created, which meant that the parties to the labor market, employers and employees, work things out for themselves without state interference.

In the 1930s, social policies developed, so the collective, the state and the municipalities, placed a safety net under everyone and saw to it that there was free schooling, social assistance, pensions, and free health care for all, rich or poor, young or old. Thus, the welfare society was set in motion; no one needed to end up in material misery. Everyone was supposed to have equal opportunities although the purpose was not to create an equal society. Redistributive and levelling tax policies have created security and smoothed out the distinctions between citizens. But at the same time they have limited or eroded personal responsibility and made it so difficult for entrepreneurs that the Nordic countries have a new form of emigration not for the wretched but the affluent.

Nordic security and welfare have had such an effect that today these Northerners, who are not known for grand emotions or passionate mood swings, are categorized as the happiest people on earth. Whether this life *is* happiness, others must judge. But many would probably decline this breed of happiness, content to be "down to earth" instead of reaching for the stars, for the Northerner knows only a few achieve them. "So, why try?" asks the Northerner, shrugging his shoulders and moving on to the chores of the day.

Helsinki:
In Search of the Optimal City

Pekka Sauri

"Cities hold the keys to the future of civilization on planet Earth."

The City of Helsinki, the Finnish capital, aims for a golden ratio between reliability and creativity. In this equation, reliability stands for availability of high-quality basic services, while creativity refers to openness to new ideas, pilots and experimentation. It is relatively easy to be reliable and also relatively easy to be creative. **The trick is combining both.** It is the optimal merger of these two prerequisites that is the basis of a successful city.

By global standards Helsinki is a modestly-sized urban conurbation. The population of the core city is 630,000 and of the metropolitan region, which consists of four municipalities, 1.1 million. Size-wise, Helsinki might be compared with Washington D.C. There are other parallels: four seasons, numerous government institutions, universities and a long coastline. On the other hand, Helsinki and Finland are among the last in Europe to face multiculturalism. Today, 12 per cent of Helsinki residents speak as their mother tongue a language other than Finnish and Swedish, but this figure is expected to reach 30 per cent by 2050. Successful assimilation of the immigrant population settling in the city is one of the main strategic priorities.

Finland is arguably the most local-government reliant country in the world. All the basic services—health care, social services, primary and secondary education including pre-school child care—are provided by the municipalities. Only the police force is the responsibility of the national government. (This arrangement is about to change as the national government is preparing an extensive reform of health care and social services which is expected to transfer responsibility from the municipalities to the provincial level, but no final decision has been taken at the time of writing.)

From Service-Production Engine to Community Partner

The strong tradition of local government as a service provider created a situation over decades where "the city" was used to refer to the local government and its service organization rather than to the community of residents. It is instructive that the City of Helsinki is the largest employer in the country with 40,000 staff providing the various services.

The division between city-as-a-service-provider and city-as-a-community has, however, changed rapidly in the past decade or so. The communication revolution has put an end to government's historical monopoly on information. Every citizen now has access to all the digitized information in the world and everybody can now run their own media channel from their pocket. This development has in a short period of time done much to bridge the gap between the city organization and the community: they are growing back together from decades of separation.

Much of this change is due to social media which, for the first time in the history of civilization, has created a platform for multi-centered, two-directional, real-time communication and dialogue between interested participants and stakeholders. The city officials, departments and decision-makers must be part of this conversation in their own best interest: public debate on city activities, services and plans goes on regardless of whether city representatives participate. And it is always better to be proactively present in the conversation before any noxious online rumor goes viral than to try to explain the situation afterwards. Social media has also worked wonders in reducing the number of individual complaints about city services: a message from City Hall, which before the era of social media reached just one citizen, can now convey the same information to 50,000 recipients on Twitter and Facebook.

Education, Education, Education

Finland is one of the best educated nations globally. Finnish schoolchildren have for years ranked high in the international "Program for International Student Assessment (PISA)" study of educational achievement, usually vying for the top slot with South Korea. Education is free from primary school all the way through to the doctorate level. Add to this free school lunches introduced after the Second World War in the late 1940s (you can choose between vegetarian and non-vegetarian options daily), and you begin to see the idea behind this: a small nation must ensure that the young receive an up-to-date and comprehensive education. The Helsinki Education Department has recently introduced a new phenomenon-based learning strategy which takes education out of the classroom: the whole city is the classroom now. It is worth bearing in mind that businesses also benefit from free education in the guise of a highly qualified workforce.

Open Data: Code Your Own Apps

It is imperative for the city, or any city, to attempt to mobilize the remarkable resource provided by education to the common good. One of the instruments for achieving this is the open data program of the metropolitan municipalities called Helsinki Region Infoshare (www.hri.fi). The idea is to publish the data created or gathered by the local government for public use and, hopefully to foster new applications and innovations.

The open data can be used by individuals and businesses alike. To date, more than 1,400 datasets have been opened, including city procurement and purchases, public transport timetables, maps and charts and so on. A recent example of innovations based on public open data is an application which shows the availability of city bikes at different bike stations in real time. This application was made public by independent coders a few days after the new generation Helsinki city bike system came into operation in May 2016.

From Public Transport to Mobility as a Service

Helsinki is a public transport city. The most notable form of public transit—and one of the most well-known landmarks of the city—is the tram (streetcar) network dating back to 1890, when the first horse-drawn tram entered service. Electric trams were introduced in 1900 and unlike many major cities the world over Helsinki never discontinued tram traffic despite opinions voiced in the 1960s and 1970s that it was an obsolete form of transport. Now the cities that abandoned trams 50 or 60 years ago are busy building new networks of light rail from scratch. The downside is that as much of the present-day tram network was designed and built a century ago, the average speed of travel in Helsinki is comparatively leisurely.

Today, 73 percent of commuting trips during morning rush hour into the inner city are made on public transport and fewer than 50 percent of inner city households actually own a car. More and more people—especially the younger generations—regard mobility as a service as opposed to personally possessing a vehicle which stands parked by the curbside 22 hours out of 24. Characteristically, the mobility priorities of the city put walking first, cycling second, public transport third and cars last.

There is also a major long-term transport infrastructure vision in the pipeline. The Helsinki-Tallinn rail tunnel across the Gulf of Finland, uniting Finland and Estonia by means of a fixed link instead of the ferries and catamarans of today, will connect Helsinki to the projected Rail Baltica high-speed railway from Tallinn via Riga and Warsaw to Berlin, Prague and the rest of Central Europe. A feasibility study of the Helsinki-Tallinn link is underway.

Recycling all Materials

There is a strong tradition of recycling in Helsinki, as in most other Nordic cities and towns. In Finland, recycling started during wartime and the post-war years of austerity when raw materials were scarce. Recycling of newsprint and a refillable glass bottle system for beer and soft drinks have been around for 70 years. Material consumption rocketed with increased prosperity and posed new challenges to recycling and waste management. Today, the recycling of materials takes place in a rather sophisticated process of domestic sorting of waste into a number of separate bins emptied by designated trucks. Paper, cardboard, brown cardboard, bio-waste, glass jars and tin cans are all sorted and collected separately and what is left over (mainly plastic packaging) is incinerated at a power plant feeding hot water into the district heating network which covers more than 90 percent of the heated space within city limits.

The system is elegant, but its strength is also its weakness: it relies principally on the diligence of the residents to put in the extra effort of sorting their waste materials. In the new district of Kalasatama (Fish Harbor), waste management is organized by means of a state-of-the-art suction-pipe network into which residents drop their sorted waste. This represents the next generation in recycling.

One City, one Planet, one Strategy

The City of Helsinki believes that an organization can have just one master strategy which encompasses all the relevant goals of the city in one document. The strategy is drawn up by the City Council every four years. Sustainable development, including climate change containment and adaptation goals, is strongly featured. The city will be carbon neutral by 2050.

The underlying idea of the city strategy is that sustainability and economic success go hand in hand and improve the quality of life of the residents. As most major targets are integrated into one strategy paper, reaching decisions on individual issues is often easier. Because the debate on values and missions takes place when the strategy is decided upon by the City Council, there is less need to go through this again during the rest of the four-year mandate. (Sometimes this does not work quite as smoothly.)

It's the Helsinki Mindset

In the above text, I have described a selection of practices and innovations characteristic of the City of Helsinki. Obviously, not everything works faultlessly all of the time, and sometimes performance falls short of targets, but that's life – the city tries to learn from experience and feedback and make improvements. As an urban community, Helsinki has made remarkable progress since the turn of the millennium and the pace shows no sign of slowing down.

At the end of the day, if information is open, if debate is free and if there is equal access to high-quality education, all problems of humankind will eventually be resolved—perhaps not tomorrow, perhaps not even next year, but eventually they will. In Helsinki, all these vital elements are in place. Cities hold the keys to the future of civilization on planet Earth. While Helsinki is a village compared with the world's mega-cities (the population of Tokyo is five times that of the whole of Finland and forty times the population of Helsinki), it has in a number of respects succeeded in providing its residents both a high quality of everyday life and a platform of creating value through creativity and innovation. Its work is in constant progress. You're very welcome to come see for yourselves.

2. 21st Century Challenges— Sustaining the Nordic Model in a Globalized Political and Economic World

These five countries, with their very distinct history, have a similar model of what it means to be Nordic. Can this model be adapted for the rapid pace of change in Europe and globally, and still be considered a success. Can this model offer a way for other countries to meet these challenges without losing sight of what it means to be a vibrant democracy? Are there inherently Nordic ways that would be of compelling interest to an American audience?

The Necessity of the Rule of Law and Transparency in Modern Society

Ragna Árnadóttir

"This lack of trust, this gulf between the public and the government, is one of the greatest challenges we face, and if worse came to worst; it could eventually erode people's faith in the rule of law."

A Flashback

The scene is a public meeting held in Reykjavík on 16 February 2009. It is attended by nearly 1,000 ordinary citizens. The chairman of the meeting asks me, "Ragna, are you going to confiscate the tycoons' assets? A short answer: Yes or No? Yes or No!" I say there is no short answer. I say consideration would have to be given to the human rights of anyone whose assets were confiscated. This is met by booing from the hall. After the meeting a number of people approach me. They are angry. A woman asks me haughtily, "What about my human rights?"

Indeed: what about the human rights of those who suffered losses in the banking collapse?

A State Based on Law

Iceland's three largest commercial banks, Glitnir, Kaupthing and Landsbanki, collapsed in 2008. While the whole world underwent a sharp recession at the time, the impact and after-effects of the banking crisis were particularly visible in Iceland. The state, businesses and households all found themselves faced with a range of urgent challenges. Shortly after the banking crisis there were calls for an investigation into what had actually happened. In December 2008, parliamentarians from all parties agreed on the establishment of a special prosecutor's office, for a limited period of a few years, to investigate suspicions of criminal actions in the period preceding, in connection with or in the wake of the banking collapse and to follow-up these investigations with prosecutions where appropriate.[1] It was also agreed by the leaders of all the groupings in the Althingi (Iceland's parliament) and the speaker to set up a Special Parliamentary Investigation Commission consisting of independent experts. Its brief was to investigate the reasons for the collapse of the banks and the subsequent economic crisis, make an assessment of the mistakes that had been made and submit a report to the Althingi.[2]

A new government took power in February 2009. Two of the ten ministers in the cabinet, those of Justice and Economic Affairs, came from outside the parliament and political parties. Entrusting such responsible positions to "externals" was a very unusual arrangement in Iceland, though some precedents existed in the other Nordic countries. When I was asked by the media what priorities I intended to pursue in my administration, my first response was that I intended to keep things at the Ministry of Justice on the same course as they had been on until that time. No doubt this seemed a feeble reply from a newly-appointed minister. As a former official in the ministry for quite a few years, I knew that in most respects matters under the ministry ran in well-defined grooves; this applied particularly to the law-enforcement system. But even though I found the answer obvious at the time, the questions put to me at the public meeting I recalled above, gave me food for thought.

---

1. Act No. 135/2008 on the Office of a Special Prosecutor. The office began operations on 1 February 2009 and was formally abolished in 2015 when a new body, the National Prosecution Service, took over the supervision of police investigations and, as appropriate, the prosecution of tax offences and economic crime.

2. See Act No. 142/2008 on the Events Leading to, and the Reaons for, the Collapse of the Icelandic Banks in 2008 and Related Events. An English summary of the contents of the report may be found at: http://rna.althingi.is/eldri-nefndir/addragandi-og-orsakir-falls-islensku-bankanna-2008/skyrsla-nefndarinnar/english/

Could it be that in all the turmoil new ideas were coming into being in society regarding how the law should operate, or about the rule of law? What lay behind these demands for the confiscation of the property of the tycoons and the imprisonment of the leading bankers? On what basis was it being alleged that it was taking far too long to settle accounts after the economic collapse?

Human rights are protected under the Icelandic constitution,[3] in addition to which Iceland, like the other Nordic countries, is a signatory to the European Convention on Human Rights.[4] The protection of human rights is never more important than in times of crisis, and human rights are increasingly at the center of our conception of the rule of law. A commitment to human rights places a necessary limit on the actions of the authorities at any given time. It is clear, for example, that whether individuals are indicted should never depend on whether the public is running out of patience; according to law, an indictment can be issued only if there is a sufficient basis for it, and the constitutionally-protected right to a fair trial must be observed.

In other words, these decisions must not be influenced by politics, public anger or pressures of other types. A prosecutor is bound by law in his or her operations and at the end of the day a court of law will examine the case presented by the prosecution and judge the defendant guilty or not guilty. Iceland's legislation in this field has evolved largely through Nordic cooperation, with a clear division between the powers of the minister and the Director of Public Prosecutions. The Director of Public Prosecutions, appointed on a permanent basis, must meet the same requirements regarding qualifications as judges of the Supreme Court, and is engaged at the same salary and on the same terms of service. The Director of Public Prosecutions exercises power of prosecution on behalf of the state; how this is done is subject to supervision by the minister, but prosecutors do not take orders from the minister unless special provisions to this effect exist in legislation.[5]

---

3. Constitution of the Republic of Iceland. No. 33, 17 June 1944.

4. European Convention on Human Rights and Fundamental Freedoms, Rome 4th November 1950.

5. See the Code of Criminal Procedure, No. 88/2008.

The general rule is therefore that the minister is not involved in any way in decisions regarding the investigation or prosecution of criminal cases any more than he or she is able to influence the conclusions reached by the courts. Admittedly it is sometimes thought that ministers have greater powers than they have, or should have: That they can suddenly decide to act in a certain way without regard to the law. That laws are just a needless formality that should be brushed aside. That a minister who bows to the law and fails to act decisively could be accused of spinelessness, which is not something to be sought after; that the electorate could punish him or her for this in the next election.

The fact is that it is not at all desirable that ministers' decisions should be subject to whims and extraneous pressures. And in the final analysis no one would want this to be so. And therefore when it comes to the crunch, most people agree that all citizens are to be treated equally and their human rights respected; that human rights are of a fundamental nature and we do not want to see them violated, no matter the individual who is involved.

There is a general consensus on this point, which is reflected in our ideas about the rule of law. The concept of a state held together by law has developed from the treatment of purely formal requirements regarding legislation to include substantive considerations regarding matters such as human rights. But it cannot be taken for granted that this interpretation will last indefinitely without a conscious effort to maintain it because the public's notion of law changes across generations, to some extent reflecting the spirit of the times.

Transparency

Nevertheless, I do not believe that the views expressed at the public meeting reflected a demand to disregard the fundamental principles of a constitutional state and that people's understanding of what constitutes a state bound by law was changing. I think that what lay behind the comments was rather a deep lack of faith in the government and its institutions. This lack of trust, this gulf between the public and the government, is one of the greatest challenges we face, and if worse came to worst; it could eventually erode people's faith in the rule of law. Public opinion polls taken in Iceland since the banking collapse[6] indicate that an effort needs to be made here. While a large proportion of people (75–80 percent) generally say they have faith in the police, the judiciary comes out far worse with just over 30 percent of respondents reporting confidence in the courts. Although there was no visible change in the levels of public confidence towards these institutions before and after the banking collapse, such a low confidence rating for the judiciary must be considered unsatisfactory. However, the Althingi faces the greatest challenge in this area: Icelanders' confidence in their parliament fell from 40 percent prior to the economic collapse to 13 percent; recent assessments put it at about 17 percent. Confidence in the banking system plummeted from 40 percent to a low of 5 percent after the collapse, though it has risen slightly since then.

A situation like this is untenable in the long run. That we have not managed to build up confidence again to higher levels than these is a matter of concern. Our parliamentarians say they are well aware of the problem, but opinion polls do not suggest that they are taking sufficient action to make the changes needed to regain public support. It seems reasonable to ask why the political parties did not go through a thorough process of soul-searching after the banking crisis to analyze the situation in full. Such an atmosphere can be an opportunity for new political parties that can bring fresh perspective to the political landscape, but could in the worst scenario also give rise to forces with extremist agendas that exclude tolerance for the rights of all citizens. Fortunately, this latter case has not occurred in Iceland. This is where we, the electors, must also indulge in self-examination: could it be that we are making unreasonable demands of our politicians? Are we taken in by false and unrealistic promises? Are we not prepared to have our politicians make decisions that are unpopular in the short term even when we know they will be of benefit in the long run? This is a vicious circle from which we need to break out.

It takes a lot of work to build up trust, and transparency is one of the essential elements in doing so. The Nordic countries have long been proud of being in the lead regarding transparency, with low levels of recorded corruption. Public access to the decision-making process is good, as far as it goes, and the public has certain opportunities for putting checks on politicians and gov-

---

6. Gallup opinion polls on confidence in institutions, http://www.gallup.is/#/traust/

ernment authorities. But it must be said that frequently, considerable familiarity and even expert knowledge of an issue is needed before one can know what materials one needs to examine in the first place, and then to understand their content. In this area we have to do better; this applies to politicians, government officials, the academic community and other experts. We have simply not made it a priority to set forth information in such a way that it will be understood. Admittedly, special attention has been given in Nordic collaboration in the legal field to have legislation presented in clear language, and most of the Nordic countries have put a lot of work into finding ways of improving the quality of legislation so as to make it easier to understand and simplify the mechanism of regulations.

Nevertheless, it must be admitted that the system is not particularly progressive in this area. This is especially noticeable when it comes to raising public awareness and giving the public access to decision-making. When I look at the texts of statutes, court judgments and rulings, I sometimes ask myself who they are written for. Is it a case of specialists writing only for other specialists? What about the ordinary citizen for whose affairs these decisions are taken? This is one of the most urgent challenges facing our society, and will play an important part in establishing trust between the public and the system.

Another challenge regarding transparency is to make information available. In the Ministry of Justice we made every effort to be accessible to the public as far as possible in order to tackle the crisis of confidence. We made a priority of providing all the information we could and talking to people and consulting them according to the nature of the case, and provided as much time as permitted. But it is not always the case that politicians or officials have the opportunity to explain what they are doing. Our society is drenched in a tidal wave of information every single day, and every second of our time is valuable. Therefore, the government must be in the vanguard of information technology and methods of communication and make a priority of reaching out to the citizens in a way that will be to their advantage.

Conclusion

Some decisions age well; others do not. We all know that decisions taken in a state of excitement are generally not good ones. In such situations, the legal foundations on which the state rests are invaluable. It cannot, of course, be taken for granted that what is understood by the constitutional structure will remain unchanged as new generations come and go. And for this reason we must make an effort to maintain our understanding of what it involves and an appreciation of why it is necessary. For this, the government must enjoy public trust. And to do this, it must deserve it.

The Icelandic Social Welfare System: Comparison with the Other Nordic Countries

Ragnar
Árnason

Gunnar
Haraldsson

Rögnvaldur
Hannesson

"The high costs of the social welfare system raise the question whether it actually generates positive net benefits. Remarkably, the answer to this question does not seem to be available."

A modern state run welfare system along the lines of the so-called Scandinavian model came into being in Iceland in the 20th Century (Jonsson 2001). It would be an error, however, to believe that this marked the beginning of social welfare in Iceland. A more accurate characterization is that the modern system evolved out of a pre-existing social welfare system that had been an integral component of the Icelandic social organization from the time of the settlement of Iceland in the 9th and 10th centuries A.D. (Larusson 1958, Byock 1990, Thorsteinsson and Jonsson 1991).

Early Social Welfare

It goes without saying that the Norse settlers of Iceland brought with them their social culture and organization. From what historical evidence is available we can gather that a part of that culture was characterized by a high degree of communal cooperation and mutual assistance (Benediktsson 1974, Byock 1990). These took various forms, some of which parallel modern social welfare systems. Two key pillars of this early social welfare system may be identified. One was the extended family system which provided support to family members in all aspects of their lives including those now regarded as social welfare matters. All family members could call upon this assistance whenever the need arose, much as people do nowadays in modern welfare systems. These mutual family obligations were supported by very strong social norms and customs. Maybe for that reason, genealogies and lineages were an extremely important part of Norse culture.

The second key pillar of early social welfare was the integrated farming system. Economic production in Old Norse culture was centered around labor intensive farming units typically comprising the owners, workers and servants and all of their families. This farming unit took care, as far as we can see, of the needs of all its members from birth to grave. It provided subsistence guarantees to everyone to the extent possible, as well as health services according to the medical knowledge of the day. It even seems to have provided education, although generally not very formal or extensive except for the children of wealthy farmers.

From what we can gather from rather meager sources, there also seems to have been a social obligation by those with sufficient means to support the needy even if they did not belong to the farming unit and there were no family ties. The Icelandic sagas applying to settlement period until, say, 1050 AD have many references to this approach (Magnusson and Palsson 1960, Byock 1990).

Later, with expanding formal social organization, these social welfare obligations were formalized. Thus, the local community (referred to as "hreppar") became by law responsible for the welfare of poor, destitute people that did not belong to a farming unit and whose small farms had failed (Larusson 1958). As a part of that system, there were laws preventing people from establishing independent households without a clear ability to sustain themselves as farmers, thus inducing people to be employed by a viable farming unit, and preventing them to marry and establish families of their own (to avoid the Hobbesian trap). Social welfare activities were also an integral part of the activities of the Catholic Church from the time of its establishment in the year 1000 AD. In 1097, a special tax (tithing) for the church was imposed, a part of which was used for charity purposes, running hospitals and establishing schools (Lindal 1974).

The fundamental organization of Icelandic society did not change much until the late 19th Century. The methods of production, the cornerstone of which was the integral farming unit, remained largely unchanged. Income levels also did not greatly improve; the level of population in the mid-19th century remained about the same as it was in the year 1000 (Thorsteinsson and Jonsson 1991). The extended family system also persisted as a social institution. As a result, there was no pressing need to alter the structure of social welfare in any radical manner.

The Emergence of the Modern Welfare System

Towards the end of the 19th century, the traditional Icelandic economic production system started to break apart (Bjornsson 1964, Snaevarr 1993, Jonsson 2001). The immediate cause was a dramatic expansion in the fishing industry, made possible by improved technology and increased foreign demand. Fishery-based villages and towns started to emerge with most of the inhabitants earning their living from selling their labor to newly established fishing and fish processing companies. In the newly established fishing towns and villages personal incomes were much higher than in the farming sector and offered freedom from the rather severe social constraints of the traditional farming community. As a result, farm laborers flocked to the fishing towns and villages (Bjornsson 1964, Snaevarr 1993). However, by leaving the traditional farming community, they relinquished the social security benefits of the extended farming system.

This reorganization of economic production in Iceland was of course just a part of the wave of industrialization in Europe and the other Nordic countries. It was caused by the same fundamental driving forces, technological advances and the opening up of new markets, and it brought with it similar social problems which ultimately led to similar solutions. The main difference is that these things happened somewhat later in Iceland than in many of the other countries.

One consequence of the process toward industrialization and urbanization in Iceland was the re-emergence of the social problems associated with personal illnesses, accidents, old age and other infirmities. The traditional farming society had developed methods to deal with these problems. These, as explained above, relied to a great extent on the social institutions of the extended family and the integrated farming unit. In the newly established fishing towns and villages these institutions were not prevalent and in many cases unavailable. Therefore, an acute social need to deal with these problems arose.

In response to this need, various new forms of welfare programs and services appeared during the first decades of the twentieth century. Most of these were initiated by the local community, labor unions and voluntary organizations such as the women's movement. It was not until the years following the Second World War that the state became the prime provider of social welfare programs in Iceland (Jonsson 2001).

The 1930s and 40s brought sweeping reforms in social policies and laid the foundations for the post-war welfare system in Iceland. The fundamental driving force for this change was undoubtedly the increased numbers of the population and, therefore, the electorate living in towns and villages and earing their living as wage laborers. This led to the strengthening of the Social Democratic Party and with it the political demand for a state-run welfare system. At the same time, rapidly increasing GDP (gross domestic product), especially during the war years, made it relatively less expensive to meet these demands.

A series of laws establishing a dominant role of the state in the provision of welfare were passed during this period. One of the most important was the Social Security Act of 1947, supposedly the first comprehensive legislation of its kind in the Nordic countries (Jonsson 2001, Olafsson 1999). It included a universal old age pension for people above the age of 67, the same rate of benefits for all people suffering from inabilities, a universal accident insurance system, and free health care for all and special benefits during periods of illness. When this was implemented in 1947, the coverage offered by this system was greater than in most European countries including the Nordic countries, but the benefits were generally lower (Jonsson 2001). Moreover, in Iceland many of the benefits were income related (lower benefits if income was higher) which was generally not the case in the other Nordic countries.

At about the same time the National Health Service was established guaranteeing free health services to all Icelandic citizens. A number of new hospitals and other health institutes were established. The state-run schooling system was also greatly expanded.

The Current Social Welfare System

The current Icelandic social welfare system may be described as a "cradle to grave" welfare system in the Scandinavian mold. Pregnancy supervision and births take place within the National Health System. Nursery and pre-schools for children from the age of nine months are operated by munici-palities and, although not free, are significantly subsidized. The state runs the entire school system from primary school to the university level. Attendance is free of charge and at the tertiary school level (colleges and universities) the state offers generous financial assistance in the form of student loans on terms that are so easy that a good part of these loans are never repaid. During adult-hood, everyone is guaranteed a minimum subsistence income.

Earning risks to labor market participants are minimized by accident, illness, disability and unemployment benefits. The state-run housing fund offers favorable rates for the purchase of private housing. There are state-run building projects to make inexpensive housing available for those worse off. To further reduce personal housing costs, the state provides rent subsidies and interest rate discounts via the income tax system. Families also receive child support at increasing rates with the number of children. In retirement, everyone is guaranteed a minimum income. In addition, there is an extensive pension system funded by labor and employee contributions that offers very generous pensions to virtually all working people. Finally, throughout every citizen's lifetime, comprehensive health services, run by the state, are provided. These health services are not entirely free. Small fees are charged. However, any individual's payments are subject to a very moderate annual maximum, so that the payments are not onerous for anyone.

The great push toward improved social welfare in the immediate post WWII period brought the Icelandic social welfare system to a level similar to that of the other Nordic countries at the time. Since then, the structure and content of the system has remained similar to that of the other Nordic countries. There are some minor differences, however. In terms of amount of benefits, the Icelandic social welfare system seems to have fallen somewhat behind the Nordic norm (Olafsson 1999, Jonsson 2000). Also, the Icelandic social welfare system is to a somewhat greater extent than the Nordic ones, reliant on private funding. This applies in particular to the pension system which is almost exclusively funded by the contributions of labor and employer, but also to the health system where partial payment by the users for services is common. Moreover, many of the benefits provided by the Icelandic welfare system are not flat rates for everyone but income related in the sense that the benefits are reduced with increasing income.

Do the Benefits Exceed the Costs?

Iceland has built up an extensive social welfare system. This system, apart from some relatively minor idiosyncrasies, is similar to the other Nordic social welfare systems. Like these other Nordic systems, the Icelandic social welfare system may be characterized as a "cradle-to-grave" system. The bulk of this system is state designed, funded and operated. An important exception is the labor market pension system which was established via collective labor market bargaining in 1974 and has been owned and operated by labor market participants ever since (Jonsson 2001, Nososco 2008). However, even this component of the welfare system is not exclusively in the private domain. It was designed in cooperation with the state and is based on legislation.

Although the benefits of this social welfare system are undoubtedly very large, the costs are also substantial. There are two types of costs: The first is simply the resources consumed by the system and the second consists of various disadvantages and drawbacks associated with the system as it is designed and operated.

The resources allocated to the social welfare system constitute a considerable proportion of total Icelandic production. Thus, between 2000 and 2014, state outlays for the social welfare system, including education, averaged about a quarter of the GDP (Statistical Bureau 2016). Adding the privately funded labor market pension system would take this share to about one-third of the GDP. Smaller additions to the general social welfare system, such as housing contributions, would take this number even higher. In short, at least every third unit of production by the Icelandic population goes to fund the social welfare system.

In addition to these direct outlays, there are several less obvious costs associated with the current social welfare system. One is the crowding out of private, often family-based social welfare services. Family-based social services are arguably the most beneficial to the recipient, not the least when it comes to health, old age and other infirmities. When these services are provided by the state and funded by taxation, families are compelled to reduce and even withdraw their support. The second cost within this category has to do with the basic inefficiency and inflexibility of services provided by governments. Moreover, state provision of services tends to be overly regulatory, bureaucratic and inflexible even in the face of social change.

Both of these factors increase the costs of the services and reduce their quality. Thirdly, the problem of cheating, inherent in all award systems, is exacerbated by the social distance between the provider, in this case the state, and the recipient. The fourth cost has to do with the often ad hoc constraints on the quantity and quality of the services that the state imposes in its attempts to meet its budgetary objectives. In Iceland, these constraints are most obvious in the health system, where they have, inter alia, led to lengthy queues for certain types of treatment and apparently sub-par services in certain fields especially for the elderly. All of these costs and others are real and, at least in the case of Iceland, they appear to be significant.

The high costs of the social welfare system raise the question whether it actually generates positive net benefits. Remarkably, the answer to this question does not seem to be available. No studies comparing the benefits and costs of the Icelandic social welfare system have been published. The same, as far as we have been able to verify, applies to the other Nordic countries. Thus, it appears that at this point in time we do not have the evidence to confidently claim that the Icelandic or the other Nordic social welfare systems produce positive net benefits.

Public Service—
More Important Than Ever

Christina Jutterström

"When large-scale TV broadcasts take place,
whether it's for news, sports or entertainment,
people still gather around the campfire."

In the autumn of 2006, Sweden received a new centre-right coalition government led by the country's Conservative party. The post of Culture Minister, also responsible for media affairs, went to the Conservatives. Just days after the government had taken office, as CEO of Swedish Television I was called in to meet the minister. She explained that the roadmap for Swedish public service was to be completely redrawn. In accordance with well-known Conservative policy, popular programming would cease and the public broadcaster would only produce content not covered by the commercial companies; in other words, news programs, current affairs and culture. Possibly children's shows as well. No more entertainment, sports, drama or films.

This was the tone after more than eighty years of public service radio, and fifty years since the arrival of television in Sweden.

But the Minister of Culture was to last only ten days at her post. It transpired that for fifteen years she had not paid her radio and TV license, which is mandatory in Sweden. A new Conservative minister was installed, but one that wasn't intent on creating a storm for public service.

The result was that the public service companies—television, radio and educational broadcasting are separate companies in Sweden—actually strengthened their market positions, rather than being hampered. The reason for this? On reflection, I think that the four centre-right coalition leaders who had initially endorsed the big change soon realized that the current public broadcaster played far too important a role for individual citizens, for Swedish society and for democracy, to be fundamentally changed. A major shift in an American direction would have caused an outcry, both among parliamentarians and in Swedish society at large. A similar event took place in 2015 in the UK (United Kingdom) when the Conservative Secretary of State for Culture proclaimed that the BBC's (British Broadcasting Communication) future range should be limited. Massive public protests resulted in a broadly unchanged charter for the BBC.

I find it very difficult to see any reason for a European country like Britain or Sweden to import and impose the American model of public broadcasting, which was originally created when the private sector in the US was considered unable to fulfil its duty. The fact that commercial companies want to avoid competition from the public sector is not a sufficiently good reason, or that private radio and TV stations would like to earn more money. If politicians wish to have reasonably well-informed citizens, then the European system is better than the American. It offers the public a comprehensive range of better quality programs and a greater diversity of content, available on all the old and new technical platforms.

How can public radio and television have acquired such a strong position not only in Sweden but in the whole Nordic region? (I'll mostly be using examples from Sweden, but the situation is similar in all the Nordic countries.) One can clearly see the influence of several factors. In my opinion, the most important one can be found in the history of the Nordic countries as public educational communities. As far back as the nineteenth century, in the wake of industrialism, growth in community organizations flourished. The founding of trade unions, adult education associations, new evangelist churches and the temperance movement were all integral parts of this movement. In addition, a number of new political parties were formed at the turn of the century; parties which also contributed to the wave of public education that surged through the Nordic countries.

In addition to this, Sweden had implemented statutory public elementary education in 1842 for both girls and boys, contributing to increasingly widespread skills in reading, writing and arithmetic. Many people were also interested in using these abilities to attain additional knowledge, not least concerning social issues.

I dare say that relatively early on, particularly among citizens in Sweden and Norway, a generally high level of education was achieved, even though the majority of students did not attend school beyond the age of twelve to thirteen years. Once they reached adulthood and started to work, they came into contact with trade unions, adult education organizations and sometimes new evangelical churches and temperance associations as well. This historical background certainly contributes to the fact that with the present large inflow of refugees, particularly into Sweden, great importance is being attached to the idea that refugees should receive educational support.

The early decision to establish a public broadcaster came almost naturally to Swedish politicians, providing a commercial-free radio that would, in the long-term, serve as a kind of well-used public education apparatus. Swedish Radio started in 1925, only three years after the BBC. Program content consisted largely of lectures, preferably by individuals from the academic world, radio plays and eventually news and sports programs. It could be argued that a part of the country's community organizations moved over to radio. To quote the BBC's founder John Reith, the intention was to, "carry into the greatest possible number of homes everything that is best." In other words: great breadth in the range of program-genres, a high level of quality and radio and television for everyone.

However, the early start for public radio was not to be repeated for television. An attitude of apprehension and scepticism prevailed, especially among the long-ruling Social Democrats. Newspaper owners also resisted, afraid that they would lose advertising income to television. In Britain and the U.S., television had been launched in the 1930s, while Sweden did not begin its first regular TV broadcasts until 1956. The Prime Minister at the time, Tage Erlander, thought that Swedes would rather buy a car than a television set. In reality, it turned out that Swedes would buy both a car and a television set, several times in their lifetime. Furthermore, public television would prove to be of assistance in raising the Swedes' general level of education.

A real boost for TV viewing came in 1958. The Football World Cup was scheduled to take place in Sweden that year, and the whole world was expecting to watch Swedish Television's broadcasts worldwide. Thanks to highly skilled and innovative engineers, recruited primarily from public radio, Swedish Television managed to create solutions for transmitting the matches from the football fields to televisions all around the world. In that year, Brazil won gold, Sweden silver. And Swedish public television has continued being technological pioneers.

Sports and entertainment came to dominate Swedish and Nordic TV in the first few years. But as time passed, the choice of programs increased and politicians became ever more precise in formulating what they expected from public broadcasting. And despite the constant debate about commercial broadcasting during the thirty years since the arrival of television in Sweden, it was not introduced until 1992. By then, 70 percent of the population wanted advertising on television. Today it's the reverse: 70 percent are against it and increasingly advanced methods are being employed to turn it off.

What, then, does the public service remit look like? Broadcasting permits are issued by the government for a number of years—currently six years—to the three public service companies: Swedish Radio, Swedish Television and the Educational Broadcasting Company. This is usually preceded by a parliamentary committee of inquiry, followed by a parliamentary decision. The preamble states that operations must be characterized by independence and integrity, conducted in a manner free from both state and political influence, as well as from economic or any other spheres of influence in society.

In the 2014 remit, the essence of program content is defined as follows: programs are to be characterized by public educational ambitions (author's note: even after ninety and sixty years, respectively), and a diversity of opinions and interests must be safeguarded when it comes to religion, culture and science. The programs must also be of high quality. The remit is to be re-evaluated annually in a number of different instances.

The state thus decides how public broadcasting should be conducted and what it should include, but it also allows for strong corporate autonomy and independence regarding programs and services. Public broadcasting in the Nordic sense cannot in my view, be called state television and radio. It is everyone's radio and television, serving the general public, as mandated by the elected representatives in parliament and from the government.

Public service funding also contributes in keeping state powers at a distance. It consists of a compulsory television fee for anyone who owns a television set, and is collected by an independent company. The money for public broadcasting is not included in the finance minister's budget. However, a few years ago this funding was subject to investigation because many viewers no longer use television sets to access content. Instead, they do so via tablet computers and mobile phones. A proposal is now on the table to introduce a media fee that all adults must pay as part of their state tax, but this will go directly to the public broadcasters, not to the Treasury. In this way, funding can be achieved regardless of how content is accessed by the public, but of course it's open to discussion whether a media fee might cause public service companies to be drawn closer into the influence of political power.

In 2006, the Swedish government's parliamentary proposal for a new public service permit was entitled "Public Service–more important than ever." Ten years later, I maintain that this assessment still holds true despite the fact that distribution methods have changed thanks to new technologies. Citizens behavior in terms of how, when and where they access public service content has also changed. The classic behavior of watching a TV set from one's couch has decreased quite drastically while strong competition comes from traditional commercial channels, Netflix, HBO (Home Box Office), YouTube and Facebook.

When large-scale TV broadcasts take place, whether it's for news, sports or entertainment, people still gather around "the campfire." This applies whenever major disasters occur at home or abroad—but also when the Eurovision Song Contest was broadcast from Sweden in May 2016. Almost four million Swedes watched the program and globally it was watched by 200 million viewers. But the challenges ahead are enormous and the outcome is more uncertain than ever.

Swedish Television's current CEO Hanna Stjärne gives her view on the current mission for public broadcasting, "Public service media will become even more important in the future. As society becomes increasingly polarized, trustworthiness is essential. Providing reliable information, knowledge and common experiences in a digital world is what we strive to do."

Will public broadcasting in Sweden and other Nordic countries be able to survive the great changes facing society today? High-quality public radio has been widely available for ninety years, and television for sixty. History provides no guarantee for the continued strength and vitality of public service in our democratic society. The future depends on three things: even in these turbulent times public service companies themselves continue to be interesting, relevant and important for citizens that politicians continue to provide public service companies with comprehensive mandates, and citizens continue to have confidence in public service companies and the programs and services they provide.

In the most recent reliable poll (2016) of trustworthiness for various public and private businesses in Sweden, Swedish Radio and Television were among the highest ranked. 70 percent of Swedes showed confidence in them. This can be a strong indicator for the future.

The Swedish Welfare State

Mårten Palme

"We are also living in what can be called the shadow of a coming crisis."

There is a renewed interest in the Scandinavian welfare state in the public policy debate in the U.S., as well as in many other countries. The obvious background to this interest is the common trends since the mid-1980s, in the U.S. and many European economies, of concentration of wealth, increasing income inequalities and social immobility. The more equal societies in the Scandinavian countries provide examples that a different development path is indeed not only feasible but also compatible with high growth and employment.

Although there are many similarities between welfare state arrangements around the world, there are two main characteristics differentiating the Scandinavian model from others. First, the level of public spending entailing both consumption and transfer payments to the households have tended to be higher than in other countries, and consequently also taxes. Second, the model is "universal," meaning that all citizens are eligible, irrespective of their income, to the transfers and services provided by the public sector.

Very few public programs are means tested and most income security programs are related to the insured earnings. Millionaires also get parental leave benefits, daycare for their children or home nursing care when they get older. This of course makes the welfare state programs more expensive compared to the means tested counterparts, but it broadens the political support for the programs. And the rich get something back from their contributions to welfare state programs. This is the cornerstone of the political sustainability of the Scandinavian type welfare state, that the self-interest of the majority of the population is captured by the design of the core programs.

It is obvious that the build-up of the Scandinavian welfare state was not consciously planned to follow any "great design." The "model" is instead a result of a historical process which continues to be extensively studied and debated in both academic and policy circles. The ability of strong labor movements to form broad coalitions with other interest groups in society has been an important and common driver behind the expansion and explains part of the resilience of the social model.

In Sweden this divergent "Scandinavian" process can be seen as taken place in two phases. The first phase, which started in the beginning of the 20th century, ending in the mid-1960s, included different income security programs. In 1913, Sweden introduced the first old-age pension program in the world with universal inclusion of all citizens. The disability insurance program, which initially was a part of the old-age pension system, became much more generous when the supplementary pension program (ATP) was introduced after a referendum in 1957. A universal sick pay insurance program, replacing forgone earnings due to temporary health deficiencies, was introduced in 1955.

The second phase, starting in the mid-1960s and peaking in the 1970s, was focused on family policy. An important starting point is the income tax reform introducing separate taxation of spouses in 1969. This radically changed the incentive for women to take up a job on the regular labor market and increased female labor force participation. Throughout the 1970s municipality daycare was built up and subsequently included more than 90 percent of all children in the age groups 1 to 6. Also the parental leave program was introduced and extended in this era.

A common feature of the policy models both in the pension area and when it comes to family policy is the employment orientation. This is important not least of all for the economic sustainability of the model. How can social policy be employment friendly? First of all, universal programs do not create the kind of poverty traps that means tested programs are plagued with. Secondly, earnings related social insurance programs create incentives to become a taxpayer simply because the more tax you pay the better insured you will be. A more meticulous analysis of the incentive structure of the Swedish pension system shows that it rewards employment much better as compared to other countries. The fact that employment levels among 60–65 year olds are higher—and on the increase—than almost any other country in the Western hemisphere should not come as a surprise. The effectiveness of universal pensions to alleviate poverty in old-age is a common Scandinavian experience.

The family policy area follows the same logic. Universal child benefits are combined with earnings-related parental leave benefits. The combination of universal access to subsidized day care for infants makes it possible for women, and men for that matter, to combine market work with caring responsibilities. The tax system based on individual taxation, not joint taxation of spouse income, provides economic incentives for what can be labelled a "dual earner model," which is nowadays part and parcel of the Swedish welfare state model. The expansion of female labor force participation may be a universal phenomenon in the world but, Swedish policy reforms not only spurred this but also helped reverse the falling birth rates that went hand in hand with women's increased presence in the workforce. Universal benefits are effective in terms of reducing child poverty, but so is having two earners in the family.

The Swedish welfare state model is subject to recurrent challenges and policy changes. The big pension reform in 1994–98 is one obvious example. While it maintained the old social policy objective of eradication of poverty and providing retired workers with income security, it strengthened work incentives further by introducing a defined contribution formula, which is in addition is a strong measure of cost control. The social services have also been reformed: while tax funding has been maintained, different choice models have been introduced accompanied by privatization of provisions. These changes can be seen as an attempt to deal with the critique of the model, but have at the same time implied new kinds of problems in terms of segregation and quality control. Popular sentiments have turned against private for-profit seeking firms.

Globalization is taking its toll in terms of tax competition and Sweden has followed the downward trends in terms of taxing capital. This suggests that the continued international economic integration is putting restrictions on how taxes can be levied. In addition, Sweden has now been a member of the EU (European Union) for 20 years. This may have led to few, but important direct policy changes. The Swedish labor market model is under pressure not only from increased labor migration but also by the friction between the Swedish model which is based on collective bargaining, and a European system that is much more guided by legislative intervention.

The Swedish model has survived several crises. In the early 1990s, Sweden experience negative growth three years in a row, employment fell by 500,000, unemployment rose from 1 to above 8 percent and moreover the share of the labor force that was engaged in active labor market policy programs increased from 2 to 6 percent. The public finances were running a 13 percent deficit in 1994. Though fiscal policies (meaning benefit cuts and tax increases across the board) helped to restore the trust in the Swedish economy, thus the architecture of the welfare state remained largely the same. The country was also well prepared when the Global Financial Crisis was hitting the economy hard in 2009. The public finances were in better shape and there was a blueprint for dealing with the financial institutions.

The refugee-crisis of 2015 is not a unique Swedish phenomenon but the number of refugees per capita has consistently been higher than in almost any other European country. This is putting new pressure on the Swedish welfare state. However, migration is not a new thing. Labor migration was of crucial importance for the Swedish growth miracle in the 1960s. The percentage of foreign born residents in the Swedish population has been on par with the U.S. for decades. These changes have not been without friction but the support for the welfare state has not been shaken by it, despite strong expectations of negative consequences from increased heterogeneity of the population.

We are also living in what can be called "the shadow of a coming crisis:" the aging of the population. The changes in the age structure will put increasing pressures on intergenerational redistribution. Migration is unlikely to solve this problem because both of the magnitude of the change and the fact that migrants also get older. Yet population aging is not a specific Swedish problem and the comparatively high fertility rates in Sweden will result in a more stable population development than in most other EU countries. This is also related to the future challenge of the Swedish welfare state model: how to secure the future tax base of the welfare state by investing in the people.

After the Tragedy:
Reflections on Norwegian Values

Henrik Syse

"…in the face of tragedy, we do say something about ourselves, and Norway tragically had the opportunity to do so after July 22, 2011."

We keep hearing of them. But what are actually Scandinavian or Nordic values? Or, for that matter, what are "Norwegian" values? Are they merely a pious figment of the imagination—a façade shown to outsiders alongside pretty pictures of fjords, valleys and mountains, but hardly representative of daily life? Or are they real, living constituents of the life actually led in the distant north?

In a modern, fast-changing and increasingly heterogeneous society, it is exceedingly hard to pinpoint such values with any accuracy or great general legitimacy, whether we are talking about Norway or any other nation. As technology, migration and political change impact all modern societies, saying that a nation "is" like this or that will inevitably be inaccurate and simplistic.

Yet Norway, along with the other Scandinavian and Nordic countries, remains relatively speaking peaceful, prosperous and stable. It is furthermore right to say that most individuals who call themselves Norwegians harbor an understanding of their own society that reflects the values of peacefulness and stability, whether or not they actively support those values.

Hence, an attempt at understanding and analyzing the values of Norwegian society, while inevitably inaccurate, does remain a study of something that has at least some kind of mental and communal existence. Let me, in my capacity as a philosopher and social science researcher, try to contribute my reflections on a few of those values, with all due humility and accompanying brevity.

Adversity and Values

My point of departure for these reflections will be the claim that moments of great adversity help us spell out our deepest values, by which I mean our most important guiding principles. We can think of many examples of "spelling out" from history, from the trials and tribulations of Abraham Lincoln and Winston Churchill, to the Nuremberg trials, or Eleanor Roosevelt and her committee's work on the Universal Declaration of Human Rights in the wake of World War II. All contributed crucial value statements that spelled out what can help us stand together, create and maintain resilience and move ahead in the midst of—or in the wake of—shocking events. Values are easily, probably too easily, taken for granted until one is called on by unusual turns of events to spell them out and hopefully also "live" them in practice.

Such a moment of adversity came to Norway on July 22, 2011. On that summer day, Anders Behring Breivik, a then 32-year-old self-styled crusader and defender of Nordic and European civilization, detonated a powerful bomb at the main government building in the center of Oslo, killing eight people and injuring many others (the death toll not being even higher mainly due to the Norwegian summer vacation). Thereafter, he traveled to the small Utøya Island outside of Oslo and massacred 69 mostly young people at a Labor Party youth camp before giving himself up to the police. The mass killings, constituting the worst armed attack on Norwegian soil since World War II, created an immediate outpouring of grief and solidarity in more or less the entire country. During the aftermath of the horrific events, political and other public figures made stirring speeches defending that society and those values, which Breivik had so brutally attacked.

In a research project I am leading at PRIO (Peace Research Institute Oslo), in collaboration with the two Norwegian Universities of Oslo and Agder and the University of California at Los Angeles (UCLA), we have attempted to analyze values that were regularly mentioned as crucial in the aftermath of the July 22 terror attacks. By calling them crucial, I think of the fact that many Norwegians in their public expressions after the tragedy saw them as foundational to the sort of society that Norway ideally should be. It was at the heart of this very foundation that Breivik's attacks had struck.

The perceived need to defend and restore these foundational values arguably represented, and continues to represent, a deeply held common intuition in Norway that without these values we stand in danger of losing the stability and peace that together are hallmarks of Norwegian society.

Democracy, Openness and Humanity

Prime Minister Jens Stoltenberg's main message in the immediate aftermath of the July 22 massacres was heavily concentrated around values. Three key values recurred in his statements: democracy, openness and humanity, as he insisted that on the one hand we should never be naïve, but that on the other, vigilance and lack of naivety must not imply that we abandon our most basic values for the sake of security and defense.

In my view, the three values of democracy, openness and humanity can be seen as serving a dual purpose.

First, these are normative ideals; that is, statements about how things ought to be. Even if we do not always live up to them or consciously let them guide our actions, they represent a set of attitudes and character traits that we want to strive for, and that we want to tell the world about as we are hit by terror and sorrow. They are part of a collective identity that Norwegians, in all their plurality and heterogeneity, should rally around.

Second, these values also, arguably, characterize a certain aspect of the everyday lived reality of Norway and Norwegians. They put into words not only the way in which Norway would ideally like to see itself, but also the way in which Norwegian institutions and ways of life actually function. A good illustration is the annual celebration of Constitution Day, May 17. On that day, these three are in many ways the core values are both celebrated and displayed.

The Constitution, while in its original 1814 form certainly not fully democratic (suffrage for instance, being quite limited), is clearly based on an idea of democratic, popular sovereignty, combined with a constitutional monarchy and separation of powers. The fact that the Constitution was modern and liberal for its time, that it has endured ever since, albeit with several amendments, and that it remains a living part of the day-to-day life of several public Norwegian democratic institutions—most importantly the Storting (Parliament)—surely makes it right to say that democracy stands as a pillar of Norwegian society, and of the May 17 celebration.

May 17, in many ways like the Utøya camp, also stands as a testament to the second of the three values mentioned: openness. One of the most natural responses to terrorist attacks in particular, and political and societal uncertainty in general, consists in security and vigilance: more checks, more stop-and-search policing, and more suspicion. "Report anything that is suspicious." "Strange behaviors must be reported." When that occurs, the openness and tolerance that ought to dominate interaction in a pluralistic, rule-of-law and rights-based democracy gradually come to be replaced by strictures and fear. The ideal that Mr. Stoltenberg wanted to stress when confronted with the July 22 terror, was one that would not fall prey to such tendencies. We see the same, at least ideally, on May 17, with inclusive children's parades and an emphasis on institutions opening up to the public (such as Parliament and the monarchy appearing in public to greet the children) and low-threshold, open community celebrations. This may all seem trivial, and it is certainly easy to make fun of (and even to feel left out of), but it is certainly reflective of something seen as highly important to many Norwegians.

Finally, humanity was put forth as a third value that ought to characterize Norway's response to the terror. This can be interpreted in several different ways: as compassion and solidarity, as the opposite of anger and revenge, or as a form of global consciousness, which makes us realize that ours are not the only problems or afflictions of the world, no matter how grave. Hence, such events as July 22 should help us remember and embrace the challenges of humanity at large, not just our part of it. On May 17, this comes out in an emphasis on rule of law and individual, universal rights, both being central components of the constitutional values celebrated.

A Nordic or Global Way?

Using this brief analysis as our starting-point, we may ask: Are these rightly to be called "Norwegian (or Nordic) values," or are they much more correctly designated as "universal values?" After all, democracy, openness and humanity (or humane behavior) are surely not Norwegian inventions or purely Norwegian or Nordic hallmarks.

The easy, yet complex answer is of course that they are both: they are Norwegian *and* universal.

That is an easy and almost obvious answer, since these values are after all taken from a liberal tradition, which is not Norwegian per se, yet to which Norwegian modern culture clearly belongs, a tradition that espouses the universality of its core values, while not denying that they are locally appropriated and formed. However, it is more complex than that, since the formulation of such values in the wake of the 2011 terror were consciously meant to say something about Norway, not about the whole world. This is especially clear in the face of Breivik's terror, since Breivik wanted to stand forth as a representative of real "Norwegianness," against immigration, pluralism and social democracy. This demanded a Norwegian response.

This tension between the local (Norwegian) and the global (universal) aspect of values is, in my view, mirrored importantly by some tensions that are inherent in each of these three values. Or put differently: In order to better understand what these values truly represent, it is useful to analyze each of these values with their in-built tensions.

Let us start with democracy and openness. In a country such as Norway, these two values represent a meeting, and indeed a tension, between modernity and tradition. On the one hand, an open, participatory democracy is subject to change and new impulses, and these are represented in everyday life as voices that may challenge and change tradition. This is an inherent part of modern life. On the other hand, these values are rooted in a tradition. They have been fashioned in particularly Norwegian ways. Constitution Day celebrations may be a possibly mundane, yet in their way an important expression of this. My colleague Marta Bivand Erdal has recently written about a local Labor Party politician who had bought a traditional Norwegian folk costume ("bunad") fitted with a matching hijab. She and the manufacturer got targeted by threats. The subsequent media storm and social media reactions came down on either side of the question about whether it is okay to add a hijab to the Norwegian folk costume. What does this strong debate about something seemingly quite unimportant say about Norwegian democracy and openness?

This tension can be likened to that of a close-knit family faced with new in-laws. All the values of the original family unit are open to the arrival of those in-laws, not least since one has always celebrated the virtues of family, marriage and inclusion. Yet that very enlargement comes with the arrival of the unknown, of new ways and of other human beings with their strong opinions and traditions. Not all will remain as it was, *but that is exactly what those values to which one expresses deep allegiance have to allow, in order to remain alive and relevant.*

Breivik's view of the Norwegian and the European is, in all its brutal, twisted and violence-bloated logic, mainly static. Nothing new or foreign should be allowed. There once existed a golden age of purity and stability, which must be regained, if necessary by terror. The arrival of foreign mores, religious views and ways of life upon Norwegian shores challenges this original and superior way of life. Real greatness thus lies in the past. That past must be recaptured, according to this view, and modernity's illusions of tolerance, pluralism, and goodwill must be dispelled.

The emphasis on democracy and openness in the wake of July 22, 2011 was meant to counter this way of understanding Norway and what it means to be Norwegian. Stoltenberg and a host of other public figures hence challenged the reactionary and deeply enclosed worldview of Breivik—and thereby the worldview of all those who attack others with violence in the name of pure ideologies.

Yet the values of democracy and openness are themselves historically and culturally situated, and they at least partially do represent something from the past that we are called upon to defend. They are, in other words, neither abstract nor purely modern or global. They are enshrined in Norwegian laws, customs, tradition and language. Even if we view them as representative of higher, transcendent ideals—and there are many reasons to do so—they are practically speaking the result of a concrete historical development. And that historical development must somehow be safeguarded. Through educational and cultural institutions, budget allocations and all manner of public statements and happenings, Norwegian values are indeed cultivated and secured, even enshrined, in monuments, laws and practices. If someone wanted to use flags of foreign nations in the May 17 parade, for example, or sing foreign national or religious hymns, they would not be allowed to do so (most likely by the local committee in charge of the parade). To be Norwegian means to accept certain common behaviors, and to take part in them or at least not to hinder them. We may, of course, negotiate about what falls within and what falls outside; a bunad with a hijab would fall within and foreign flags and hymns would fall outside of those boundaries. Where those boundaries lie is not a given and must constantly be renegotiated, but that does not mean that the underlying values are unimportant or arbitrary. Most would say that they are indeed important. And they would add that if there is no willingness to back them up and defend them, there is also no way in which they will remain alive and meaningful.

And hence we are confronted with what we may call a basic tension within those values that make up Norwegian and Nordic ways. They are universal in the sense that, to a large extent, they come from and find close parallels in other parts of the world. And they are open to the manifold differences that our pluralistic, ever-changing world exhibits. But at the same time they are particular and local in the sense that they are stamped by decades and centuries of "Norwegianness." Hence, they cannot simply be changed at will or be removed from their context without losing some crucial part of their meaning.

This leads us to the final of the three values that I have focused on: humanity. As indicated above, it is a value with many aspects to it. It stresses our common humanity as human beings—that we are humans first and nationals of a country second. It stresses compassion and solidarity and asks us not to be brutal or in other ways inhumane towards others. In what ways does this value characterize Norway? In the wake of July 22, the emphasis when talking about this value was clearly on togetherness and on taking part in of and respecting the grief that so many felt vividly and personally. However, I would claim that this value is just as much about "not losing oneself." In the face of tragedy, an angry wish to exact revenge easily and naturally comes to the fore. Rejecting such feelings and not losing one's essential humanity can thus be a hard task. Stressing the value of humanity is a way of saying that we must not lose ourselves to rash and hateful emotions in the face of terror and brutality.

It is often said of Norwegians, accurately or inaccurately, that we are somewhat Stoic, to use a designation from ancient Greek philosophy (or decidedly Lutheran, to use a designation closer to home). We are not prone to huge mood swings or outbursts of emotion, for good and ill. In this context, maybe what Jens Stoltenberg wanted to express after July 22 was that even in the greatest sorrow and deepest tragedy, during which we weep and cry to the heavens, we still maintain that basic humanity which makes us what we are, and which stops us from descending into actions or feelings that we will afterwards regret. This may be a universal aspiration, yet there is also something decidedly Norwegian about it.

Conclusion

The aim of this short article has in no way been to glorify certain Norwegian or Nordic values or character traits. Every quality described can be found in various shapes and forms across cultures and nations. Yet, in the face of tragedy, we do say something about ourselves, and Norway tragically had the opportunity to do so after July 22, 2011. Therefore, the aftermath of those events did say something about Norway.

My theme has been values. What is a value? A value in the sense of this article can best be defined as something that has action- and emotion-guided meaning; that is, something that guides how we act and think, and I would add, something that in order to qualify as a value proper, has a certain stability and longevity.

Norwegian and Nordic values, like all values, are constantly being negotiated and subjected to change and challenge. They are not unique to one country, nor are they given for all time. But the tragedy of July 22, 2011—a tragedy sadly repeated around the world many times over—helped Norway formulate some of those values more explicitly than what would otherwise have been the case. It is too early to say whether this has had a lasting effect on our society; many fear that it has not. But either way, the thought processes and ideas surrounding these values are worth revisiting and analyzing. Through such an analysis we come to see the tensions inherent within each of these values, and how important they remain to a living, tolerant and peaceful society.

How to Make It in the Nordics

Petter Stordalen

"It was humiliating. Humbling. Horrible. I was a failure, and I hated it. But, I did have something to show for it."

My hometown, Porsgrunn, is a small city a few miles outside of Oslo. In 1974 I was 12 and working in my dad's grocery store. I scrubbed the floors, worked the cash register and sold strawberries at the local market. I loved selling strawberries, but sometimes I would look at the other sellers and envy them because they had larger berries and nicer sales stands than mine. One day when the unfairness of this hit me particularly hard, I did what every ambitious businessman would do. I went to my dad to complain.

"Son," he said, "you have to sell the berries you have, because they are the only ones you can sell."

Lying in bed that night I had my first "Eureka" moment. I realized that if I spent my time and energy focusing on what other people were doing with their given opportunities, I would never improve. What I needed to do was focus on getting the most out of the opportunities given to me. I needed to sell the berries I had, because those were the only berries I could sell. Later that summer, the local newspaper gave me the unofficial title of Norway's best strawberry salesman.

Since that day my father's words, which I call the Strawberry Philosophy, have guided my every move in business. The Strawberry Philosophy is not revolutionary. But it is genius in explaining in a simple way (that even a 12-year-old can understand) the concept of working with what you've got. And the people of the Nordic countries understand this concept well.

You have probably heard of brands like Statoil, Jotun, Yara and of course Norwegian Salmon. Norway has a strong engineering tradition and was blessed with an abundance of natural resources such as oil and fish. We have been extremely lucky, there's no denying it, but we have also managed our assets very well. The Swedes, on the other hand, did not strike oil, but their knack for design and tech development has proven to be a goldmine. Ikea, H&M, Ericsson, Spotify and Volvo are just some examples of their success. The Danes can claim shipping mastodon Maersk; "Probably the best beer in the world," Carlsberg; and one of the world's biggest pharmaceutical companies, Novo Nordisk. Meanwhile, the Finns have revolutionized communications technology with Nokia.

In many important ways, the Nordic countries differ. But we have all become wealthy nations. I believe this is because resourceful inhabitants have assessed the opportunities available and created their own competitive advantages. Or, as my father would say: we have sold the berries we have.

Failing is the First Step to Success

In 1992, at the age of 28, I was presented with a historic opportunity: Steen & Strøm. Steen & Strøm is the oldest department store in Norway, so old and prestigious it could have fathered Harrods in London. Triple-A location. Smack in the middle of the Norwegian capital. It had Norway's first coffee bar, first escalator and first high fashion store. The whole building was oozing with that sense of prestige that only more than 200 years of continuous success can give you. There was just one problem: Steen & Strøm was bankrupt and desperately needed saving.

Bringing Steen & Strøm from failure to success was the biggest turn-around operation of my life. It was also my first real breakthrough in the Norwegian business world. Soon, Steen & Strøm was the largest listed shopping mall company in Scandinavia. I was CEO and president. The employees were thriving. We had fun. And we made money. A lot! And right at that time, the richest man in Norway and the majority owner of Steen & Strøm called me into his office, and fired me.

It was humiliating. Humbling. Horrible. I was a failure, and I hated it. But, I did have something to show for it. I had some money, a bankrupt hotel, and a choice. I could take my money and retire with my family, or I could invest some of it. Both, very real alternatives. But there was a third option. I could risk it all. I made a plan and I went to investors and the press to present it. I told them, "In ten years we will be the biggest hotel business in Scandinavia." The room went quiet. Then a reporter asked this one simple question: "How many hotels do you actually have?"

"One," I said.

"Which is bankrupt," he answered. And everyone laughed.

But, not for long. Today, Nordic Choice Hotels is one of the largest hotel chains in the Nordics. We have 185 hotels in six countries, 13,000 employees and annual revenue of about 1.2 billion USD.

Failing is a part of business. Risking everything is a part of business. At the same time, risking it all is extremely daunting, especially if you have a family to take care of. Most people won't do it. Human psychology suggests we are risk-averse, and generally speaking, we will accept a lower payoff that is certain over a higher payoff that is uncertain. On an individual level, that is fine. But if everyone played it safe, there would be no growth.

My story is in no way unique, you can scale it up or down, but the prospect of losing everything is intimidating no matter how much you have to begin with. People who are willing to take risks are crucial for growth, and in my experience, failure is inevitable on the path to success. The social safety nets and welfare systems of the Nordic countries provide *some* insurance should everything go wrong. This might explain why Sweden is the second most fruitful tech start-up hub in the world per capita, or why, according to Creandum's Nordic Exit Analysis 2015, in the last 10 years the Nordic region has accounted for almost 10 percent of all global tech exits, trailing only the U.S. and China. Lessening the ramifications of a worst-case scenario—where you lose everything—encourages more people to take risks, invest more and grasp opportunities.

In the Eyes of the World, We Are All Vikings

Foreign media have spent a surprising amount of time covering Norway lately. The world is curious about Norwegian music, art, architecture, history, nature—even our capital, Oslo. Swedes and Danes are experiencing the same thing. The explanation is simple. What is in style are the Nordic countries, not Norway in particular. In the eyes of the world we are all Vikings and, luckily, Vikings are more popular than ever.

Swedish and Danish actors have opened the door for Norwegians, just as Swedish and Danish music and architecture will be vital for establishing international interest in their Norwegian counterparts. The same concept goes for tourism. International travellers do not want to spend their holiday in either Norway or Sweden or Finland. The Nordics as one destination, on the other hand, can offer top international attractions such as Santa Clause, fjords, the northern lights, geysers and saunas. Similarly, foreign investors are hesitant to invest in a market of five million people (like Norway's), but the Nordic region's 25 million are far more interesting.

And yet, there is surprisingly little cross-border cooperation. When Nordic Choice Hotels became a Nordic company in 2003 with its first Swedish hotel, Clarion Hotel Stockholm, many commented that it would be difficult for a Norwegian company to get ahead in "big brother's" market. Today, Sweden is our biggest and most profitable market, and I am certain I did the right thing by not listening to the sceptics. Scandinavians are more alike than we think, and we need to take advantage of that. Three words describe what we have in common. We are honest, honourable and effective. Those qualities are a competitive advantage in international terms. Also, the flat structure of Nordic companies enables us to make quick decisions, and Norwegians, Swedes, Finns and Danes work well together. The Danes say what they mean—no filter, no fuzz. The Swedes value process and have a strong meeting culture, while the Norwegians are more impatient and want things done fast. Yes, we are different, but there is great potential in combining these differences and making them pull in the same direction.

Conclusion

The Nordic countries are special. We are among the wealthiest and most educated nations in the world, and have an abundance of natural resources that would make any nation envious. We have managed these resources well, but we have also successfully exploited windows of opportunity in areas that cannot be ascribed to geographic luck.

Our political systems are built on social democratic principles and a robust welfare system. These institutions provide social safety for inhabitants of the Nordic countries, which may increase individual willingness to take risks, and in turn help explain the region's high number of start-ups.

Finally, people of the Nordic countries have unique, different and complementary strengths that combined are a great source of untapped potential. We work well together, but we need to see ourselves as one to a much greater extent, at least in a market perspective. Cross-border consolidation is inevitable, and future business successes will come from actors who are able to take advantage of our similarities and ability to cooperate. These actors might be Nordic, and they might be foreign. One thing is certain, if the Nordic countries do not think in a Nordic perspective international companies will do it for us.

Industrial Foundations—
The Danish Model

Steen Thomsen

"Industrial foundations are socially responsible by design in that most have a charitable purpose, and in principle aim to own their companies in perpetuity."

In this short paper we take a look at a governance arrangement that is unique to Denmark: charitable foundations that own business firms or *"industrial foundations"* as some call them. Other terms in the literature are *"enterprise foundations," "corporate foundations" or "commercial foundations,"* but note that these are not entities established by a company for Corporate Social Responsibility (CSR) purposes, but controlling owners of those companies. Throughout we will use the example of the brewery Carlsberg, which is majority-owned by the Carlsberg foundation.

What are Industrial Foundations?

Industrial foundations are foundations that own business companies. The foundations are independent legal entities governed by a board under a charter written by the founder and supervised by a government regulator, known as the foundation authority. Most have a charitable purpose but some aim for the benefit of a particular company or founding family. They are created through donations by wealthy entrepreneurs motivated by the same ideals as Bill Gates, Warren Buffet or Mark Zuckerberg; although in practice most of them are quite small. The main difference with the U.S. is that Nordic industrial foundations continue to hold shares in the founder's former company. Dividends from the company fund the philanthropy.

Some world-famous companies like Robert Bosch, Ikea, the Tata Group or U.S. Hershey are owned in this way, but the structure is particularly common in Denmark, where the three largest Danish companies—Novo Nordisk, A. P. Moeller Maersk, Carlsberg—and many other prominent businesses—have a foundation as the main controlling shareholder. Foundation-owned/controlled companies account for about 70 percent of market capitalization, 50 percent of research and development (R&D), 10 percent of value added, and 5 percent of employment in Denmark. In Sweden, foundations control the two leading business "spheres" (loosely connected business groups) – the Wallenberg and Handelsbanken Spheres, which at one point were said to own half of the country.

Industrial foundations also play a role in Norway where foundations own DNV (a large insurance company), a number of savings and loans associations (including Gjensidiga, an insurance company), the Thon Group (a hotel and property Group) and Kavli (a food producer). To the best of our knowledge we have not been able to find examples in Finland or Iceland, which appear to be closer to the U.S. in this respect. Therefore, it is probably more correct to define industrial foundations as a Danish phenomenon than as a part of a generic Nordic corporate governance model.

One may wonder why industrial foundations are so common in the Nordics but virtually unknown in the United States. Actually they were quite common in the U.S. until 1969 when it was decided to put a stop to them through heavy fines on foundations with controlling influence on companies (Thomsen 2016). Today, U.S. corporate governance reflects political decisions rather than economic fundamentals. The prominence of industrial foundations in the Nordics (Denmark, Sweden) may have been partly motivated by high wealth taxes, which founders of these companies could avoid by establishing foundations. However, a strong desire to give back to society also played a prominent role. In fact, most of the large industrial Danish foundations were established before wealth taxes were introduced and rose to very high levels in the 1970s. Visionary founders creating new institutions were evident in the early history of many industrial foundations. Of note, is the early example of

Carlsberg, one of the world's oldest industrial foundations, which created a role model for other entrepreneurs to follow.

The Example of Carlsberg

In 1876, J.C. Jacobsen, the founder of Carlsberg, donated his brewery to a foundation that he established. This donation was motivated by his belief in science and innovation and his wish to give back to society. He asked the Royal Danish Academy of Science and Letters to select five professors to govern the foundation and thereby also the Carlsberg brewery. The purpose of the Carlsberg Foundation was, and is, twofold: to ensure that the Carlsberg Brewery Group is well managed; and to support basic research within the natural sciences, social sciences and humanities. Today, the Carlsberg Foundation still owns 30.3 percent of the shares and 76.5 percent of the votes in the Carlsberg Group (the difference being attributable to a dual class stock structure in which one share class has more voting rights.) J.C. Jacobsen also established the Carlsberg Research Laboratory as a research department of the foundation.

This type of visionary leadership would be necessary if the United States were to adopt industrial foundations by changing the law. However, the recent example of Mark Zuckerberg and Facebook shows that U.S. business leaders have what it takes. Facebook comes as close as possible to foundation ownership within the confines of U.S. law. According to the plan, the voting rights (control) of Facebook are to be held by the founding family, while the cash flow (dividend) will go to a foundation.

How Does Foundation Ownership Work?

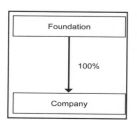

In principle, foundation ownership is simple: the foundation owns a business company as shown in this diagram.

Of course many nuances and variations exist. For example, the foundation may not own all of the stock, some may be owned by other / minority investors and part of the shares stock may even be listed and publicly traded. The foundation may (or may not) retain voting control by dual class shares by holding on to shares with stronger voting rights, while shares with few or no voting rights are issued to the public. This is particularly common in Sweden and Denmark. In some cases, like in the Tata Group, the stock may be held by several independent foundations. There may also be a holding company in between the foundation and its operating company, and there may be more than one operating company.

Industrial foundations will typically have two objectives: to be a responsible owner/principle controller of a company and to use company dividends to give back to society for philanthropic and charitable purposes. Industrial foundations distribute less than other foundations per dollar of assets, but in the long run this is more than compensated for by the growth of the asset base. Most of the donations are given to research and education, but art and social projects are also important causes. Because of the industrial foundations, private Danish foundation support for R&D is the highest in Europe.

Depending on the charter, it may be that the business objective outweighs charitable giving, which may be secondary or altogether absent. However, it may also be that the foundation is formally purely charitable and just happens to own a business. In any case, industrial foundations tend to take their ownership obligations very seriously, as often requested by the Founder, and its goals are clearly spelled out in the charter of the Foundation.

A Long-Term Ownership Model

Industrial foundations are true long-term owners. They rarely, if ever, sell their shares. Thus foundation-owned companies are not plagued by the increasingly ephemeral nature of stock ownership, which has led to a rapid decline in average holding periods along with the associated risks.

Occasionally, of course, foundations in distress may be forced to dilute their shares to attract outside equity, or the foundation may be persuaded that a merger is in the company's best long-term interest. Carlsberg is a good illustration of this. A series of charter changes in the Carlsberg foundation enabled Carlsberg to take part in a joint venture with Norwegian company Orkla, and to participate in a joint venture with Heineken to acquire the Scottish brewery group, Scottish & Newcastle. This enabled the company to become much larger. It is now the third largest in the world.

Research and Development

Another indication of the long-term approach is research and development. Foundation-owned firms tend to be more research intensive, both because they tend to do more research than their competitors and because they cluster in research intensive industries.

The Carlsberg Research Laboratory was created as an integrated department of the Carlsberg Foundation. It was at this laboratory in 1883 that Professor Emil Christian Hansen produced the first pure yeast for lager beer in the world. However, it was decided not to patent this invention, but to make it available to everyone. This open innovation approach meant that the lager yeast, named—you might have guessed it—Carlsbergensis, was shared with brewers around Europe. Today 90 percent of all lager beer in the world is based on the pure yeast from Carlsberg.

Foundation-owned companies tend to survive longer. While financial owners are concerned mainly with financial returns, foundations value the survival of the company as an independent entity. Carlsberg is now close to 170 years old. Few companies survive that long.

Surprisingly, the foundation-owned firms are able to combine their long-term approach with good financial results. Profitability in foundation-owned firms is comparable to, or better than, other privately owned companies, especially in large firms and for the sector as a whole (Thomsen 2016). However, small foundation-owned firms tend to underperform, presumably because the benefits of a long-term approach are modest if they are too poor to invest in the future.

Social Responsibility

Industrial foundations are socially responsible by design in that most have a charitable purpose, and in principle aim to own their companies in perpetuity. As philanthropic institutions, they sponsor research, education, the arts, social projects and other worthy causes. Except for distributions to minority investors, profits in foundation-owned firms are either reinvested or paid out as donations. For example, all dividends paid out on the Carlsberg Foundation's shares in Carlsberg are given back to philanthropic activities by the Foundation to support basic fundamental research, art, cultural and voluntary activities and the environment.

To be sure, this does not mean that they do not face the same moral dilemmas as other corporations. For example, some tobacco companies are also foundation-owned. Carlsberg, the company, produces alcoholic beverages which some would see as immoral. However, as argued by Professor Henry Hansmann of Yale Law School the absence of a personal profit motive may make foundations and their companies less likely to pursue short-run, opportunistic strategies.

What Are the Weaknesses?

Despite the many important advantages to foundation-ownership, industrial foundations are real world institutions with weaknesses as well as benefits.

First, they are relatively rare since they require the ultimate economic sacrifice by the founder-entrepreneurs who voluntarily and irrevocably give away most or at least a substantial part of their wealth to the foundation. Not everyone is so philanthropically inclined.

Second, renunciation of the personal profit motive places great responsibility on the foundation board. Industrial foundations require first-class board members to succeed—people who are not primarily motivated by money, but still have a talent for business. The structure is relatively robust and not all board members have to be geniuses, but it can be difficult to replace a board that is malfunctioning.

Third, foundation ownership may slow the growth of the company because foundations desire to retain control, which makes foundation-owned companies reluctant to issue new equity. Their financial conservatism may in turn result in risk aversion and reluctance to borrow. Some would claim for example, that Carlsberg fell asleep for a while and let its grasp of the global brewing industry slip.

Fourth, most companies are started by entrepreneurs rather than foundations. The foundation structure is less appropriate for start-ups, i.e., the creation part of creative destruction. And foundations are not too good at closing down the companies they are designed to sustain. So, they are probably at their best in the middle-adult stage of the corporate life cycle, which is the continuation and growth of the company.

Fortunately, despite a few bad examples, most industrial foundations manage this phase well. And it is important to remember other ownership structures have weaknesses of their own, for example the succession problem in family businesses which the foundation structure solves in an elegant way, or the short-term approach and free rider problems of companies with diffuse ownership.

A Model for the Future

Industrial foundations are a blueprint of what capitalism can become, if it is freed from the ideology of shareholder value. It could be more responsible and sustainable, provide better checks and balances and control the problem of executive pay. It could have broader vision and contribute more to society. It can even paradoxically generate higher returns to shareholders. All that is required for legislators is to allow high-spirited founders to set up foundations that own business companies.

This will not, and should not, change society overnight. The vast majority of businesses will always remain owned by individuals, families or financial investors. Few people have what it takes to give away most of their wealth. But this approach can introduce a modicum of altruism into the business community and create role models for other companies to follow.

3.

The Nordic Social-Economic Way to Ensure Childhood Development, Quality Education and Healthcare

What is social democracy and how does that define and institutionalize the unique Nordic relationship between citizen and state? How has this commitment across all sectors of society to universal and quality education and healthcare been instilled into the very fabric of Nordic society? In an era of increasing heterogeneous populations and an aging society how will education and healthcare adapt and find new ways to address new challenges?

Language and Culture Link Us Together

Auður
Hauksdóttir

Jørn
Lund

Ulla
Börestam

"In recent decades the growing use of English as a lingua franca in an international context and the prominent status that the language enjoys in Nordic universities has become to some extent a threat for the Nordic language community, as shown by the fact that many Nordic youngsters tend to use English at the cost of neighbor languages."

The Nordic countries or "Norden" include the five nations Denmark, Finland, Iceland, Norway and Sweden as well as the autonomous territories of the Faroe Islands, Greenland and Åland, plus the Saami regions. Within this area three linguistic families are represented, if we limit the scope to "native" languages and their standard forms.

1. Nordic languages include Danish, Faroese, Icelandic, Norwegian (bokmål and nynorsk) and Swedish,

2. Finnish and Saami are Finno-Ugric languages,

3. While Greenlandic is classified as an Eskimo-Aleut language.

A total of over 27 million people live in the Nordic countries today, and this article deals with their intensive language and cultural contact, which is characteristic of the area. The Nordic region comprises a multilingual community, where some 200 non-Nordic languages are also spoken (Declaration on a Nordic Language Policy 2007:11)[1]. The majority of the population knows one of the Nordic languages; Danish, Norwegian or Swedish, either as a mother tongue, as a second language, or as a foreign language. These three Scandinavian languages are closely related and therefore potentially mutually intelligible. Each of them is referred to as a *neighbor language*, for example, Danish and Norwegian are neighbor languages for a Swedish speaker. When we speak of a *Nordic language community* and *understanding of neighbor languages* it is therefore the use of these three languages to which we refer.

The Declaration on a Nordic Language Policy

Article 8 of the Helsinki Treaty of 1962, the original basis of Nordic cooperation, stipulates a number of obligations on each country's educational authorities. "Educational provision in the schools of each of the Nordic countries shall include an appropriate measure of instruction on the languages, cultures and general social conditions of the other Nordic countries, including the Faroe Islands, Greenland and the Åland Islands." Although the Treaty has only been implemented to a limited extent, it also forms the background for the adoption of the Nordic Language Policy in 2006, the most important document in this field for decades.

According to the Declaration, Nordic residents are entitled "to acquire an understanding and knowledge of a Scandinavian language and comprehension of the other Scandinavian languages enabling them to participate in the Nordic language community." In addition, they are entitled to acquire a language with international diffusion, enabling them to participate in the development of the international community (Declaration on a Nordic Language Policy 2007:12). There are large variations as to whether and to what extent instruction in neighbor Nordic languages is offered in Nordic schools. In those schools where neighbor language instruction is provided in Denmark, Norway and Sweden, it is typically part of language arts, i.e. mother tongue instruction. In contrast, Danish is a mandatory foreign language subject in the Faroes, Greenland and Iceland, while Swedish is a subject in Finnish schools. However, the actual role of the target language in these countries varies greatly. Due to their links with Denmark, Danish plays a key role in

---

1. http://norden.diva-portal.org/smash/get/diva2:700895/FULLTEXT01.pdf

Faroese and Greenlandic society, while it is seldom used in everyday life in Iceland. Swedish is an official language in Finland along with Finnish.

Foreign languages, especially English, have high priority in the Nordic school system, both at the compulsory school level and in secondary education. This emphasis on foreign languages has been of major significance for individuals and for the possibilities of these countries to make their voices heard in an international context.

Historical background

The Nordic countries' long history, going back to medieval times, has included both conflicts and confederacies. Historical ties are strong between Norway and Denmark, which shared the same monarch from 1380 to 1814, and between Sweden and Finland which had the same sovereign until 1809. From 1814 to its full independence in 1905 Norway was in a personal union with Sweden. Iceland belonged to the Danish monarchy from 1383, was granted autonomy in 1918 and became an independent republic in 1944. Two other former Danish dependents, the Faroe Islands and Greenland, were granted Home Rule in 1948 and 1979 respectively, but remain part of the Danish realm. Since 1921 Åland has the status of an autonomous territory in Finland. The Saami population native to northern Scandinavia are spread over four countries: Norway, Sweden, Finland and Russia.

It is in fact impressive that the Nordic community has managed to survive despite asymmetries of power, oppression, conflicts and even wars between various states.

- Relations between Sweden and Finland through the centuries have been charged with drama.

- Denmark and Sweden have repeatedly waged lengthy wars and for centuries were "archenemies."

- As recently as 1905, Sweden and Norway were on the brink of conflict over Norwegian independence.

- Finnish Åland is Swedish-speaking.

- Denmark lost Norway, which step by step gained control of its affairs and ended up with several official written languages. The most widely used *bokmål* has its roots in written Danish, while *nynorsk* is based on Norwegian dialects.

- From 1383 onwards Iceland was part of the Danish kingdom and to a large extent was administered from Denmark for centuries before it gained statehood in two stages, in 1918 and 1944.

- The Faroese, Greenlanders and Saami do not have full sovereignty in all areas.

Individual Nordic countries often refer to the group as "the countries we use for comparison." While each land has its own culture, traditions and current political position, they can be compared precisely because each country can find features it recognizes in others and traits which may differ without being foreign. Even if sympathy between the countries is often more implicit than explicit it is nonetheless a reality.

Despite opposing interests and confrontations in the recent past, politicians, businessmen, NGOs, students and young people in service sectors find common cause, and as a tourist destination for Nordic residents, the Nordic countries have never been more popular.

However, there appears to be a widespread misconception that Nordic cooperation is a thing of the past. It was established and institutionalized in the 1800s and 1900s, in the recent past—and today is based on three, not necessarily congruent, criteria: historical, geographical and linguistic. Danish, Norwegian and Swedish are mutually comprehensible while Icelandic and Faroese share the same roots.

Most significant, however, are the shared values, to which all of the above criteria are subordinate. Nordic countries have developed a set of related approaches to and applications of concepts such as authority, democracy, minority and equality. These values have attracted notice well beyond the countries' borders, most recently by President Obama, increasing the countries' foreign policy influence and creating a certain respect.

Language Comprehension and Communication Between Nordic Neighbor Languages

Danes, Norwegians and Swedes can quickly learn to speak to each other in their native languages, so that in only a short time they become accustomed to understanding each other. For those Nordic residents who have to learn their neighbors' languages as a foreign language, the Faroese, Finns, Greenlanders, Icelanders and Saami, participation in the language community requires both receptive and productive ability in one of the Scandinavian languages. This is a major challenge, not least for Finns, Saami and Greenlanders, where the difference between their mother tongue and neighbor languages is significant.

Danish, Norwegian and Swedish are so similar that sometimes we have difficulties ourselves in distinguishing them. For a Swede encountering a neighbor language in written form it is sometimes not easy to determine immediately whether this is Danish or Norwegian bokmål. The latter partly originates from Danish, which is why the two languages have so many words in common. As far as pronunciation, however, the opposite is true; Norwegian and Swedish are most similar. Sometimes a Dane can initially have difficulty in determining whether it is a Norwegian or Swede speaking.

As far as vocabulary, a majority of words are similar, but there are also words which are completely different. This is true for numbers. While the number 50 is expressed as femtio in Swedish and femti in Norwegian (literally five tens, like fifty) in Danish it is halvtreds (literally half three times twenty). Then there are the words which look or sound the same but have different meanings, a faux amis or false friends. An often related anecdote is about a Swede visiting Copenhagen who asked his taxi driver to take him to a roligt spot. He ended up in a cemetery, which he found not at all roligt. The joke being that roligt means "fun and lively" in Swedish but "quiet and calm" in Danish. Frokost means lunch in Danish, but not in Norwegian and Swedish. The verb grine/grina means "to cry" in Norwegian and Swedish but "to laugh" in Danish.

As Faroese and Icelandic have the same roots as Danish, Norwegian and Swedish, there are some similarities in their vocabulary, especially in words of traditional character. Lengthy cultural contact with Denmark has also contributed to the lexis of Faroese and Icelandic. Written Danish, Norwegian and

Swedish are the most easily accessible to Faroese and Icelanders. As is the case between Danish, Norwegian and Swedish, neighbor language homonyms can prove tricky when Faroese or Icelanders speak Danish. An Icelander, invited to spend the weekend, asked if he should bring his sæng along. In Icelandic the word sæng (pronounced "saing") means "duvet", while seng in Danish means "bed" (rúm in Icelandic). To confuse things even more, the Danish for "duvet" is dyne which in its Icelandic form dýna means "a mattress". Because of extensive structural and lexical differences between their mother tongue and the Scandinavian neighbor languages, communication with these neighbors is a major challenge for Finns, Greenlanders and Saami.

Nordic Languages as Neighbor Languages

As previously mentioned, comprehension of neighbor languages among Scandinavians (Danes, Norwegians, Swedish-speaking Finns and Swedes) is based on their being able to understand Danish, Norwegian or Swedish with the help of their mother tongue. Those Nordic peoples who have to make use of a Scandinavian language which is a foreign language (Faroese, Finns, Greenlanders, Icelanders and Saami) have to be able to both understand the languages and express themselves through oral and written means in one of them.

Empirical research on Nordic language comprehension was pioneered in the 1950s by Haugen[2], and other researchers have followed. Maurud's 1976[3], "Reciprocal comprehension of neighbor languages in Scandinavia" and the 2005 Delsing & Lundin Åkesson[4], "Does language hold the Nordic countries

---

2. Haugen, Einar, 1953: Nordiske språkproblemer – en opinionsundersökelse. [Nordic language problems - an opinion survey] I: Nordisk tidskrift 29. pp. 225-249.

3. Maurud, Øivind, 1976b: Reciprocal comprehension of neighbour languages in Scandinavia. In: Scandinavian Journal of Educational Research 20. pp. 49-72.

4. Delsing, Lars-Olof & Katarina Lundin Åkesson. 2005. Håller språket ihop Norden? En forskningsrapport om ungdomars förståelse av danska, norska och svenska [Does language hold the Nordic countries together? A research report on how well young people understand Danish, Norwegian and Swedish] (TemaNord 2005: 573). Copenhagen: The Nordic Council.

together," show how well young people understand Danish, Norwegian and Swedish. Both of these reports are based on actual testing of neighbor language comprehension, not just self-reporting. In contrast to previous studies the testing in 2005 was carried out in all the Nordic countries and even included second-language speakers (immigrants) in Denmark, Norway and Sweden.

The research shows unequivocally that Norwegians understand the neighbor languages best, particularly Swedish; almost comparable to mother-tongue comprehension. They also understand Danish better than the Swedes (Norwegian developed from written Danish). Norwegian speakers are highly accustomed to linguistic variation, as dialects have high status in the country. Swedes, however, are not as good in Norwegian, and many Norwegians are surprised when they travel to Sweden and are not immediately understood. It is also more difficult for the Swedes to understand spoken Danish. Reading comprehension is a different story. As written communication through electronic media has replaced oral contact, the premise for well-functioning inter-Nordic communications will continue to improve, and encounters will be more successful when written exchanges serve as the first point of contact.

The results of Delsing & Lundin Åkesson's research show that the Faroes do best of all the survey groups when it comes to understanding of Danish. In addition, they understand Norwegian better than either Swedes or Danes. Finns have the greatest difficulties with neighbor language comprehension and Greenlanders and Icelanders manage Danish better than Norwegian and Swedish. Knowledge of Danish gives Faroese, Greenlanders and Icelanders a key to Norwegian and Swedish. The Finns understand Swedish best, especially the written language, but have problems with both Norwegian and Danish. Faroese and Greenlanders understand spoken Danish better than written Danish, while Icelanders understand written Danish better than spoken.

Almost thirty years elapsed between the two critical neighbor language comprehension studies and in the interim a wide-reaching internationalization has occurred. Large numbers of immigrants have moved to Scandinavia and now live with Danish, Norwegian or Swedish as their second language. Testing showed that immigrant understanding of neighbor languages was much less than native Nordic language speakers. However, even in this group, Norwegian participants performed the best. In another study (Börestam 2008)[5] immigrants of non-Nordic origin who moved from Denmark to Sweden or vice versa were interviewed. They were faced with two second languages, a situation they chose to deal with in one of two different ways. One strategy was aimed at keeping the two languages separate, either by actually becoming bilingual or by changing from using Danish to Swedish or the reverse. The other option was to combine the two languages without worrying about mixing them together. The result became some form of "Scandinavian," an unpretentious mixed language, which turned out to function well in many situations. Such a flexible mixed language, in fact, is something many people in Nordic countries say they use.

Another consequence of internationalization is the use of the English language at various levels of society. English comprehension was also part of the Delsing & Lundin Åkesson study. In oral comprehension, young people had a better understanding of English than their neighbor languages, and other research (Hauksdóttir 2012: 37-43[6], Börestam 2015[7]) shows that Nordic youngsters often use English as an auxiliary language in their contact with other Nordic people, especially when their neighbor language competence is not great. Among some young people, English seems be a more effective language option than Scandinavian languages.

There are, however, many indications that this research does not reflect the whole picture. A number of studies suggest that neighbor language com-

---

5. Börestam, Ulla. 2008. Samma skjorta—olika knappar [Same shirt —different buttons]. Icke-nordiska invandrares erfarenheter av dansk-svensk språkgemenskap i Öresundsregionen. [Experience of immigrants of non-Nordic origin of Danish-Swedish linguistic co-habitation in the Øresund region]. (TEMANORD 2008:535.) Copenhagen.

6. Hauksdóttir, Auður. 2012. Dansk som fremmedsprog i en akademisk kontekst : Om islændinges behov for danskkundskaber under videreuddannelse i Danmark. [Danish as a foreign language in an academic context: On Icelanders' need for knowledge of Danish in tertiary study in Denmark] Københavnerstudier i tosprogethed. [Copenhagen Studies in Bilingualism] Copenhagen: University of Copenhagen

7. Börestam, Ulla. 2015. Excuse me, but can you tell me where the Nordic House is located? Linguistic strategies in inter-Nordic communication in Iceland illustrated through participant observation. In: *Linguistics* 53:2. 2015. pp. 219-254.

munication functions more effectively in real life than in laboratory testing. Currently a pilot project is underway, initiated by Nordic Language Cooperation (NOSK) and financed by the Nordic culture ministers, aimed at mapping through interviews the linguistic situation among young adult Nordic residents (under age 30) working in a neighboring country. The research is being conducted by Eva Theilgaard Brink (2016). Some preliminary results indicate that linguistic adaptation is common, but that the extent varies greatly. English is used intermittently but seldom is completely dominant, and in a social context, many appear to avoid English. The Nordic languages continue to be the social cement that binds us together.

In Closing

Neighbor language comprehension and cross-border communication in Nordic languages has a very central role in Nordic cooperation. For the majority of Nordic residents, although not for all, this means that they can speak the language for which they have the best command while at the same time understanding their neighbor languages. Receptive multilingualism appears to be a pragmatic and even linguistically sustainable solution, not only for the Nordic countries but perhaps for other regions of the world where languages are genetically/typologically related. Linguistic cooperation reflects a close and lasting cultural contact between Nordic nations and studies show that knowledge of Danish, Norwegian or Swedish can function as an effective key to contact and communications with other Nordic residents. How much effort is required to reach the stage where neighbor languages can be used in speaking and writing, however, depends to a varying extent on the mother tongue and the distance between neighbor languages.

In recent decades, the growing use of English as a lingua franca in an international context and the prominent status that the language enjoys in Nordic universities has become to some extent a threat for the Nordic language community, as shown by the fact that many Nordic youngsters tend to use English at the cost of neighbor languages. In other contexts they use English in tandem with the neighbor languages or as an auxiliary or access language to the neighbor languages.

The Child's Right to Culture and the Arts

Karin Helander

"…children and young people are dependent on the benevolence, values and choices of adults."

In the Nordics, childhood in the postwar period was impacted by the growth of the welfare state and the perception of children as citizens. Cultural traditions and social patterns are largely consistent between the Nordic countries; but this essay highlights Swedish child culture policies and child perspectives as well as how Sweden has worked for children's cultural rights.

Historical background

In the postwar period, the previously dominant image of good children's culture which was characterized by a nostalgic, idyllic, romantic and innocent view of children and childhood was renegotiated. As early as the 1930s, children were described as competent participants in society in school radio programs and the like, which was in tune with the goals of the state apparatus and the political debate. Educational reforms, which had their breakthrough in Sweden in the 1940s and 50s, asserted children's creativity and independence. The aim was to liberate children's competence and raise them to be democratic capable individuals. Schooling was to be influenced by a greater degree of student activity and the legal rights of children and young people were strengthened. This perspective of children was also shaped in children's culture. The new postwar perspective on children focused on the playful individual and the creative, constructive child.

New winds blew through the Western world in the late 1960s. The Swedish social debate was radicalized. Environmental equality and redistribution issues held a dominant position on the political scene. The desire to democratize culture had a strong bearing on children's culture. It was stressed that children's opportunities to encounter art and culture had been heavily dependent on their parents' economic and social backgrounds. Commercial culture was identified as a threat and there was a seeking out of knowledge about how cultural products affect children's lives. The democratic aspect was emphasized; culture should be available to all children regardless of where they live or their economic situation. Children should be brought up to be politically aware of social injustices and work to achieve solidarity, justice and equality. The view of the child as responsible and competent took a new turn in the 1970s, when the inner worlds and complex emotions of children were taken seriously in children's culture. Children's existential questions, philosophical musings and intractable dilemmas have been portrayed very often on stage as well as in literature and films for young audiences ever since.

The UN Convention on the Rights of the Child

Since the UN (United Nations) Convention on the Rights of the Child was adopted in 1989 and ratified in 1990, its Article 31 has had a major impact on children's culture in Sweden through culture policy discussions and decisions as well as in thematic and artistic choices. Article 31 of the Convention formulates the child's right to participate fully in cultural and artistic activities.

"States Parties recognize the right of the child to rest and leisure; to engage in play and recreational activities appropriate to the age of the child and to participate freely in cultural life and the arts.

States Parties shall respect and promote the right of the child to participate fully in cultural and artistic life and shall encourage the provision of appropriate and equal opportunities for cultural, artistic, recreational and leisure activity (Convention on the Rights of the Child)."

Ideas on the rights of the child were developed and legitimized. Besides Article 31, Article 12 in particular brought to the forefront a child's right to be heard in matters affecting them from a cultural perspective.

"States Parties shall assure to the child who is capable of forming his or her own views the right to express those views freely in all matters affecting the child, the views of the child being given due weight in accordance with the age and maturity of the child. (Convention on the Rights of the Child)"

Article 12 includes incentives to ensure the child's right to participation, involvement and influence, and thus strongly influences Swedish policies towards children's culture in theory and practice. Concepts such as the child's perspective, participation and best interests of the child have permeated children's and young people's culture.

Children's Culture Policy in Sweden in the 2000s

In the 2000s, children's and young people's rights to culture are based on the Convention on the Rights of the Child. The large-scale cultural policy venture *Skapande skola* (Creative School) was launched in 2008 in order to take a long-term approach to integrating cultural expressions in school learning. *Skapande skola* is seen as a tool that can be used to achieve the school's proficiency goals and is aimed at students from preschool to ninth grade for personal creativity in projects with cultural educators or encounters with professional artworks. For several years, all municipalities in Sweden have been granted project funds and more than half of all students in the relevant age group have participated in the *Skapande skola* project.

The current culture bill from 2009, *Tid för kultur* (Time for Culture), formulated a new cultural policy goal, which is to, "pay special attention to children's and young people's right to culture." This is motivated by the supposition that since children are less able than adults to assess, choose from and influence cultural offerings, society must ensure that all children and young people have equal opportunities to participate in and have access to high-quality cultural activities. The spirit of the Convention emphasizes that children and adolescents should be given the opportunity to influence and participate in the activities that concern them. The Ministry of Culture has instructed the state cultural institutions to integrate a child perspective and develop specific child and youth strategies for their organizations.

It is remarkable how children's cultural policy in the 2000s is permeated with ideas about children's rights in the spirit of the UN Convention because of the desire to formulate the child's perspective and invite participation. This shows an awareness that children and young people are dependent on the benevolence, values and choices of adults.

The View of Children and Childhood

The view of children and childhood is currently shifting from the child as a development project to the child as a capable citizen and social partici-pant. Today's child culture policy includes both of these positions: an active and competent child with rights, as well as a child in need of protection and assistance. In the Swedish child cultural policy of the 2000s, the child is seen largely as a learning subject, but also as constructive and creative. Children's participation in cultural activities is considered meaningful from a societal perspective; the young generation must be able to meet tomorrow's challenges and expectations. The child is of national interest and is seen as the key to the future. Some of the adult-produced culture for children still includes images of the nostalgic angelic child alongside the exposed, vulnerable child and the curious, inquisitive child.

The Convention's Article 31 also applies to the very youngest. The range and availability in terms of artistic expression for ages 0-3 has increased sig-nificantly during the 2000s in the wake of the Convention. Sweden and other Nordic countries rely on modern infant research and also see the youngest children as an audience with the need for and capacity to absorb artistic expe-riences. In the many projects in which artists have collaborated with psycholo-gists and childhood researchers, it was discovered that young children have a developed a sense of form and aesthetic expression. What is striking in the research done on performing arts for the very youngest audience is the desire to manifest "the useless necessity" and give the small children sensual, artistic experiences, without narrow educational motives.

Technological developments have changed the perception of children, childhood and cultural practices. Today the everyday digital lives of children are discussed as either part of the 2000s version of the good childhood or as a passivating threatening risk factor for children, who need to be protected. The current discussion and child culture research highlight topics such as how today's children navigate the virtual world, consumption's role in the media worlds of children, new technology in relation to pedagogy and play, and what form of identity creation that the digitalized childhood entails.

Children's right to culture is expressed in, for example, professional Swedish children's theater productions by the desire to make the young audience involved as bearers of ideas and participants in interactive projects. Many theaters are involved in letting young audiences actively participate in the performances. Children have frames of reference and associations that add depth and a child's perspective to the performances.

The UN Convention on the Rights of the Child has influenced, inspired and permeated both child cultural policy discussion and child cultural practices. Adults wish to nurture children and youth with culture and the arts, but also give them the opportunity to create, participate in cultural activities, and experience high-quality artistic expression. The result has been a strong focus on children's and young people's own creativity in cultural processes and aesthetic projects and that adult-produced professional culture for children is influenced by concepts such as participation, children's perspective and the rights of the child.

Child Health in Sweden

Hugo Lagercrantz

"…despite good somatic health, many Swedish children, particularly teenagers seem to be less happy and psychological problems have increased. This is an enigma of the welfare state."

Historic Aspects

The Swedish author Ellen Key declared in 1900 that the 20th century would become the century of the child. This wish could at least be fulfilled in Sweden, more than in most other countries, in part because Sweden was neutral and did not suffer from the two world wars. Infant mortality decreased from 10 to 0.3 percent and child mortality below 5 years also decreased. The mortality rate due to accidents is one of the lowest in the world.

There are several reasons why child health has been promoted in Sweden. Child mortality was very high during the 18th and 19th century since Sweden was less populated than the Continental countries there was more concern about decreasing nativity. Rosén von Rosenstein (1706–1773) contemporary with Linnaeus wrote one of the first textbooks in pediatrics. It was actually first published in the Swedish calendar (Bondealmanackan), the only literature which was read by the Swedish farmers besides the Bible and the hymnbook. The book in pediatrics was translated into 11 languages.

In 1845 Fredrik Theodor Berg (1806–1887) was appointed as professor of pediatrics at the Karolinska institute, probably the first in the world. He continued as head of the statistical bureau and said prophetically, "that the health of the nation is related to the survival of infants."

In the 1930s Swedish nativity was decreasing which concerned the politicians, therefore important reforms were initiated. Antenatal clinics and childcare centers were introduced and poor mothers could receive child benefits starting in 1937. Ten years later all children sixteen and under would receive child benefits. Parental allowances were introduced in 1962. Reducing social inequalities has been one of the main goals of Swedish politics since the 1930s, which is of particular importance for the promotion of children's health.

By the 1950s home births had become less frequent and nearly all deliveries took place at lying-in clinics. Children's health clinics opened in all counties. During the 1960s and 70s many pediatricians were trained and the ambition was that most children at least in the urban areas should have access to pediatricians if necessary. This changed during the 1980s when the training of many pediatricians was substituted by an increase in General Practitioners.

Infant Mortality

The infant mortality in Sweden became one of the lowest in the world, alongside Iceland, Finland, Japan and Singapore. One important reason is the nearly 100 percent attendance at the antenatal and child health clinics, which is free. Women with gestational diabetes or hypertension of pregnancy (preeclampsia) are identified at an early stage and treated. Teenage pregnancies are usually terminated by abortion. Nearly all deliveries take place at lying-in hospitals usually situated in close proximity to children's clinics. Women with complicated pregnancies are referred to university hospitals.

There have been some worries that the extensive immigration of women from Africa, Afghanistan and now Syria would lead to a higher perinatal mortality. However, this has not occurred. First of all most of these women attend the same health services as those women born in Sweden. Furthermore, they are often younger between 20–30 years, which is the optimal child bearing age, while mothers born in Sweden tend to postpone their first pregnancies to a later time which increases the risk of complications.

About 10 percent of all newborn infants need special care due to asphyxia, jaundice and breathing problems, particularly prematurity. Most of the neonatal wards are situated near the delivery wards to avoid transports. The standard of these wards is fairly equal around the country.

Premature Infants

The incidence rate of premature birth (before 37 gestational weeks) in Sweden is about 6 percent which is much lower than in the U.S. This is mostly due to the general antenatal care and the small numbers of teenage mothers. There is also devotion to the care of extremely preterm infants (infants born before 27 gestational weeks with birth weights below 800 grams). In a national study of Extremely Preterm Infants after active Perinatal Care in Sweden the so-called EXPRESS study (2004–2007) the survival of these infants was more than 70 percent. This is higher than found in corresponding studies in England and Wales (Epicure) and France (Epipage); although the incidence of neurological sequels was about the same.

The rational for the proactive attitude to resuscitate infants at the border of viability is based on the United Nations (UN) convention on the Rights of the Child. Preterm infants should be treated as well as older children and adults. However, about one third of these micro preemies become severely or moderately disabled and even more develop cognitive problems. And it can be questioned whether this proactive lifesaving is in the best interest of the child. On the other hand follow-up studies have indicated that most of these ex-preemies feel that their quality of life is as good as others. Swedish neonatologists are probably less worried about disabilities, possibly because a good organization exists to take care of these children.

Sudden Infant Death Syndrome (SIDS)

The main causes of infant mortality, aside from prematurity, are malformations and infections, which have remained fairly stable during the last decades. SIDS was previously the most common cause of infant death after the newborn period. By putting the infants in a supine position (on the back to sleep) and cutting out maternal smoking, the incidence has decreased in most countries. In Sweden it dropped from twelve in 10,000 in 1990 to two in 10,000 in 2014. This impressive decrease is probably due to effective public campaigns and that medical advice is being followed.

Preventive Health Care

Childcare centers play an important role for the health of children. A few weeks after delivery, a nurse from the childcare center or barnavårdscentral in Swedish (BVC) visits the home of every newborn infant. She inspects the homes, checking the bed, gives advice about breast feeding and tells the parents how important it is to put the baby in a supine position. Afterwards, there are regular visits at the BVC to follow the growth and development of the child. Vaccinations are given according to a program and are accepted by most parents, although there have been some worries during the last years due to the occurrence of narcolepsy among children after the general vaccination against influenza in 2012.

The prevention of accidents has also led to low child mortality; five per 100,000 children in 2009 was the lowest in the world. By comparison in the U.S. it was nine per 100,000 and in Brazil 18 per 100,000. Professor Ragnar Berfenstam in Uppsala did some seminal studies on accidents among children leading to a series of preventative actions. There are now strict regulations to prevent home accidents with regard to electricity, stoves and use of hot water among other things.

During the 1960s several new suburbs around the big cities were built, the so-called Miljonprogrammet. One idea was to separate pedestrian walks from the streets.

A number of safety rules were introduced. Children below ten years old are not allowed to sit in the front of cars. Bicycle helmets were made obligatory in 2005 for all children 15 and under. Communities are responsible to have swimming lessons and all children are encouraged to swim at least 200 meters.

Chronic Diseases and Rehabilitation

Finland and Sweden have the highest incidence of juvenile diabetes (type I) in the world. Allergic diseases particularly asthma among children are common in all the Nordic countries, much more than in Estonia and the other Baltic countries. This led to the so-called hygiene hypothesis; children growing up in clean urban societies develop allergies more easily than in a less modernized environment. There are special pediatric outpatient clinics for diabetes and allergies which function well and are free of charge.

Disabled children have free access to special rehabilitation centers with teams of neuro-pediatricians, psychologists and physiotherapists. The parents of these children can receive extra child-care allowances to be able to spend more time at home with their child. There is also a special law directing that communities must provide resources so the disabled children can lead as normal lives as possible. If a child is severely disabled and needs help on a daily basis, the parents can engage personal assistants free of charge.

Child Wellbeing in Sweden

According a report from UNICEF 2007 Sweden was ranked as the second best country in the world with regard to the wellbeing of children (after the Netherlands) among the world's wealthiest countries. All the Nordic countries were ranked in the top ten, while the average ranking for the U.S. was 18.0 and the United Kingdom 18.2. Sweden was ranked as number one with regard to material well-being, health and safety. However family and peer relationships and subjective well-being did not do as well in Sweden. Although this study was done about ten years ago, it is probably still valid today.

Other studies have demonstrated that the psychological health of Swedish children has deteriorated during the last decades. Conditions like ADHD (attention deficit and hyperactivity disorder) and autism spectrum disorders (ASD) have risen, although this could be due to an increase in the diagnosis of these conditions. Depression and anorexia have increased particularly among girls. Additionally, suicides have not decreased among youngsters as they have in the general population.

It is a paradox that the general improvement in physical health has not lead to a corresponding increase of subjective well-being. Many youngsters seem to be less optimistic about their future. Swedish children are probably provided with more computer gadgets than in any other European country. The extensive use of social media and related technology has not improved the well-being of children; rather it is the other way around. Many children, particularly boys are involved in athletics, but only the elite athletes are truly supported.

Most pre-school children after one-two years attend day-care centers. Although this seems to have mainly a positive effect on the development of the children and their social adaptation, there is some concern that the groups of children are too big with only three or four staff persons per 18 children. The school situation seems to be less good, with a shortage of competent teachers and discipline problems. And compared to Finland, Sweden receives a lower education ranking.

Conclusions

The physical health of children in Sweden as well as in the other Nordic countries is excellent and probably among the best in the world. The pediatric care in general is well organized and thanks to excellent preventive programs the mortality as a result of accidents is lowest in the world. But despite good somatic health, many Swedish children, particularly teenagers seem to be less happy and psychological problems have increased. This is an enigma of the welfare state.

An Education System Where Quality and Equality Go Hand in Hand

Pasi Sahlberg

> *"Schools must have measures to better cope with the harmful consequences that disadvantaged family backgrounds have on teaching and learning in many schools."*

Since the release of the first results of the Program for International Student Assessment (PISA) in December 2001, Finland has become the mecca of education pilgrimage. Some visitors wish to discover the secrets of Finland's high scores in international reading, mathematics and science. Others hope to find out how great teachers are prepared or what successful schools look like. Among these visitors are also scores of U.S. educators who want to take a first-hand look at an education system that can exist without private schools and frequent standardized testing of pupils and teachers.

When I ask these visitors what is the most important souvenir of the Finnish education system they bring back home, a common answer is: the widespread trust exhibited by Finns in their public education system, especially in their teachers and schools. They also wonder how only a few Finns seem worried about whether teachers do what they are expected to by authorities and parents. What becomes clear during these school visits is not often found in other education systems: Finnish parents seem to think that if there are schools that do not perform according to expectations, local authorities will find ways to help them get better rather than urge that bad teachers should be fired or failing schools should be closed.

The Finnish Way of Change

In the global perspective, the Finnish education system doesn't fit into any conventional model of schooling. In some ways it seems to be a paradox—doing less but accomplishing more. When much of the rest of the world is implementing more oversight of schools to assure teachers meet specific externally set goals, lengthening the school day to extend formal learning time, toughening academic standards for all students and increasing homework, Finnish children continue to enjoy a relatively short school day, a whole-child focused curriculum and a reasonable homework load. Moreover Finnish children do not attend private tutoring sessions in addition to their regular schooling or spend any time preparing for standardized tests, as so many of their peers around the world today must do.

Perhaps the most surprising part of the Finnish educational philosophy is the central role of play in children's lives both in and out of school. Formal learning doesn't start before the first grade when children are seven years old. Before that, children spend their time in play to develop a sense of independence and responsibility and to learn about themselves and others. In the early years of elementary education, children learn to read and do math through various forms of play, music and drama. Indeed, the old adage of "less is more" is carried out every day in Finnish schools, as I describe in Finnish Lessons 2.0: What can the world learn from educational change in Finland.

In many other countries, formal schooling is replacing informal childhood play earlier than ever. Standardized tests are introduced in kindergarten when children are as young as three years old to make sure they are ready for school. But that hasn't happened in Finland. In the U.S., for example, in many states preschool has become the new First Grade. The Finns regard play as not just a break from academic work but as an important and useful skill, like any human ability, that one hones through experience. Much as the Swedish psychologist Anders Ericsson has famously concluded that mastery of any complex skill requires approximately ten thousand hours of practice, Finnish educators and authorities alike consider play a skill that necessitates sufficient time over many years to develop. As children spend more and more time at play, they sharpen their capacity to imagine, improvise, remain curious and then collaborate. If Ericsson is right, it takes about ten years for children to achieve such heightened ability to discover their minds and then use imagination to create new ideas. This may be one reason behind widespread creativity and innovation in Finnish society—in arts, design and industry as well.

Outside of school, Finnish society's public policies lay the foundation for proper educational development. Child wellbeing, happiness and the political empowerment of women are some of the conditions that help Finland's school system work well. Finland, together with its Nordic neighbors, is also a leading nation in economic competitiveness, good governance, scientific inquiry and technological innovation, all in turn generating a climate of constant learning. Indeed, Finland is a great place to be a mother, as Save the Children annually concludes in its global survey of health, well-being, education and family care. All these social and economic factors create a productive context for formal education in Finland.

Finland's educational success is a result of finding its own way of change, not doing more of the same than others. This is particularly true in enhancing both quality and equality of education outcomes. Some foreign observers claim that Finland's success story results from the country's smallness, cultural homogeneity and evenly distributed wealth. Those thinking this way often fail to distinguish the Finnish way of educational thinking from what I have coined the "global education reform movement" (GERM). It sees competition between schools, standardization of teaching and learning, frequent high-stakes testing and associated punitive accountability and the privatization of public schools as the most effective means of educational improvement and turning around failing schools.

Myths about Finnish Education

But there are also many myths about Finland's schools and education system in the United States. In 2015, one of the UK's trusted newspapers run a story titled "Finland schools: Subjects scrapped and replaced with 'topics' as country reforms its education system." This story became viral in world news and social media creating an impression that soon Finnish children would not study mathematics, music, reading and science, or any other subjects at all. "Stay calm" was my advice then and now. Finnish schools will continue to teach these subjects now and in the future.

It is important to underline two fundamental peculiarities of the Finnish education system in order to see the real picture. First, education governance is highly decentralized which gives Finland's 320 municipalities a significant amount of freedom to arrange schooling according to local circumstances. The central government issues legislation tops up local funding of schools and provides a guiding framework for what schools should teach and how. Second, the National Curriculum Framework (NCF) is a loose common standard that steers curriculum planning at the level of the municipalities and their schools. It gives educators freedom to find the optimal ways to offer good teaching and learning to all children. Therefore practices vary from school to school and are often customized to local needs and situations.

So what is happening in Finland's school reform now? The next big thing is the introduction of the new NCF effective August 2016. It is a binding document that sets the overall goals of schooling, describes the principles of teaching and learning and provides the guidelines for special education, well-being, support services and student assessment in schools. Although project and problem-based pedagogies have a central place in this new NCF, teachers' professional autonomy guarantees that each teacher has the freedom to choose the most suitable teaching methods.

Integration of subjects and a holistic approach to teaching and learning are not new in Finland. Since the 1980s Finnish schools have experimented with project-based learning and it has been part of the culture of teaching in many Finnish schools since then. The integrated approach that blends different subject matters together has been a normal practice among primary school teachers for a long time.

You may wonder why Finland's education authorities now insist that all schools must spend time on integration and project-based teaching when Finnish students' test scores have been declining in the most recent international tests. Educators in Finland think, quite correctly, that schools should teach what young people need in their lives rather than try to bring national test scores back to where they were. Many educators argue that what Finnish youths need more than before are more integrated knowledge and skills about real world issues. The integrated approach, experience suggests, enhances teacher collaboration in schools and makes learning more meaningful to students.

What most of the stories about Finland's current education reform have failed to cover is the most surprising aspect of the Finnish way of change. NCF 2016 states that students must be involved in the planning of these project-based study periods and that they must have a voice in assessing what they have learned from it. This is a concrete response by policy-makers to enhance student behavioral and academic engagement in schools and thereby improve their learning outcomes.

Some teachers in Finland see this current reform as a threat and the wrong way to improve teaching and learning in schools. Many other teachers think, on the contrary, that breaking down the dominance of traditional subjects and reducing the isolated nature of teaching provide good opportunities for more fundamental change in schools towards deeper learning and teacher professional collaboration. While some schools will use this reform to advance further redesigning of teaching and learning to more student-centered learning and professional collaboration guided by the NCF 2016 in schools, others will choose more moderate ways in implementing project-based studies in their schools. In any case, teaching subjects will continue in one way or the other in Finland's basic schools for now.

Finnish Challenges

No country has a perfect education system and Finland has its challenges too. Having spent decades on the top of the world as an envied model has made it difficult to continue progress in the improvement and renewal of education. As a consequence, Finland's performance has begun to slip, learning gaps between students have widened and the equality of outcomes has weakened. Finnish students have improved foreign language skills but at the same time reading and mathematics performance have declined especially among adolescent boys. These all are serious signals of deeper problems that educational policies must address for the school system to continue to serve all children equally.

Many have argued that it is not possible to achieve excellence in student learning and equality in education simultaneously. The experience in Finland—as well as of those in Canada, Japan and The Netherlands—show that with smart social policies, sustainable education reform efforts and professionally committed personnel in schools, most children can succeed. Even many Finns, who thought such success once seemed unlikely, have been silenced by the PISA results. Perhaps the most valuable lesson that the United States can learn from Finland is how to build an education system that offers equal opportunity for all children to succeed regardless of their family backgrounds.

Lessons for Americans

Many people have asked me, "What are the main reasons that prevent American students from achieving the kind of success that Finnish students attain?" In my response I stress the following three things that have positively affected the quality of Finnish schools which are absent in American schools.

First, Finland has built a school system that has since the 1970s systematically strengthened and invested in educational equality. This means early childhood education for all children, funding all schools so that they can better serve those with special educational needs, access to health and well-being services for all children in all schools and a national curriculum that insists that schools focus on the whole child rather than narrow academic achievement.

Second, teachers in Finland have time to work together with their colleagues during the school day. According to the most recent data provided by the Organization for Economic Cooperation and Development (OECD) the average teaching load of middle school teachers in Finland is about 40 percent less than what it is in the United States. That enables teachers to build professional networks and share ideas and best practices with their colleagues. This is an important condition to enhance social capital among teachers and thereby improve teaching quality in schools.

Third, as mentioned earlier, play constitutes a significant part of individual growth and learning in Finnish early education and schools. Every class in all Finnish schools must be followed by a 15-minute recess break so that children can spend time outside on their own activities. School days are also shorter in Finland than in the U.S., and primary schools keep the homework load to a minimum so that students have time for their own hobbies and friends when the school day is over. Research evidence is clear about the positive benefits of play to children's health, well-being, happiness and education.

Should U.S. schools adopt all the ingredients of Finnish education to get better? Transferring practices and policies from other education systems is always risky, but there is a lot to learn from the paradoxes, policies and common sense thinking behind an education system that nine of ten Finnish taxpayers approve today. One of the most urgent lessons would be to learn how the teaching profession is one of the most wanted career choices among young Finns year after year. For the Finns, that is the most important accomplishment, not the top tier on international exams.

The ultimate test for the American education system will be whether it can bring equality to the forefront of education policies. When poverty explains up to half of student achievement in the U.S. and beyond, schools must have measures to better cope with the harmful consequences that disadvantaged family backgrounds have on teaching and learning in many schools. The key Finnish lesson is that with smart and sustained policies education quality and equality can indeed coexist.

4. The Nordic Creative Process – Central to Innovation in the Arts, Technology and Business

Why quality of life, arts and design, are so much part of the Nordic model. How have innovative approaches to art and design defined life and lifestyles, and economic progress in Nordic societies, and international creativity and competitiveness? What are the challenges to maintaining this high quality of design in a world of mass production, and what is the new thinking in art, design and technology that gives this Nordic approach the competitive edge?

May the Future Be With You

Nicklas Bergman

"We see the emergence of a new understanding and acceptance of the fact that different perspectives on uncertainty and ambiguity are essential for future success."

My grandmother, Selma Olsson, was born in 1900, and gave birth to seventeen children between 1920 and 1944. Quite apart from that marvelous achievement, by the time she passed away in 1992 she had also experienced close to a century of amazing technological development. She witnessed the: mainstream adoption of the telephone and electricity; arrival of radio and television; new means of transportation by car and airplane; conquering of space; and invention of the computer. She lived her whole life in the countryside on the Swedish west coast. Although she was a curious and open minded person, she never really embraced all the new technologies and instead was content with her way of living. The lives of my children, born at the beginning of the 21st century, could not be more different. We are entering an era in which technology will redefine who we are. It is no longer just a question of what technology can do for us, but what should we allow technology to do.

Starting in the 19th century, Sweden was well positioned for the arrival of the industrial revolution. Vast natural resources, access to rivers for both power and transportation and all within relatively easy reach from populated areas, formed the basis for industrial innovation and growth. For the past century and a half Sweden has been a technology test bed innovation powerhouse and product guinea pig. Despite the fact that we are a small country up north with less than 10 million people, midnight sun in the summer, cold, long dark winters and a complicated relationship with pickled herring, this special environment created many companies that still thrive today as global market leaders. They thrive despite geographical proximity and a minuscule domestic market because Swedish companies with ambitions have always been forced to have a global perspective from day one.

Emerging technologies can be seen as both opportunities and/or threats, depending upon your existing position, viewpoint and mindset. For a startup, a new technology can be its entire reason for being, but there is still a need to understand what is happening in the field. For established companies, or incumbents, emerging technologies are often seen as complicated, time consuming, risky and quite frightening. The reaction to this new reality is often a defensive response where the incumbent believes that the new technology poses a threat to its core business, and secondly a sense of possibilities when the technology shows promise and is too tempting to ignore.

The examples of Kodak, Blockbuster and Borders are illustrative; despite intense efforts to innovate and stay relevant when facing changing customer needs. They failed to survive in this new technological reality. Today technol-

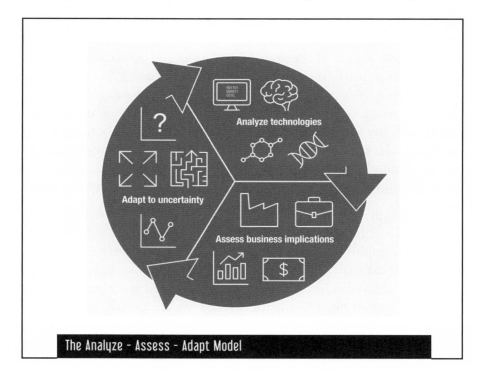

The Analyze - Assess - Adapt Model

ogy and business development intersect and create interesting and a highly complex environment. Not only do companies have to cope with a new reality of the increasing speed of technological development, they also have to face the challenge of designing new business models that can better cater to the ever-changing needs of consumers.

Based on my experience and background as an entrepreneur and early stage investor, I realized that all major corporate decisions, whether a strategic move in one of my existing companies or an investment decision in a new venture, are based on a number of factors. These are, first, an understanding of well-known mega trends (in this case technology); second, the notion that these trends will change the way a company or industry works; and third, the company's ability to adapt to this volatility, uncertainty and complexity.

Analyzing Emerging Technologies

Critical business decisions often need to be made in situations where information is scarce and filled with uncertainty and ambiguity. With today's constant flow of information it is difficult to set aside time to inform yourself of the potential "next big thing" when you have more pressing matters to deal with in running your daily business. But staying on top of current and future technology trends does not have to be complicated or time consuming. The challenge is to create a new mindset for how to relate to the constant flow of information. Do not for a second believe that it is possible to cover everything; instead be content with the fact that something is a lot better than nothing, and make following a number of technology news sources a part of your daily routine. Scan articles and aim for a good overview and then go deeper into a few specific areas. Use fresh perspectives, find new sources that are not necessarily aligned with your world view, ignore trigger warnings and try to move outside of your comfort zone.

Once you have identified relevant technologies, the next step is to estimate their respective approach velocity. Timing is often extremely difficult, but nonetheless of high importance. For this, three technology adoption level milestones are useful to consider: First, when the technology makes it onto the radar the first time and when the press is focusing on the "enormous" potential. At this point it is possible to create a brief initial strategic assessment, which tries to understand the implications of this new uncertainty. Second, when the technology has passed the hype, seen some negative press and is on its way to reach an early commercial audience. Third, when the technology has "crossed the chasm" and reached mainstream adoption. At this stage, media is covering the positive transformation angle, and now (at the latest) it is time to launch a full scale effort to handle this new technological landscape.

Spotify, the Swedish music industry disruptor, is a great example of a company that has managed to get the technological timing right. Already in 2006 when Spotify was founded, the entrepreneurs behind the company saw what was coming: That listeners would move from desktop to laptop to mobile as their primary device, that we would go to cloud based storage, from downloading to streaming music, and that advanced algorithms would be used to analyze our behavior and deliver better music recommendations. The success of Spotify, together with several other unicorns in the Swedish start-up scene, has paved the way for a more positive view on technology and business innovation. Politicians are now fighting to be seen at start-up events and entrepreneurs are considered to be one of the main future drivers of economic growth.

Assessing Short and Long Term Situations

The next step is to assess how your shortlist of emerging technologies will affect your future business from different perspectives. Just as with analyzing technologies, it is not possible to get a full overview and understanding of the business implications of a new technology. Instead, this whole approach is aimed at creating a new mindset and overall understanding of the intersection of business and technology.

Emerging technologies have an impact in all areas of business, ranging from how an industry changes, to how customers react, to the inner workings of a company and new operational challenges and opportunities. Based on this, and in an attempt to simplify but not over simplify, we can list a total of nine areas that need to be considered *(see table)*:

INDUSTRY	
Existing and new competition	What are existing competitors doing, and are they early adopters or laggards? Are other industries already using this technology? Will we see new entrants in the industry?
Partners and collaborators	Will this give more power to our existing partners and/or collaborators? Will this give us new partners and/or collaborators? Are your partners and/or collaborators expanding into your area?
Standards and regulations	What new standards will emerge? Will new regulations emerge? New legal requirements? Who will lead this work? The government? Large industry players?
CUSTOMER	
Value Proposition (and offering?)	What new value can you deliver to your customers? How can you deliver it? How will customer needs and expectations change? What parts of your existing value proposition will be less important or obsolete?
Products and services	Can your product or service be digitized and automated? Can you add products to your services or vice versa? Can the customer take part in the development and/or production of your offering?
Markets and segments	Are your markets or segments open to new innovations? Which are the most affected? Can you take your offering to new markets or segments? Areas where you see high (even exponential) growth from low levels?
COMPANY	
People and processes	Will this change the way we organize work? What new competencies will we need? What old ones will disappear? Can this improve your operational excellence?
Marketing and sales	Will this improve understanding of your audience? Will this provide new ways of reaching and interacting with your customers? Will this change your brand and/or positioning?
Supply chain	Will this give more power to your existing suppliers? Moving up the value chain? Will this open up for new suppliers? Will this mean new production processes? Warehousing? Logistics? Other?

By mapping each of the technologies according to levels of urgency and business impact, and plotting them in a matrix, the result is a visual representation of the relative importance of each technology. Now it is easy to gain a good overview of the strategic technology landscape for your organization. By keeping it close at hand, you will have updated alerts as the business and technology environment changes.

Performing this exercise and keeping the changing technological landscape in the back of your mind, will give you two perspectives on emerging technologies; technological urgency and business importance, which should result in four views of strategic technology priority. By mapping each individual technology from the two perspectives, it is easy to set priorities between technologies. Also, mapping progress over time highlights trends in which direction and at what speed a specific technology is heading:

ACT. You must act when a technological threat or opportunity is imminent, and it will have significant impact on your business environment. If you are not already embracing this technology, and unless you have a very good reason not to, now is the time to act;

PREPARE. These are the technologies that you need to understand thoroughly and for which you need to plan once they take off;

MONITOR. These technologies are, by definition, not relevant for your business – as of today, that is! As technology evolves and goes from experimentation through expansion and then eventually transforms society, the use and implications of a technology are bound to change; and

WATCH. You want to watch when technology disruption is imminent but not relevant to your industry or business. That said; do not fully discard the technology, since the landscape might change rapidly.

Adapting to a New Uncertainty

In recent years, organizations have become increasingly aware that "uncertainty is the new normal." It is a fact that the business world we used to know, where strategic planning was simply extrapolating a trend based on the past couple of years, has come to an end. Instead we see the emergence of a new understanding and acceptance of the fact that different perspectives on uncertainty and ambiguity are essential for future success. As with many other management approaches, this field has its roots in the military. In the 1990s, the acronym VUCA was introduced, short for vulnerability, uncertainty, complexity and ambiguity. The original purpose of this approach was to address strategic foresight and insight as well as include a behavioral perspective on groups and individuals.

Part of the uncertainty involved in a new technology relates to the likelihood that it will succeed on its own, and on how quickly that success will occur. For any business dealing with the old technology, there will come a time when they have to make a decision to continue in their current direction, jump ship and invest in the new technology, or find a balance between the old and the new. Take the music industry, for example. When digital music and file sharing first made a big splash, record companies had to make a decision either to embrace the new technology or to continue to produce and release music in the ways it had done previously. While all companies struggled through this transition, the ones that embraced the newer technology and found a balance between both were the ones that succeeded. Others held on to the old technology out of fear of the risk and uncertainty of the new.

From the uncertainty perspective, Sweden is unusual. It has a long history of stability, and has not participated in a major war for more than 200 years. Of course an intact industrial infrastructure after World War II was a huge strategic advantage when the rest of the Western world was rebuilding and in great need of almost everything. Moreover, this stability in combination with well-established legal frameworks and a consensus approach to the labor market has proven to be very fruitful for creating stability in an uncertain environment. This will most probably prove to be very useful in the coming decades when companies have to put all their energy into coping with ambiguity in all areas, from technology to business to environmental and geo-political challenges.

Conclusion

To summarize using the findings from the Global Information Technology Report 2016, where the World Economic Forum places Sweden among the top three countries in the world when it comes to the ability to leverage ICT (Information and Communications Technology) for increased competitiveness and well-being. The four key findings from the report translate well to the successful Swedish approach to technology, innovation and entrepreneurship.

First, the nature of digital innovation today is more about business model innovation than technological innovation, and in Sweden there is a long tradition of using technology to fuel business development. Just look at Skype and Spotify to mention two recent examples.

Second, there is today an increasing pressure to innovate continuously. Here Sweden has a long tradition of innovation and R&D (Research and Development), year after year ranking among the top countries in patent applications.

Third, the rapidly growing digital population is demanding new products and services. In Sweden, the digital user base is rapidly approaching 100 percent of the adult population. This creates a great test bed for businesses, which of course attracts talent as well as money.

Finally, the digital economy is requiring urgent innovations in governance and regulation. With a highly developed IT infrastructure, Sweden is well positioned to stay in the forefront of eGovernance, but all nations, including Sweden, can definitely improve.

Thank you for your attention and May the future be with you...

The Food Culture Revolution

Claus Meyer

> *"Instead of running around like a maniac trying to repair every single imperfection of our food culture, I could take a top down approach and share a simple idea: that one day Danish food culture could be counted amongst the greatest in the world."*

I am from a country where Ascetic doctors and puritan priests have led a 300-year-long crusade against the pleasure-giving qualities of food and against sensuality as such. For centuries the idea of preparing wonderful meals for your loved ones was considered a sin, in line with theft, exaggerated dancing, incest and masturbation. The philosophy so successfully communicated by these fine people was if you want to live a long and healthy life on earth and avoid going to hell eat something of inferior taste and get it over with in a hurry.

It was in this spirit that I was brought up in a middle class family in the 1960s—the darkest period in Danish food history. My mother represented the first generation of Danish women who worked outside the home. It was an era of canned meatballs and potato powder; of artificial sauce coloring and of the stock cube.

My parents raised me on a diet of fatty and cheap meat and frozen vegetables, pre-boiled years before in Kazakhstan and stocked in massive chest freezers in our basement. Most of the meat was coated in toasted bread crumbs three or four times and deep fried in margarine packed with trans-fat acids. We used the extra margarine for dipping.

My parent's generation had lost the connectivity to our landscapes, and the sense of seasonality. They had lost the language through which we capture the nuances of different food items, and, more broadly speaking, they had lost any interest in the more subtle qualities of our food and food systems.

At the age of 15, I weighed 94 kilos (approximately 207 pounds); one of the three fattest kids in the region. Eating was not a way to reach out towards the beauty of life. It was a matter of economic efficiency. Food should be cheap; it was to be prepared and eaten in less than 30 minutes. And I was not the only kid in the Nordic countries exposed to this. It's fair to say that we grew up with a range of indistinct, if not terrifying, national cuisines with no hint of greatness and devoid of coherence or any sort of regional sense of community. Until 2003, "Nordic Cuisine" didn't exist, not even as a linguistic construction.

I ended up spending the first 25 years of my adult life trying to improve the food culture in my home country, Denmark. I did this with a certain amount of success, but with a limited impact on the bigger food picture.

Then, at the beginning of the millennium, I co-authored a book about the Spanish food revolution and came to the realization that Spanish chefs such as P Sub, Martin Berasategui and Juan M Arzak had actually sat down in 1973 and made a conscious decision to revitalize Spanish cooking. 25 years later, with San Sebastian as the city in the world with the largest number of Michelin stars per capita and El Bulli selected as the Best Restaurant in the world in 2002, Spain had won its place as a global hegemon of gastronomy. This discovery made a certain impression on me.

Along with this discovery, I was inspired by a number of Danish film-makers under the leadership of Lars Von Trier, who launched their dogma manifesto that for more than a moment, at least in Europe, changed the dynamics of film making in the late 1990s. Finally, I met an expert in plant biology, Niels Ehler, with whom I entered into a long and extremely inspiring discussion about the impact of the land on the biochemical makeup of plants, as well as their aromas and health promoting attributes.

Influenced by these experiences I got the very simple idea that instead of running around like a maniac trying to repair every single imperfection of our food culture, I could take a top down approach and share a simple idea: that one day Danish food culture could be counted amongst the greatest in the world.

This was my sudden realization, and for me it was a revelation. So I decided to do three things: The first was to open up a restaurant that would explore ancient Nordic cooking techniques and work solely with local produce, which at that time was a totally outrageous idea.

The other was to start exploring if one day our food culture could be counted as one of the most admirable in the world, and which values should define that culture and guide our journey.

My third task was to form an idea, the vehicle through which we could efficiently disseminate this belief system into the lives of people. Now we were talking systemic change, a shift of paradigm, so I had to find a way of engaging the most important stakeholders in that agenda before this could grow on its own from the bottom up.

In 2003 I picked Chef Rene Redzepi as head chef for the restaurant that would embody these ideals. We called it Noma, and I proposed to him a partnership. And then, he introduced me to chef Mads Refslund. That encounter changed our lives and looking back, I could not possibly overestimate the impact of this choice. Rene Redzepi and I saw the same light- we found that the time had come for chefs to raise their voice.

Luxury at that time was about foie gras, truffles, lobster and caviar, hand-ironed table-cloths, expensive stuff—fine dining for the elite. We wanted to redefine luxury. We felt that ingredients, picked or caught and treated with passion, humble ingredients like weeds, beet roots and herring could be considered luxurious as well. We wanted to emphasize seasonality and the idea of "terroir" in cooking, to restore the link between the chef and their surroundings in nature.

We also wanted great food to be compatible with healthiness and sustainability; and at that time, a position taken by no food culture in the entire world.

The reality, however, was that we were on a suicide mission. Our colleagues doubted that we could run a restaurant relying entirely on local produce – what would we do in the wintertime when nothing could be harvested in our region? People made fun of us and said we were serving seal penis, the rotten intestines of arctic birds, baby whale and other endangered species. In those days a dinner reservation at Noma sounded more like a threat than an invitation.

A few months after the opening of Noma we invited the gastro-intelligentsia to a Nordic Kitchen Symposium. The basic idea was to unite chefs and farmers in all of the Nordic countries: small and big companies, politicians and private individuals around a common vision to define the contours of a New Nordic cuisine.

Noma was not meant to be the best, and the purpose of the New Nordic Cuisine was not to build an introverted elitist brotherhood reserved for biodynamic farmers and wannabe Michelin chefs. We wanted to find a way of coming up with food that would blow people away and profoundly impact their lives. But we also wanted the values from the manifesto to live not just in a fine dining context but in our everyday lives, and in people's hearts.

Today, 12 years later, cabbage is worshipped and rye is the new black in a cook's proverbial closet. Wild herbs are collected and sold in supermarkets, and festivals celebrating our food have emerged all over Scandinavia, and even in the U.S. thousands of restaurants and chefs have followed in the footsteps of Noma and left their French, Spanish or eclectic menus behind them in search of more original expressions of their surroundings and context. A huge and growing number of young vibrant food companies have been born, a handful of Nordic restaurants have entered the list of the world's 50 best, and most of the culinary world is asking, why did it all happen?

To answer that question, we will leave aside timing, human talent and the success of Noma. From the very beginning, we thought of the New Nordic Cuisine as a benign virus, an informal movement of consumers driven not by desire for short-term profits, but by the joy of learning more, and of building true value together. The journey has been characterized by openness, knowledge sharing, a democratic perspective and a wish to include everyone down the road. No one can really be against the New Nordic Cuisine Movement.

As with all things in life defined loosely, in the end the New Nordic Cuisine will of course be whatever we make it out to be. For me, the truly compelling and valuable aspect of this movement is the redefined role of the chef in the modern society and with everything it implies for our food cultures and the concept of using deliciousness as an instrument for solving some of the most important problems of our time.

Now that the chef community has been awakened, food journalism globally has risen to an unprecedented level of refinement, but also ruthlessness with regards to inadequate ethics. I have come to believe that we are getting there; that there is a fair chance that my kids will one day live in a world where the ideas we stood up for in the past few years will have become "the new normal." And now living in America, I am particularly happy to see how many U.S. chefs, foodies and food entrepreneurs share this perspective, are moving in this same direction and are pursuing it with great eagerness. I look forward to seeing how this progresses on a global stage and am proud that what started as a simple idea in Denmark has brought about change that we never could have imagined.

From Design Studio on a Norwegian Mountain to World Stage

Carlos Zachrison Arne Nerjordet

"The best way to create something modern, exciting and new is to look back into your past, your own history, your culture and your heritage. Just look around and take the very best elements of the things you love and make them relevant for a modern audience."

Officially, we started ARNE & CARLOS in 2002. A few years earlier we had decided that we wanted to have our own business, but didn't have enough capital or knowledge for how to achieve this. At the time, Arne was working as a teacher in fashion design and pattern construction at the Esmod school of fashion design in Oslo and had received a job offer to teach in Jakarta, Indonesia. I had received a job offer to go work for IKEA in Beijing, China at the same time. Neither one of us actually wanted to take those jobs, far away from Norway, and also far away from each other, and so we decided that we would start a design company together.

Without any funds to start a business, we only had one option: to sell the small apartment that we owned in Oslo and move to the countryside. This happened in the year 2000. Arne had an acquaintance who told him about a disused railway station in Etnedal, which is located in the inland region of Valdres, about 170 km north of Oslo, 80 km east of Lillehammer and 149 km from Oslo Airport. Tonsasen Station, as it is known locally, is a small, traditional looking wooden house, built around 1902 and part of the Valdres railway network that was in use until 1988. The train station, next to a small lake, is located 682.5 meters above sea level. In addition to the station building, there are three additional houses on the property.

We immediately saw huge potential in this property. Inside the main house, were three large rooms with high ceilings and huge windows on the ground floor and upstairs an apartment that had been used by the stationmaster. There was plenty of beautiful light, with sun from morning to evening and sunsets over the lake in the summer. The air was pure and crisp and there was lots of sun, blue skies and snow in winter, as well as a big system of cross country skiing tracks, one of which was laid out on the old railway tracks that passed by our house. It was perfect! We knew we would have a lot of work to do, but the location was idyllic and peaceful, not too isolated nor far away from Oslo Airport, so we decided very quickly that it was doable to renovate the houses, create a residence for ourselves, as well as a design studio, and establish ourselves in this area. So we made an offer and got the entire property for a very small amount of money. The idea was to do the most immediate renovations, such as upgrading the electrical system and reintroducing running water in the main house, and then use the rest of the money from the sale of the apartment to fund the start-up of our business. Then we would continue the renovation of the houses slowly, over the coming years. We saw this whole process as a "life style" project and it actually inspired us from the beginning to include the story of our house in our business model.

Neither Arne nor I knew much about starting a business, but we did have some ideas of what we wanted to do, we would start a fashion business, specializing in women's wear and use our Scandinavian esthetics in both the designs as well as in marketing strategy. We spent the first couple of years preparing ourselves to set this up and in the meantime we took local odd jobs and attended "How to start your own business" courses offered by the government. We learned a lot about the practical things, like how to register a business in the official register, how to make a budget and how to make a business plan.

In the beginning, we felt that no one really took us seriously, as we always were pretty clear about what we wanted to do and how we wanted to achieve it. We always knew we wanted to address an international audience straight away, as we felt our concept might be "too Norwegian for Norway" and would therefore not work as well in our own country. Many people thought that our business idea and model was a bit far-fetched, we could see it on people's faces as we were asked many times if we were really serious about starting "an international design business, from a small railway station, on top of a mountain, 682.5 meters above sea level, in a remote area in inland Norway." Usually, when people asked this question, we would just smile and reply: "Sure, why not? We have electricity at home, there is a phone line, we have an internet connection and we also have a fax. And the airport is not that far away."

Looking back at this now we realize that we may have been ahead of our time in our way of thinking. Today, 16 years later, it is very common for a lot of people to work from anywhere in the world. All you really need is a computer and a Wi-Fi connection! Today, we also know there is an ongoing global trend, where creative people all over the world, who do not have to go to a physical office to work, settle in the countryside, making the areas outside the cities more innovative and exciting. There weren't many like us in the early years, but this is more common now. We identify with that group of people. And I think our life style has also become a big part of the Nordic "good life" with which our fans and readers associate us.

In August 2002 we launched our first women's wear collection. It was a series of sewn and knitted garments, inspired by our personal universe and Scandinavian heritage. We showed our collection in Oslo and it was an instant success with the press, landing us the cover of VG, the largest newspaper in Norway, the next day. We immediately became known as "the designers that live in an old railway station in Valdres." Ever since that day, the press has been fascinated by our work and our way of life. It started in Norway, but 14 years later we are interviewed and written about on a regular basis all over the world: from South Korea and Japan to Europe to the USA and Canada. I think the fascination people have with us is very connected to our way of life. We have chosen to remain in rural Norway and continue to get our inspiration from the place we live and work, and choose to travel around the world to promote our work and our Scandinavian life style. It's our daily life that interests people, and the fact that it is very down to earth, and real.

The launch of our brand may have been very successful with the press, but the next years were still quite hard. We didn't manage to sell anything in the beginning and we were running out of money very fast. Luckily, we did have a press book that started filling very quickly, and people's skepticism towards our idea was slowly changing into admiration and excitement, so we tried contacting a series of people who worked with developing our region and the local communities in Valdres, to see if they could help us move forward and help us solve the financial issue that we were facing. And maybe help us find an investor, or something like that. Within a few months we were referred to an advisor in Lillehammer who specialized in working with innovative concepts and people like us, and who helped them set up companies and finance them. Our local community even sponsored the initial fee of 20,000 NOK that we needed to get the 20 hours it took to set up a new business plan, a budget and an application to Innovation Norway, a governmental company in Norway that gives out grants to people who start their own companies.

We will always be immensely grateful to Innovation Norway. Without their help, we would never have been where we are today. It started with a simple grant, to establish our first company. We sent an application to them, which we wrote together with our advisor and after a few months we received a phone call from their office in Lillehammer, giving us the great news that our application was accepted and that we had received a grant of 200,000 NOK to finance our idea. Since then and for the next few years, Innovation Norway helped us by continuing to help fund our company and projects.

But Innovation Norway knows that not all companies they fund will last long enough to prove themselves. We faced this situation in 2007. After many years of designing a series of women's wear, travelling to, and showing our products in showrooms during fashion weeks in Copenhagen, Paris and New York, we were still getting a lot of press and attention as well as establishing our brand. But there were not enough sales, no money coming in and things were not looking very good for us. We were very aware that we were at a point where something serious could happen to us, where we would have to give up on our idea.

At a meeting with Innovation Norway, we explained our situation and told them our prospects were not looking very good. We were then told by them that they had many different ways of helping out companies. There were grants, loans with low interest, and there was also the possibility to get a grant that would help fund a Mentor for us. Innovation Norway felt that we had potential, but we were not very business minded, only creative, and perhaps getting a person with deep business knowledge to help and guide us could be the best way to move forward. Arne and I started discussing potential mentors and we quickly realized that getting all the media attention was also getting us a great network of highly skilled people, and when we started looking into who we'd met, we realized we had an incredible list of potential candidates. On the top of our list was a strong Norwegian businesswoman who we had met through mutual acquaintances, and with whom we already had a great personal relationship. At first, we were a bit afraid of asking her as we didn't think she would be interested in helping a business such as ours, but we decided we had nothing to lose, so we asked her. We were very surprised and excited when she answered YES immediately! And so, she became our mentor.

The next few years were incredible. Our mentor helped open our eyes, she told us to focus on our strengths and she truly helped both Arne and me to find our own roles in our business. I think most of the really useful things we've learned about business we learnt from her. The years between 2008 and 2010 where the most exciting and productive years in our company. We looked at what we were doing and realized that the women's line wasn't working because it wasn't commercial enough. We had been ignoring the fact that it was our Scandinavian inspired sweaters that had most potential and were the items that were getting the best feedback. So from one day to another, we simply decided to focus on our knitwear and get rid of the rest in order to create a line of sweaters and accessories for men and women. We showed our first knitwear collection at the Paris men's fashion week and suddenly we were writing orders constantly for the duration of the whole show. Looking back at this today, I think there were a number of factors that contributed to this sudden success. Our mentor's help in rethinking our strategy was one of those factors, naturally, but also, we tapped in on the beginning of a new trend, where stores were looking for unique products that were not mass produced in China. They were looking for unique products that told a story, preferably made by small family run companies, in remote locations. And we fit in perfectly with this trend. I don't think we would have had the same impact, if we would have launched our knitwear line the year before. In our business, timing is of crucial importance.

We went from selling our line in a few stores to around 200 of the most high-end and prestigious fashion stores in the world. It was an exciting time for us and we felt like we were finally getting everything together! Still, we had a feeling that the knitwear line that we had established could be one of those fashion trends that were "hot" today and "out" tomorrow. We were looking at our situation and realizing that perhaps things could change from one day to the other. One clear indicator of this problem was all the other brands that suddenly started doing "Scandinavian Knitwear." When H&M put a series of Scandinavian looking sweaters on their window display, we knew we were in trouble. And then, the financial crisis hit the world, including Norway.

In the beginning, we were scared of the financial crisis. But our Mentor would say to us: "Don't worry; we have control over the situation." Our order books remained more or less unchanged in 2009 and we were still doing business just as we had done in 2008. But we couldn't help noticing there was something in the air around that time, things were changing very quickly in the world of fashion. People had less money, things weren't selling as they used to and everything was on sale. I remember having a meeting with a German agent that wanted to represent us and sell our line all over Germany. He said to us that the whole point of people changing their wardrobe after fashion trends, every six months, was so that people like him and we could "sell more clothes." We never really thought that we were part of that society of mass consumption until he uttered those words. For us, the end product wasn't really the most interesting thing. We loved the design process, the way we used our culture and heritage to create unique pieces and the desire to share the entire design process with the people that bought our products.

In January 2010, we knew there was going to be a big change for us. After the men's shows in Paris and Copenhagen Fashion Week, Arne and I had a meeting. Living together, as we do, we usually don't have meetings. This was the first and only time in our professional life that we sat down to have a serious talk. We sat there, looking at our order books, sales were still okay, although they were going down due to the financial crisis, but we were realizing that we were getting tired of the fashion industry and we also felt that fashion was becoming unfashionable. The whole concept of changing your wardrobe every six months was becoming ridiculous, for many different reasons. So, we decided to cancel all our orders and leave the fashion industry for good. By February 2010, we had let our two employees go and spent the greater part of spring selling the stock of knitwear that we had accumulated during the earlier years. We opened a pop-up shop in our house during Easter. We put an ad in the newspaper aimed at everyone who came to spend their Easter holidays in the mountains where we lived and we managed to sell most of the stock we had during that one week.

In 2008 we collaborated with Comme des Garçons, a very exclusive, high concept brand from Japan. We designed a collection of knitwear and because the theme of this collaboration was for the Christmas holidays, we decided to propose to the owner of the brand that we should decorate all their concept stores with knitted Christmas Balls, with Norwegian patterns, designed by us. The owner of the brand, Rei Kawakubo loved the idea so much that she ordered 400 balls to be designed by us. We had them produced in the factories we collaborated with in Peru and in December 2008, all her stores carried the line of knitwear that we had designed for her, as well as the balls. We visited the shop in Paris and the collection looked amazing there, but to our horror, we discovered that the balls that we had designed and made for them were not used as decoration, but were being sold for $100 each. We found that to be insane and provocative, as these little Christmas Balls were so easy to make and should be accessible to anyone. That provocation made us contact a publisher in 2009, Cappelen Damm, which is Norway's largest publishing house. We pitched the idea of the Christmas Balls to them as a DIY book with knitted patterns and they signed us straight away. Our idea was to collect a series of Scandinavian patterns and adapt them to a knitted ball that anyone could knit. There was a one problem though, they already had a DIY Knitting book with a Christmas theme to publish in 2009 and therefore asked us if we could wait until 2010. We accepted this and started to work on our very first book.

We knew the book was going to be published in September 2010, but we had no idea of how well it was going to do. The few people we told about the book smiled and didn't quite believe this was going to be our big break. We weren't sure ourselves, but we just didn't want to go back to the fashion industry again and so we hoped things would turn out for the best. We spent the summer of 2010 in our garden with nothing else to do than work on our flower beds and enjoy a very long and relaxing summer. Within days of the publication of our book, it had reached Number 3 on the best seller lists in Norway and after a few weeks it was Number 1 and stayed there for the rest of that year. We were everywhere that Christmas! Eventually, the foreign language rights to this book were sold to more than 15 countries. Since then we have written seven books which are enjoyed by a wide audience in English, Danish, Dutch, Estonian, Finnish, French, German, Icelandic, Italian, Japanese, Korean, Russian, Spanish and Swedish. We have landed an extremely successful collaboration with one of the largest yarn companies in the world and do consulting for them on a regular basis. We are also sought after speakers and travel the world to meet our fans and promote our books.

The past six years have taken us to so many new countries where we connect with people and tell them about our life in rural Norway and our passion and joy for crafts like knitting and crochet. It has been amazing and we could have never dreamed of living the life we live now.

Experiencing this from our perspective we sometimes struggle to understand what the big deal is. Why do people from every corner of the world connect with Arne and me? Everywhere we go, there are always crowds of excited fans who want to meet us. But it's just us, two normal Scandinavian guys, who live on a mountain in rural Norway and who have a passion for gardening and knitting. What's so special about that?

We have many theories on this and there isn't just one straightforward answer. I think that for us, design is very emotional, and our designs come from the heart. We put a lot of ourselves into our work and we love referencing our childhood and our culture. So regardless of where people come from they seem to understand where we are coming from. Of course, we are also benefiting from the huge and never ending Scandinavian trend that people just can't seem to get enough of.

Now that we write books we are not just showing people our products, as we were doing in the fashion industry. With our books, we can also share with them our design process and our unique universe which is deeply connected to all the things we do and love as well as our house and the garden.

Or maybe it is as simple as this: The best way to create something modern, exciting and new is to look back into your past, your own history, your culture and your heritage. Just look around and take the very best elements of the things you love and make them relevant for a modern audience. Not only will you be able to create something fabulous, you will also be preserving and passing your culture on to the next generation.

Creating a Future for Scandinavian Movie-Making

Elísabet Ronaldsdóttir

"It is a telling fact that if you surf the internet in Europe, Scandinavia included, films are usually listed under Art and Culture. In America, they are listed under entertainment."

Every country has many cultures. Every mind that is corralled within that culture, good or wicked, has an interesting story to tell or to suppress.

The visual mediums are trading in virtual reality that can offer us a better sense of what lurks under the surface. When personal stories expose the hidden shackles that are causing real pain, a single moment can alter the idea of what is acceptable among vast swaths of the population. And as our perceptions change, the call for new stories continues, as does our need to tell these stories to set us all straight.

One year after I was born, Iceland got its first national TV station that broadcasted twice a week for the first year. This later became daily except for Thursdays. During the short Icelandic summer, every able hand in the country was needed elsewhere and TV was off the air during the month of July. In spite of that, I grew up with lots of TV because we were exposed to a clash of cultures; we could ride piggy back on broadcasts from an American military base.

From a very early age, I delivered newspapers. This might be called child labor today, but decades ago I was just pulling my weight. Every month I was rewarded with a film screening in an abandoned World War II army barrack; always with American features on the screen. Although a film enthusiast, I was already 15 when I got my first chance to see an Icelandic film. The point of all this is that I grew up in the culture of American film and TV, not because these were better than Scandinavian stories but because they were more accessible.

Today, I cannot even imagine cinema or TV without American, European, Asian and Scandinavian influences in a refined blend. Through all these decades we have influenced each other copiously. This is the beauty of cultural mingling and, with any luck, it will bring us forward to a common cause.

The Nordic countries have had a blooming film and TV industry for a long time. There is no lack of stories in this part of the world and no lack of quality, but the limited distribution continues to be an Achilles heel and even European budgets never match those of Hollywood studio films. In Europe, Hollywood dominates the cinema scene. On average, 80 percent of all films shown in cinemas across Europe are products from Hollywood. Even in countries like France, with large film industries, the American films continue to dominate. There is no question that North America has a grounded tradition and has gained superb craftsmanship in story telling through moving images.

But easy access to financing plays a big role in all film production and the vast distribution networks, including American military bases, can make or break the success of a new movie or a TV program.

It is a great privilege to have worked on film in Denmark, Iceland, England and America. While the goal is always to tell a good story, European and American film appear worlds apart. In my mind it is mainly because American cinema is deeply rooted in entertainment while European and Icelandic cinema have stronger roots in literature.

The culture industry of films, whether they are made for entertainment, has become a world supermarket that seeks to satisfy demands of acquired customer taste. A few Icelandic films are more like fresh produce sold over the table in a farmers market. They have an only locally acquired taste, but are unsullied by industrial ingredients to enhance the flavor.

Indeed, most European films are labeled as art films in America and only reach a limited audience in the larger metropolitan areas. It is a telling fact that if you surf the internet in Europe, Scandinavia included, films are usually listed under Art and Culture. In America, they are listed under entertainment.

Nothing crystallizes this notion better than the different approach in financing a film. American film and TV are financed, more or less, through private funds while public funds make up the budget on the other side. The director is on the top of the pyramid as the storyteller, rightfully or not, except in America where the producers govern the top. My experience is that in Europe, and especially in Iceland, the focus is still on the director's vision. In America, the focus is on what the target audience is willing to pay for a ticket. The more money in the pot, the more pressure for solid returns. There are pros and cons with attitudes; the focus on what sells may gather a bigger budget to work with, but the end result may become a hot monotone mess in the attempt to accommodate as many viewers as possible. The focus on a director's vision can bring out originality and push a film as an engaging piece of art, or it can end up as a piece of self-indulgent crap.

Please don't get me wrong, I respect the work of filmmakers on both sides of the Atlantic. They move within different frameworks but they all work hard on telling their stories. Money has always been a powerful influence as it takes a lot of it to make a full length feature film. But money alone cannot buy originality or even a good story, but it can buy a good film in order to remake it. America has a tendency to remake the foreign films that they like, not only because they don't like reading subtitles, but because they know they can make more money by taking the story and the style through the traditional grinder. I am of course generalizing; America is extremely diverse and there is more in the American mix than Hollywood.

With new technology filmmakers can engage in their art at lower costs, which bodes well for Scandinavian cinema. And the advent of digital overtaking photochemical film has had a great influence in Iceland as we no longer need to seek film developing abroad with its attendant significant financial cost. Even the historic advantage of American film distribution is being challenged by new distribution technologies.

In the last decade, the borderless world of cyberspace has changed the way we watch and listen to our daily dose of entertainment. We are gaining access to works that we never before had a chance to enjoy. We are just realizing the enormity of a digital shift. Soon the fresh produce of our farmers market will be but a click away. Scandinavian films have broken out of the local cultural pen and there are no limits to the influence we can spread. We all gain from a healthy film industry, its positive economic impact is well documented, and it is imperative that policymakers understand what's at stake and take decisive steps to secure its existence.

There are many challenges in store for the future of Nordic cinema. Europe has made its own blockbusters while we in Scandinavia sometimes fall into the pit of pretending to be American. I hope we will have the good sense to embrace diversity while retaining our courage to honor local heartfelt stories. That of course requires financial support and solid government backup. One can always hope.

From the Abstract to the Concrete: The Danish Approach to Design

Kasper
Salto

Thomas
Sigsgaard

"We often talk about a relay race when we explain our relationship to earlier generations of designers. We are obliged to know our history in order to be able to define where we are headed."

When at the beginning of the 1950s Finn Juhl was given the task of designing the Danish Hall in the United Nations (UN) building in New York, better known as the Trusteeship Council Chamber (TCC), there were a number of things about which he wanted to have an imprint of in his proposal. One of the first things we know he did was visit the site; the first thing an architect does! He went to the building site in New York to sense what we are still taught in architecture school today: the genius loci—the spirit of place.

Finn Juhl sensed that the ceiling in the hall, which was under construction and therefore pretty much only a raw concrete framework, felt too low in relation to the space. The space, in his eyes, was out of proportion, and he straightaway went about finding a solution to this problem. Today, we know that this observation would form the basis for the spectacular ceiling, one of the things for which the hall is best known.

The interior design of the TCC was later proven to be his real breakthrough in Danish design and is today one of the most important cultural edifices in Denmark.

It is one thing to say that the interior design of the TCC would be the high point of Finn Juhl's career. It was something else, a bit more fortuitous, that in connection with the creation of the TCC he ran into a certain gentleman by the name of Edgar Kaufmann Jr. Kaufmann not only introduced an array of Finn Juhl's furniture to the American market, but also furniture from other prominent Danish designers which started the great interest in Danish and Scandinavian design. In the decades that followed, one of the greatest Danish and Scandinavian export successes slowly took shape. Today Denmark is still known as one of the most important leaders in design in every aspect of the discipline.

In 2010, we were invited to participate in the competition to refurbish the TCC, which was next in line for a comprehensive renovation in the UN building. The hall was quite shabby and did not live up to modern requirements for technology and lighting. The layout of the hall had also been changed since Finn Juhl's project from the 1950s. In Denmark, the project was administered by the Danish Ministry of Culture in close collaboration with the Danish Ministry of Foreign Affairs. The Danish Arts Foundation was responsible for the competition itself.

Five experienced designers from Denmark were invited to the competition. They were five designers who all had great insight into the production of furniture. This was important for the task since time was short. It was also important that the designers were from Denmark, since we were dealing with Danish cultural heritage on a world-class level. Each of the designers was to submit a proposal for new tables and chairs for the hall. At the point when we were introduced to the project, the hall was pretty much as raw and empty as that time in the 1950s when Finn Juhl went across the Atlantic to inspect the site.

Taking a trip over there was also one of the first things we considered doing, but as mentioned, there was not much to see in the hall and time was short. Our task in relation to Finn Juhl was to execute new furniture that would fit in with Finn Juhl's design of the hall. Whereas Finn Juhl in his time wanted to relate to the spirit of place, we wanted just as much to relate to Finn Juhl's "spirit." We began a journey into the universe of Finn Juhl, a journey that meant not only getting inside another man's way of thinking but also connecting it to a completely different time in the history of Danish design.

There was no doubt that because the TCC is such a significant piece of cultural heritage for Denmark, there would be a focus on this project beyond the professional interest in our success of adapting this new furniture; there would also be attention from the media. We would come to experience this interest at close range even from the start of the process. The Danish national television station DRK followed all five teams very closely throughout the entire competition period up until delivery, in particular, the announcement of the winner of the competition. This took place at MOMA in New York with Her Majesty Queen Margrethe of Denmark hosting.

We won the competition, and soon after began one of the greatest experiences and challenges in our professional life. This period led to a lot of self-examination and internal debate at Salto and Sigsgaard, but the debate primarily took its starting point in the public space with the press and among colleagues, since there was a great interest in the thought process behind our proposal.

Denmark is a democratic country; therefore, daily discussion takes up a lot of space in the lives of Danes. We are constantly on the lookout for an alternative way of doing things. We engage in doubt where others toe the line, and we are generally interested in getting our mitts into things. For us at Salto & Sigsgaard, we talk a lot about not going for inspiration but rather engaging in abstraction. Inspiration is often used in design and architecture and represents an immediate and unexplained idea that suddenly arises. Whereas abstraction is "the slate that is wiped clean," and the necessity of complete emersion starting from the beginning in order to get everything in. We are obsessed with starting our process with research, in which every imaginable thing that has influence on the future product is found. This is vital before any decision is made. In this way, we have a greater opportunity to hit the bulls-eye. We often say that, when we have done proper research, things almost design themselves. The most important thing is the research in order to avoid getting into a situation later in which we have to say, "Oh, we didn't think of that."

However, if we are to be honest, we experienced such a situation at MOMA in New York in front of the Queen of Denmark after she had announced us as winners of the competition for new furniture for the TCC. It happened at the reception afterwards, where she in a painterly way described the situation around the front edges of the delegate tables, which we had designed rounded, that made it possible for, as she put it, 'secret documents to slip over the edge and be revealed.' Her Majesty has a good perspective on art, design and architecture. We could see no way around admitting that we had not thought of this and asked whether we might use this excellent observation in our ongoing process. We could. She is also a very accommodating person. The Queen's focus on the situation with the rounded edge ended up becoming a detail in the design of the tables where we combined two challenges: one was the situation in preventing things from rolling over the edge and the other was the challenge of "spring back" in the molded tables. We had a rather large, molded veneer front on the delegate tables that gives a bit over time. If we did not do anything, this would appear as a fissure in the assembly between the table top and the front. The solution was to let the front overlap the table top a little, thus solving both challenges. This detail today goes under the name "the Queen detail."

This story relates a very essential component of what we believe characterizes Danish design, which is also the reason Danish design has become so well-known and valued. Today, anyone can design, render and 3-D print things that look handcrafted and finished, but are not. Design requires an insight into materials, finances, logistics, production methods etc., to make things into reality, something that should involve a number of different fields.

Many designers in Denmark do not see themselves as people who design products. They place great store in their honor to finding a principle, and only in the subsequent dialogue with the producer, developer, or other relevant professional input, does design arise. Therefore, the principle that we invent must not be fixed by a form, because then there is little room for adjustments when the, in our eyes; true design process begins.

What a designer is educated in, is to imagine things. To a high degree, it is to find things that have a relevance in this world: to find the right problem and then find the right solution for it. Unfortunately, there are too many examples of "right solutions, but for the wrong problems." And this is something that we at Salto & Sigsgaard focus on in much of our approach to design, to find a "good problem." And then the right solution.

One of our recent projects at Salto & Sigsgaard is, in our eyes, a good problem/challenge that we are all familiar with, and which a lot of solutions are found but lack the essential ingredient. The problem takes its starting point from the fact that there are more and more people in this world and, as if that weren't enough, many of us really want to live in large cities. In fact, the idea came into being after a visit to the Danish art museum Louisiana, where there was an exhibition that took up the subject of the extent to which we must relate to numbers like; in 2038 half the world's population will live in metropolises. Taking this as our starting point, we saw many interesting challenges in everyday life and in the subsequent days we spoke a lot about how living quarters will take shape in accordance with these facts.

The project we ended up throwing ourselves into, had to do with how we tackle having guests in a small residence. How do we quickly and easily adjust our living space so that it can relatively quickly transition into holding a larger or smaller party?

Relative to earlier generations, our living quarters are already in the process of a transformation in which, among other things, the permanent dining room with room for 8-12 guests is exploited for other purposes or is not part of new construction at all. More and more people today go out to eat, but there is still a widespread and good tradition in Denmark to visit each other; family and friends, work colleagues, etc. What we wanted to solve was how to conjure up seating quickly and easily! So we ended up with a seat that was close at hand – but not in the way. We were both tired of having to drive into the office to get extra chairs or going up to the attic to find chairs that were filthy, cold and possibly ruined by weather. You can find many types of folding chairs that are quite fine and functional, but they do not take into account the storage situation when they are not in use.

We picked up the baton with one chair—it was Mogens Koch's folding chair from 1932, for which he designed a stand so that when they were not in use, they could be stored upright and folded. However, they still took up space in the house, and we wanted to have chairs that would "disappear," so they were just as much out of the way as a chair in the attic or the cellar.

The first thing we did was to scout our homes and workplaces to find a suitable place for these extra seats when they were not in use. Quite quickly our interest fell on the bookshelf, the bookshelf that everyone has and is also found on a large scale at most workplaces. Now it was just a matter of getting a chair in there! This we realized would require it to be folded. We saw it as an absolute necessity that the chair should end up having the same seating height as an ordinary dining table chair.

If you imagine an ordinary box bookshelf approximately 70 x 70 x 30 cm., divided into 4 spaces, then we have a space for storage that is about 30 x 30 x 30 cm. If we imagine a block to sit on in these measurements, then we 'lack' about 18 cm. in height. These 18 centimeters were a big reason that the project remained for many years an idea/a principle. It was, in other words, not easy to solve, and the project changed design many times until, with the Danish furniture producer MONTANA, we set about developing GUEST in 2012.

MONTANA is mostly known for its large shelf system in a sea of colors. So, the fact that we had gotten hold of Denmark's best and largest producer of shelves could not have been more relevant for the project. Today, GUEST is a piece of furniture that fits naturally into MONTANA's portfolio— particularly, since books are moving off the shelves and into tablets etc. GUEST is also a piece of furniture that challenges the traditional view of a folding chair. It is folded together; the same size as a thick book, and therefore fits into most bookshelves, and also especially the Mogens Koch shelf that, in its time, inspired MONTANA.

Perhaps, Mogens Koch had toyed with the same ideas of putting a chair in a bookshelf since in his day he designed a folding chair but lacked the "good problem."

The two examples we have emphasized here—the TCC in the UN building in New York and GUEST—take their starting point in the surrounding context/space. They are two very different spaces, but common to them is that in these two spaces there are necessary things that have decisive influence on the products that are going into them. We view the process itself of finding these things and generally getting the things to take shape as a sort of tool, something we take with us from task to task. A tool that we can maintain like, for example, a good knife. The tasks are different from project to project, but our process/tool, this is something we refine and hone on a running basis.

Working

Karsten Dybvad, Paving the Way for a Wealth of Ideas:
Embracing the 'Flat' Model, Chapter 5

Montana Chairs

Salto and Sigsgaard, From the Abstract to the Concrete:
The Danish Approach to Design, Chapter 4

United Nations Design

Salto and Sigsgaard, From the Abstract to the Concrete:
The Danish Approach to Design, Chapter 4

Game Graveyard
Ilkka Paananen, Supercell, Sisu and the Importance of Failure, Chapter 5

Children's Theater

Karin Helander, The Child's Right to Culture and the Arts, Chapter 3

Sustainable Fisheries

Thor Sigfusson, A New Utilization Movement, Chapter 6

Archipelago *(Ivana Helsinki)*
Paola Suhonen, Nordic Light, Chapter 4

Teamwork

Pasi Sahlberg, An Education System
Where Quality and Equality Go Hand in Hand, Chapter 3

Photo Credit: Mari Paavola

Urban Transport

Emmi Itäranta, In Our Nature: The Case for the Future of
Sustainable Transport, Chapter 6

Photo Credit: Mads Pihl

Faint northern lights over Tasiilaq Mountain Hut

Minninguaq Kleist, Greenland—An Up and Coming
Arctic Island Country, Chapter 6

Fuuse Films: Banaz—A Love Story

Khan and Payton, Minority Women and Nordic Values, Chapter 8

Fuuse Films: World Woman Conference

Khan and Peyton, Minority Women and Nordic Values, Chapter 8

Meet in the Street along Denver 16th Street Mall

Jeff Risom, The Nordic Urban Design Model, Chapter 6

Christmas Balls to Knit

Arne Nerjordet and Carlos Zachrison,
From Design Studio on a Norwegian Mountain to World Stage, Chapter 4

Sled Dogs Pulling Uphill

Minninguaq Kleist, Greenland—
An Up and Coming Arctic Island Country, Chapter 6

Helsinki Seaside

Pekka Sauri, Helsinki: In Search of the Optimal City, Chapter 1

Spin Me

Jeff Risom, The Nordic Urban Design Model, Chapter 6

During the Golden Age in Danish design, which began between the two World Wars, we see a clear starting point in the dialogue between designer and producer. But there was also a fundamental desire to make good, solid furniture for all social strata. Design rings in the ears of many as something that is expensive, but we know today that this is not the case. The task is almost always to find the easiest and cheapest way to produce a product. At any rate, you can say that we in Denmark are known for simple design and that we are finished with design: When you cannot "take more away" and not, "when you cannot add more." In our eyes, the simplicity in our everyday design can easily stem from the previously named desire. In fact, we almost demand that things be transparent and easy to grasp and understand.

When, we set out on the task of developing new furniture for the TCC, we had to put ourselves into another human being's thought-process, not to do design like Finn Juhl, but to harvest valuable knowledge to continue the process. Moreover, we had to get into a design universe that took place over 50 years ago, a universe that, as mentioned before, was designated as the Golden Age of Danish design.

For good or ill, this part of design history has had a great influence on the subsequent generations of designers and architects. And we have to say that, every so often, it has been a challenge to get out from under the shadow of the great pioneers and get the eyes of the world directed toward new design.

Of course you can ask yourself why there has to be something new when what is on the market sells well. But the question is whether it also functions well? Have people simply gotten used to things and settled into a sort of comfortable existence with a lack of desire to get into something new and alien? It is entirely clear that the challenge for the new generation of designers, and the designer in general, is to take on what people are used to. The designer must imagine whether there might be a better way of doing things. This is not a critique of the classics and earlier designers but rather shows a great respect for them, particularly during a time in which there was an infectious desire to take on the classics of that earlier time. People wanted to further new techniques and materials that unfortunately a couple of world wars were a powerful part of creating.

Therefore, we often talk about a relay race when we explain our relationship to earlier generations of designers. We are obliged to know our history in order to be able to define where we are headed. As Larry the cable guy said in the film "Cars" to McQueen who does not like to go in reverse and has no rear-view mirror: "If you don't know where you've been, you don't know where you're going." When you look back, it is also easier to see who was onto something.

The lucid light of hindsight clearly demonstrates that Finn Juhl was on a mission inspired by such artists as Henry Moore and the Danish sculptor Erik Thommesen, where his design had more to do with making comfortable chairs than furniture that was subject to a limited set of rules from which many of the well-known designers of that time worked. This approach to design was a part of what inspired us when we wanted to put our imprint on the UN job. In short, we wanted to make furniture in a way that we were sure Finn Juhl would have loved being a part of, had he been on our team. We were convinced that our furniture should be suited to the TCC. At the same time, however, we were not interested in doing a project that took us backwards.

We wanted people to have a clear view of the hall as a totality: An alternative to making a new set of furniture that was faithful to the time that clearly defined what was there originally and what was added.

Yet we had a strong belief that, just as Finn Juhl had, that we should work toward a "gesamtkunstwerk (a total work of art)." And this belief was reinforced even more as we spoke with the everyday users of the hall. They stressed again and again how good the acoustics, scale and atmosphere were in the hall. Things that had undoubtedly been Finn Juhl's intention and which, therefore, were also very high in the hierarchy of things that we believed should have an influence on the future design. To work towards something that seemed like a totality only made it much more challenging to hit upon the right materials, form and scale. The collaboration with the American architects and craftsmen made it possible for us to achieve this goal. The common language that dominated the different professional groups came into its own and was reminiscent again that the adjustment of the UN on several levels left a deep respect for design history but also history in general.

The Danish producer ONECOLLECTION, which has the rights to produce Finn Juhl's furniture, was to produce a new batch of the original Finn Juhl chairs that were in the TCC hall, but also produce our delegate table, the central secretariat table and the secretariat chairs. Through this entire process, from the start of the competition, after the conclusion of the project and the opening of a new UN, ONECOLLECTION has been our steadfast companion around the world to help us to talk about the project, Danish design and about Finn Juhl.

Today, they produce our secretariat chair, which is called the Council Chair, and they are at the moment our most important partner in a number of new interior design projects. We are entirely certain that the old pioneers would nod with approval at the collaboration and friendship we have with them and be reminded of the many good and passionate discussions there undoubtedly were in the Golden Age of Danish design: Always with respect for each other and in a good tone, but with the lanes clearly outlined and ready to challenge each other and design.

It is one thing that Finn Juhl went to New York and got a sense of the place, but perhaps the most important thing is that he had a message in his project, something that he certainly thought he would have, and now had the chance to affect the world just a little bit. He wanted his furniture to make a mark on democracy, that everyone must be heard before a decision was made. His original proposal for the position of the tables and the way they are positioned today is a horseshoe arrangement of the delegate tables so that everyone can see each other. Moreover, he wanted everyone to be on the same level in the hall and able to look one another in the eye.

This is art that has a kind of patent on having a message behind the object. But we believe that design can borrow from this field when it makes sense to do so. Art may sometimes have a point in that the creation does "not work," but designers should always strive to make things better than they are each time we set out to do something.

Music is More
Than What You Can Hear

Signmark

"I feel that society should not treat the deaf as handicapped people but as a linguistic minority with their own culture, community, history and heritage."

26th of June the day I was born
I learned to speak in a whole entire
different form, my parents didn't budge
the fact I couldn't speak, instead embraced me
with care, signs they started to teach back in
my school times, life felt far from fair kids got
curious, gave me the daily stare they couldn't
understand, why am I using my hands?
Never asked for sympathy, on my two I stand
never got fed up, always kept my head up
few times got knocked down but my pride
made me get up
I couldn't speak, but that didn't make me weak,
I only got stronger when they ridiculed week after week

It's about time for you to open your eyes,
open your mind

It's there for you to find, no longer time to decline
The jokes on you, so what's it gonna be
This is our life unheard and as you've never seen

As I get older, made it to the university even
though the rest doubted, no one believed in me
slowly the attitudes changed, my life was
re-arranged people no longer looked at me as
I was strange could you believe, that not until '95

The rights of the deaf man by law was not
identified but now sign language was our native tongue so even my father
could show where he's coming from he used to tell me if he got caught using
his hands the teacher would take those hands and give him them a wham
Docs drilling holes in our heads tryin' to be
heroes but if you look into their eyes you can
see the sign of euros but really they don't care
they just trying to make a profit out of makin'
the deaf hear implants and wires, let 'em know
we tired how the hell that gon' change us and
make us admired?

Damn right we can't hear, but I don't care
we ain't disabled here, I use sign language
We got our own language yeah, proud of that
I am
We got our own culture yeah, I'm bi-cultured
here
We got our history yeah, I'm part of history
We got our society, this is my community

(Signmark - Our life)

Music is more than what you can hear. I share my message over strong beats where hard, low frequencies and bass are playing a crucial part in my performance. These elements help me adapt to the rhythm. Hip-hop culture has the tradition of stretching boundaries of art, culture, politics and society. Rap goes beyond music, lyrics, culture and languages and has helped different social groups and communities to find their own voice. With my music I want to change attitudes towards the deaf. I feel that society should not treat the deaf as handicapped people but as a linguistic minority with their own culture, community, history and heritage. Appreciating all diversity is exceedingly important in today's increasingly multicultural world.

Like in many other countries, the history of the deaf in Finland has been difficult. When I give lectures around Finland and in other countries, there is one piece of deaf history that shocks people every time. In the 1930s eugenics came to Finland as the legislation was passed that deaf people could not marry unless the woman went through sterilization first. This continued until the mid-1960s and there are still people alive today who remember and lived through this time period. My parents have friends who had to experience that. Another internationally important event for the deaf community happened a lot earlier and had an even longer lasting effect on the whole community.

A progressive development of sign language, education of the deaf and enabling the deaf to become a part of the society, which had risen earlier during the 19th century, came to a sudden stop in 1880 at The Second International Congress on Education of the Deaf. The congress, more commonly known as The Milan Conference, was, despite the name, the first international conference of its kind. In that conference a resolution was made that oral education was better than sign education, starting the period of oralism and from then on, also in Finland, all education of deaf people was focused on learning how to read lips and to use voice. This lead to drastic deterioration of the education that deaf people received for a long time. When my father was in school, signing was banned completely so if he was caught using sign language in the school area, even during the breaks, he would get beaten on the hands with a stick.

Oralism in the education system went on for a long time, but eventually it was understood that it just doesn't work. All research results showed that the method was successful in only a very small minority. Still, somehow the lesson was not fully learned. Today in the deaf community there is a lot of talk about audism. The discussion has risen from the development and generalization of cochlear implants which are small electronic devices that mimic the sense of hearing. Nowadays, there are children, often of hearing parents, who have the implant and as the implant is considered a "cure," these children do not receive any training in sign language. Of course, this does not apply to all children who have the implant—only to part of them. The problem here is not the implant itself, it's the lack of information that hearing parents of deaf or hard-of-hearing children receive. This has risen a discussion about history repeating itself.

Like I mentioned in the beginning, deaf and sign language users are a linguistic minority with their own culture, community, history and heritage. However, for outsiders, the hearing majority, it is all largely unknown. That's why it is a sad situation that there are children who will grow up without getting a chance to live within both hearing and deaf cultures just because of the lack of information. I would love to see that in the future, deafness of a child would not be seen as something that needed immediate fixing but as an opportunity to embrace a new culture and community.

One main key to bridging the gap between the two cultures, or any cultures, is media. Minorities are often under-represented in mainstream media and for a long time the deaf have been at the tail end. Besides news and documentaries, there are occasional visiting characters in series, sometimes even recurring roles and, once every blue moon, a full series around people who differ from the general norm. Commercials are still a minority-free void, unless comic relief is needed, because it is commonly believed that only "normality" sells. All this makes the situation worse when it comes to facing differences in real life. When media doesn't familiarize us with diversity and people different from us, we don't learn how to face that diversity when we encounter it on the street in real life.

We as people are quite lazy and don't want to bother ourselves with things that don't influence our lives directly. Only when we are forced to face the situation, new language, religion, injury or whatever it may be, do we start to look around for help. Only after the initial shock has passed do we start to comprehend. It is a cliché but each person is an individual with their own story. That's why it is important that we do not judge before we get to know the story. Getting to know is the only road to understanding, and understanding enables change.

I was born deaf into a world where music is for the hearing. My career in music started with translating Christmas carols to sign language so our whole family could sing together. I fell for hip-hop and rap music, both because of the beat and the possibility to talk about important issues through the music. Ignoring those who doubted me, I kept pursuing my childhood dream. With the help from my friends and other volunteers, I released the world's first sign language hip-hop album and DVD in 2006. My second album "Breaking the Rules" was released by Warner Music and I became the first deaf person in the world to get a record deal with an international music label. My third album came out in 2014. I have performed all around the world, approximately 1,000 shows in over 40 countries so far. Since 2010 I have been working with the Foreign Ministry of Finland to promote the rights of disabled people. I tell my story through my music, which is why I began this story with the lyrics of my song "Our life," about the deaf community and my part in it, and I am going to end this with "Talk the Talk," a song about what working hard has brought to me.

I always wanted to work hard and it paid off
My dreams grew bigger, as I grew strong
But while I keep on defeating, a fear in me grows Living with the loneliness
nobody knows Creeping and scratching, inside my head
With whom will I be standing,
after the lights are dead
working my fingers to the bone,
so you could hear my Silent Shout
Signing in the dark is like covering my mouth When my daughter grabs my
hand, I'm home You are the reason I stay strong
Now put your hands up
Now put your hands up
Now put your hands up
Get ready, and here we go

I talk the talk
and I walk the walk
talk the talk, walk the walk
I talk the talk
and I walk the walk
talk the talk, walk the walk

I do what I want - this flow, I got it!
I set up a band, three albums, I got it!
Walked through university, got my own company been to Eurovision, there's
a book about me Olympic medal, I've met your president
Forty lands, hundred trips,
my people represent!
Hands up! Have you seen a rocking UN?
Hands up! Have you ever rocked the UN?
I educate, I entertain,
I share what's right 'n' wrong
Look at my family of a hundred million
Been around, around, the world so
Doctor, doctor, should I slow down the tempo?
I'm always giving my all, and it pays off
Being a father that my daughter can be proud of Opening letters statin' to
kill me
None of the hate will ever touch the real me walking through these storms
carrying my faith gotta keep believing, sharing, relate
to the man I am deep inside
little man with dreams full of pride

(Signmark - Talk the Talk)

Nordic Light

Paola Suhonen

"The Nordic light is both natures' own remedy for the weary souls, and also an empowering spirit, a mindset that is shared between all of us Finns."

Today tonight is the longest day of the year.
Last night was the full moon and solstice,
shining, competing with each other's.

There is nothing to compare the midnight sun. Its white light, its powerful, its proud and clear. As the magically light, Nordic summer nights are here again I feel inspired to explore the contrasts of the Finnish summer season. A special type of tranquility is present in the land during this season. It's the never setting midnight sun, white nights and the magic hours where long shadows linger quietly into the sceneries, which continue to inspire me to capture these moments both into moving images and physical objects. The lightness of the summer also underlines the contrasts which occur in the Nordic climate: from the darkest of the long winters to these beautiful, carefree summer nights.

Nordic Contrasts

Throughout the year we balance between contrasts that affect our everyday lives. The lightness of the summers makes us feel alive and wild while the darkness and coldness of the winters makes us hide quietly at home. Contrasts are also present in the traditionally utopian image of the Nordic countries where this area is seen as a picture perfect home for quiet and peaceful nations who enjoy their clean nature, good healthcare, high level education and clean design. "Nordic-ness" both as a trend and a lifestyle keeps on collecting global popularity and Finland has become an interesting travel destination for adventurers and travelers. Finnish culture is attractive especially for its calmness, practicality and sustainability which occur both in our design and values.

Fennofolk

The pure lines of traditional "Finnishness" has its conspicuous elements of backwoods, primitive charisma and tranquility. These aspects blend beautifully with Northern oddness that shifts between absurd combinations of east and west, harmony and dissonance. It is a culture where David Lynch meets Björk: a Twin Peaks setting with something twisted that appears in enchanted formations. The mythological image of the North, which paints it as a dreamland-like landscape of the mind, culminates in new Nordic oddity, Fennofolk, which defines this style, concept and aesthetic phenomena.

Fennofolk is not a movement or a school. It does not emphasize or romanticize nationalistic values but instead mixes aspects of the modern media in variable contexts and openly dares to rely on its nationally created self-confidence. It is a mix where culture, experience and perspectives come together. In these ways, Fennofolk gives the traditional form of Finnish design a twist where it combines elements of modern Scandinavian style with a traditional Slavic touch and with something unexpectedly odd. This popular cultural phenomenon gives the modern, clean, almost over-simplified Nordic design a new form where all these previously mentioned elements are combined successfully together. Fennofolk creates worlds where Slavic melancholy blends with pure Scandinavian moods and the contrasts of our four seasons.

Finnish Oddness

Finnish oddness is one of the most influential parts of the Fennofolk. This oddity springs from the quiet and somewhat awkward nature of us Finns and relies on a line of traditional values, phenomena and moods such as "sisu." Sisu means the way in which we Finns "have guts," a so called inner stoic determination to display courage in the face of adversity and the way in which we stick to the previously decided course of action until we have reached our goal. Sisu is something that all Finns have, an inner flame that keeps us going against all the setbacks and gives our otherwise quiet character an unexpected boost. It is a part of our own inner Nordic light that makes us shine during tougher times.

The Diversity of the Nordic Nature

The magic and diversity of the Finnish nature is an important aspect that keeps on inspiring me throughout my work. Whether this inspiration comes from the archipelago landscapes, northern lights on a dark winter sky, magical forests or the wild north itself, there is always something new and unseen to explore and to get inspired by. Our clean tranquil nature is something that we take for granted and one of the most appealing factors that attracts international travelers to visit us. The aesthetics of the Nordic nature are also present in our everyday lives in the form of design objects that take both physical and spiritual material out of its variability. Through combining the diverse line of contrasts, Northern legends, the thin lines between the past and the present, and *naïve* mind-landscapes, I aim to create art that works both as souvenirs of my very own soul world and also as a part of a personal story line.

As the summer season approaches its bittersweet end and days become darker and longer I will be reminiscing of the lightness of this summer. The Nordic light is both natures' own remedy for the weary souls, and also an empowering spirit, a mindset that is shared between all of us Finns.

5. Management and Economics—Embracing an Integrated Economic Model for Partnership Between Management and Labor

How has this flat model, broadly characterized as a mutually respectful relationship between managers and workforce achieved such great success? What are the uniquely Nordic features that ensure not only prosperity, but a deep and abiding commitment to global responsibility that has earned them international respect and success? How are these businesses preparing for a far different future than the one envisioned even a few short decades ago?

Paving the Way for a Wealth of Ideas: Embracing the 'Flat' Model

Karsten Dybvad

"Denmark is founded on liberal market ideals. But our capitalist society has soft edges so that the quest for growth and prosperity does not come at the expense of social cohesion and equality in society."

In the heart of provincial Denmark lies the town of Sjølund—a small town with around 500 inhabitants. The town has a church, a school and a small supermarket. It enjoys a scenic location, surrounded by rolling fields near "Skamlingsbanken," which is a national historic monument symbolic of the civil battle for Southern Denmark.

Americans are unlikely to have ever heard of it. In fact, few Danes are probably even familiar with the place. Sjølund is not somewhere you visit unless you have a very specific reason to do so.

Sjølund is, nevertheless, not misplaced in an essay about the strength and characteristics of Danish companies. Besides the scenic location of the town, it is also home to the company "Sjølund," where metalworkers and engineers work with the rolling of steel and milling of aluminum extrusions.

Put very simply, they make linear steel and aluminum extrusions into round, organic shapes, as seen on wind turbines, complex building structures and high-speed trains. Wherever there is a demand for design, Sjølund produces steel and aluminum parts with precision and strength.

The company might be located in a small town, but its ambitions are far from small: Sjølund wants to be best in the world at what it does!

In Sjølund's case, it is broadly speaking a question of investing in two things: The first is an industrial park geared up for even the most demanding of tasks. The second is people. They find that if you want to be the best in class at what you do and compete globally, you need engaged and motivated employees at all levels of the company, be they metal workers, salespeople or management.

A few years ago, the CEO of Sjølund received a call from one of its business partners, the German industrial giant Siemens, which needed special aluminum extrusions for new high-speed trains in China.

The CEO asked workers to look at the project and come up with a solution. Days later, they presented a solution that worked. From one day to the next, they had a foot in the door of the Chinese market.

Sjølund is a reflection of some of the factors that have unlocked the competitiveness of Danish companies; a strong correlation between production and innovation. The company operates in a way that there is only a short distance from the helm to the machines. Danish companies hold the basic belief that employee involvement paves the way for a wealth of ideas that make it possible to create customized high quality products for which customers are willing to pay a higher price.

These are just some of the characteristics that make Danish companies competitive internationally; this despite Denmark being one of the most expensive countries in the world in which to run a business.

Is Danish Competitiveness a Paradox?

From the outside, Danish competitiveness and prosperity might seem paradoxical to an observer of the Danish economy who only looks at individual economic indicators such as taxes, wages and the size of the public sector (Mandag Morgen: Fra velfærdsstat til velstandsstat). Thankfully, competitiveness is not equal to the sum of these costs, even though these are important parameters in any nation's quest to compete globally. But there is more to a country's competitiveness and prosperity; there are societal factors and these may explain how Danish companies are able to compete in extremely competitive global markets.

The social factors that highlight Danish competitiveness are two-fold and wide ranging. There are the hard factors, which explain why Denmark is a stable country in which to run a business—a strong economy, public finances, AAA-credit rating, among others. And there are the soft factors that highlight Danish value-based strengths. Danish companies have successfully translated social factors, equal rights and opportunities, a balanced society and government transparency into commercial strengths and competitive advantages.

Regardless of the size of companies, type of industry or geographical boundaries, the majority of Danish companies base their strategy on such values. And it is not because the values look good in a corporate social responsibility (CSR) report, but that values help generate innovation, draw in new clientele and create new jobs in Denmark.

To understand why Denmark and Danish companies are doing well, you have to look beyond individual economic figures and consider a broader picture.

Short Distance from the CEO's Chair to the Factory Floor— The Danish Management Model

If you had to pinpoint the strength of Danish society, it would be the concept of "trust." Danes trust one another, the authorities, government, parliament, civil service, police and even the tax man! Private sector confidence in the public sector is a prerequisite for success, as is the mutual trust between employers and employees which make the Danish labor market one of the least regulated labor markets in Europe and one of the most flexible.

This high degree of trust is imprinted in the Danish management model, where there is a short power distance from the CEO to the employees on the factory floor. In this management model, it is perfectly natural for the CEO at Sjølund to delegate important tasks directly to his metal workers. In turn, the workers deliver because they are motivated by a high degree of autonomy, which shows that influence and responsibility make for better results.

The management model is followed by many Danish companies including the major technology group Haldor Topsøe, where engineers installed a new robot on the production line. The robot involved a sizeable investment, required specialists to operate it, and shortly after the first robot was set up, three workers (two unskilled and one skilled) approached management with another proposal to reorganize working procedures for operating the technology. The proposal required less investment and was far more efficient; management listened, trusted their employees and changed the procedure.

This mutual trust in the workplace enhances employee responsibility and encourages them to approach management with suggestions for improvements. This mutual trust means, for example, that management will listen and admit that new and better solutions can be found. European Commission studies measuring interesting tasks, workload, autonomy in relation to problem-solving, engagement and work-life balance, show that Denmark is the frontrunner in job satisfaction compared to other European countries. And satisfied managers are also a byproduct of this flat business model, benefiting from employee ideas and spending fewer resources on control and monitoring.

Better to Create Jobs than to Protect Jobs—the Danish Labor Market

The unique style of management is closely linked to the collective agreements in the Danish labor market. In many countries, it is difficult for employer representatives to meet with trade unions to discuss and reach agreement on labor market factors including pay and working conditions. In Denmark they do. The Danish model is based on voluntary agreements between employers and employees, with little interference from the government. The model obliges the parties to ensure market stability by resolving disagreements without outside intervention. Conflicts are handled peacefully, making it possible to settle disagreements with regard to termination, for example, in the course of just a few months. This flexibility is one of the strengths of Danish companies, as it is a common understanding that it is far more important to create jobs than to protect them. Remarkably this model withstood the recent economic crisis even when wage restraints were implemented to improve Danish competitiveness.

Although the system has a high degree of autonomy, close cooperation between the labor market's partners and politicians is vital. Labor market issues related to unemployment benefits, training and re-training and even integration of refugees into the workforce, are matters requiring government concurrence.

The Danish model is not only a forum for flexible hire-and-fire practices, but also a place to find ways to improve the training and competencies for Danish workers with public education, in part paid for by employers. It is a worthwhile investment because it results in greater productivity and more qualified employees. Underscoring this point is the prevailing notion in the industrial sector that Danish companies have to compete. If not, production is in danger of being outsourced to countries with lower production costs, or the companies go out of business. This focus on productivity: upgrading workers' skills and the ability to move production into specialized, high value and higher cost products, is critical.

Is the Danish Model Fit for the Future?

The world is evolving, and there is no guarantee that even the best social models will endure. As with many other welfare states, Denmark is facing challenges from the speed with which many other countries are growing their economies. While it is convenient to blame these new challenges on globalization, the answer is not for companies to cut themselves off from the outside world and turn their backs on the global economy.

An active role in the global economy is crucial, an absolute cornerstone if Denmark is to continue its economic success. This requires a positive approach to globalization, whatever challenges it presents and whatever pressure it places on the Danish model. In fact as a small open economy, Denmark has no choice.

As a nation, Denmark has built its prosperity by trading with other countries. Almost half of the private production of goods and services created in Denmark are sold to customers abroad. And around 40 percent of private jobs in Denmark have been created thanks to the ability of Danish companies to reach out to people and markets all over the world to meet labor demands.

Denmark's policy and external relations must reflect this, now and in the future. It is therefore crucial for Danish companies and Danish politicians to maintain a global mindset, one that dares them to seek out global opportunities and dares them to exploit them. It is possible to address the challenges faced by Denmark: Too little investment, a high tax burden, comparatively high wages and a public sector which is too large. In a globalized economy it is important to address these concerns not least to constantly ensure that the cost of doing business in Denmark allows companies to be profitable. Aside from high production costs, new challenges for future Danish prosperity have arisen, particularly the major challenge of recruiting qualified employees.

Employment needs have risen constantly over the past two years, and unemployment is close to the structural level. Danish companies already lack specialized, skilled labor, from industrial technicians to engineers. If Denmark is too fully exploit the global economic recovery, which is underway, its companies must first and foremost have better access to qualified employees.

This means that Denmark has to be an attractive country for skilled foreigners in which to live and work. It means that more attention is required to ensure that Danish worker qualifications match corporate demand. Likewise, greater effort is required to move people who are on social benefits into permanent jobs, and for people in jobs to stay longer in the labor market.

There is no need for social upheaval in Denmark to adapt to new challenges. But there is a need to revitalize and adjust the social model, with a sharp focus on the qualities that have made Danish companies amongst the best in the world. This does not mean that Denmark has to compete with China or Vietnam on their terms and blindly cut prices and wages; far from it.

One of the absolute positions of strength for Danish companies is their ability to thrive in well- defined niches and to produce "up market" products. These are typically relatively common types of products that are high quality and therefore allow companies to charge a higher price. These upscale products already represent 40 percent of Danish exports, and can be found in almost all sectors. Such products are so unique, they can bear higher prices and justify high Danish wages and production costs; these products must continue to be developed in Denmark. The only way Denmark can do this is by being better, more productive and innovative.

For companies, this means no cutting corners. It takes investment in machinery and in people. And as observed in Sjølund, there can be no cost-cutting on the part of society either. Denmark must invest in future growth, particularly in education and research, because it is necessary to boost the skills of Danish employees across the board. It is both about hatching more skilled talents, and about training the many professional workers that companies will be lacking in the years to come if Denmark is to succeed in the global innovation race.

Capitalism with Soft Edges

Denmark has ranked first in six of the ten annual editions of Forbes Magazine's "Best Countries for Business List." This position is difficult to achieve for a country with a socialist structure, a characteristic Denmark is regularly labeled with in the United States. There is just one problem. The label is skewed, and to a large extent, mistaken.

Denmark is founded on liberal market ideals. But our capitalist society has soft edges so that the quest for growth and prosperity does not come at the expense of social cohesion and equality in society.

Denmark has low income inequality when compared to other developed countries. Behind that ranking are factors such as a high tax burden, a widespread allocation of wealth in society and a generous system that helps unemployed workers find new work and get retraining. But the output is something that everyone benefits from, companies included. Because of the flexible model, Denmark has a well-educated workforce, a result of free education, a high degree of unity and stability in society because of strong national ties, an almost total absence of corruption, and lest we forget, the lucky title-bearer of the happiest country in the world according to the United Nations.

In the Confederation of Danish Industry our vision is, "an open and affluent society in growth and in balance. On this foundation, Denmark must be the world's most attractive country for businesses to work in and from."

Balance is a key word here. It refers to multiple objectives: The correlation between how much money governments earn and how much money governments spend; the balance between the public and private sector; and the balance in society where companies do not act as isolated islands independent of the society in which they operate, but also take responsibility for the environment, safety and the development of their employees. But just as important, society should not take the dynamic development of companies for granted.

Balance is not easy. But when done correctly, there should be no contradiction between a relatively large public sector and competitive capitalism. Striking the right balance in the future will determine whether the Danish Model is sustainable into the future.

Supercell, Sisu and the Importance of Failure

Ilkka Paananen

"We like to think that every failure is a unique opportunity to learn and every lesson will ultimately make us better at what we do. That's why we have a tradition of celebrating these lessons by drinking champagne every time we have a major failure."

In Finland we have a word—"Sisu."

It's actually more than a word; it's a national characteristic, a kind of patriotic self-identification like the "British Bulldog spirit" or the "American Dream."

It has no clear English translation, but is generally accepted to encapsulate things like determination, resilience, bravery, guts, courage and perseverance in the face of failure. For example, Finns often credit Sisu with our country's ability to resist invasion during World War Two.

I immediately thought of Sisu when I learned of this "Nordic Ways" project. Although the individual values included in this project are embraced by entrepreneurs the world over, it occurred to me that only someone coming from Finland would describe the combination of these values as Sisu. In fact, when defined this way, I believe that Sisu goes a long way to explaining the success of many successful start-ups. It certainly explains a lot of ours at Supercell.

I've spent my entire career working in the games industry, co-founding the studio Sumea in 2000 before selling it to Digital Chocolate in 2004 and working there as a President until 2010. In that time I saw a lot of what was great about the industry (namely, great people and great games) and a lot of what was frustrating for the best creative people—bureaucracy, artificial deadlines, the sacrifice of quality and long-term success for short-term financial gain. In 2010, myself and five other veterans of the sector—Mikko Kodisoja, Lassi Leppinen, Niko Derome, Visa Forsten and Petri Styrman—decided to found a new kind of games company on a simple motto: "the best people make the best games."

In this kind of model, the sole mission of the founders and management would be to acquire the best talent for every single position, create the best possible environment for them and then get out of the way. It would be an environment with zero bureaucracy, no top-down mandates and a culture of independence and responsibility for those making games. A place where the best people could have the biggest possible impact and nothing would stand in their way. Everything else, including financial goals, would be secondary.

We all believed from past experience that people, particularly creative people such as artists, developers and designers, achieve the most when they come to work every day with a deep passion and excitement for what they do; when they feel that there is nothing that can stop them from developing the next hit game and that they are in complete control of their own destiny. The most effective way of achieving this is to give them complete independence and responsibility over what they do; allow them to pursue the projects they care about, follow their own timetables and, crucially, empower them to make the difficult decisions of when those projects have to end. In essence, they need to act as entrepreneurs and to do this they need to embody Sisu.

At Supercell, we achieved this through a structure of small, independent "cells" that conceive, develop and launch (or kill) their own games. These cells act as start-ups within a start-up, entirely autonomous of management and each other. Together, these individual cells form Supercell. Today, I think of Supercell as a company of 190 entrepreneurs, all full of Sisu!

Our hierarchical structure, to the extent one exists at all, has the role of CEO very much near the bottom, overseeing acquisition of new talent, forming it into new cells and supporting them where necessary but otherwise getting out of their way. Often, I'm one of the last to know about major decisions on our projects and it is almost always after the decision has already been taken. In fact, the vast majority of the best decisions at Supercell have happened exactly this way. Therefore, I like to say that I'm the world's least powerful CEO. What I mean by that is that the more decisions the cells themselves make, and the fewer decisions I need to make, the better and faster we operate as a company. Our organizational model has been optimized for passion and speed, not for control.

Although we set out with this vision, remaining true to it in those early days was sometimes difficult. We had a bold dream of creating games that people would play for years, if not decades, and that would become part of the rich history of gaming. Games that would be so intuitive and accessible that literally everyone could play, but would also provide a deep and rich experience that would keep players engaged for years. We viewed games not as products but as services that would become part of the everyday lives of our players.

Our first attempt at achieving this was a game called *Gunshine.net*, an online multiplayer title for Facebook that we ultimately hoped would be available across browser, mobile and tablets and become the first truly cross-platform game service. An early version of the game launched on Facebook in February 2011 and soon found a passionate base of players online. At its peak in the summer of that year, *Gunshine* had around 500,000 players every month. However, inherent problems in the game soon became clear.

In the first instance, despite our best efforts, *Gunshine* clearly was not a game that people would play for years; the long-term engagement we envisioned simply wasn't there. Secondly, it was too difficult for novice players to understand and engage with, severely limiting its growth potential. This was not a game that everyone could play. Finally, and perhaps most importantly, it proved impossible to make the game work on mobile devices and tablets. It simply wasn't the kind of game we wanted to create.

In autumn of that year we came to realize a few things that ended up being pivotal for Supercell. First we started to believe that mobile and tablets were the future of gaming. Second we were convinced that games that were going to succeed would have to be developed specifically for tablets from the ground up and not altered from other platforms. Our vision of "cross-platform" would not result in optimal experience on mobile devices. Third because of these realizations, the game on which we had worked so hard, *Gunshine*, simply had no future.

This was the first critical moment in our history and a moment where Sisu was vital. To stay true to our vision we realized we would need to make our company "mobile first" and in the course of doing so, abandon every single project we were working on and begin again.

We had to go back to a state where the company would not have any products out in the market and therefore no revenue. What made this decision even more difficult was the fact that we had received €8m from the venture capital firm Accel Partners less than six months earlier, by far our biggest external investment at that point. Now we had to tell them and our other early investors that the strategy they had backed was being jettisoned completely.

Yet perhaps the most difficult part was talking to our people about this new vision we had, because it essentially meant that they would need to abandon projects they had poured their hearts and souls into for months. But we knew it was what we had to do to have a shot at success in the long term. Everyone agreed to pull the plug and start all over.

That, let me tell you, took determination and courage: Sisu. When I think about that period today, I am still in awe of the courage the team showed.

I would also like to note that the Finnish government has shown some Sisu in how they support start-ups like us. When we founded the company in 2010 it was a time of economic difficulty and private investment was not easy to come by, but our government stood by its pledge to support Finnish tech enterprise. Tekes, the Finnish Funding Agency for Technology and Innovation, provided us with a vital loan of €400,000 that allowed us to recruit our first people and get the business off the ground.

Nordic governments are often wrongly perceived internationally as not being friendly to business but I truly believe that we could not have built

Supercell anywhere other than Helsinki. The Tekes loans did not require personal guarantees, meaning that we could take the risks we needed to take without having to gamble our homes. And the limited bureaucracy involved in starting and scaling a business has allowed us to hire more talent without burdening ourselves with unnecessary process. We've also been able to find much of that talent on our doorstep because decades of investment in Finland's education system have created an abundance of talented, creative people.

But to come back to that moment in late 2011, expanding our team was not in the forefront of our minds. We needed to begin again. So staying true to our vision, by early 2012 we had five small teams working on new games, all for tablets and mobile devices. We knew that one of those games would have to be at least moderately successful for the company to have a future. One of the things about which I am still very proud is that despite the seemingly difficult situation, we had the Sisu to continue to kill projects we didn't feel were up to our standard; one called *Pets vs Orcs* in February and then *Tower* later in the spring.

Neither of these were "bad" games—they were fun for a period and would have likely generated some revenue had they ever launched globally —they just weren't the games we wanted to create. Nobody in the company was willing to compromise on "OUR" goal, even when our backs were against the wall.

In May, we launched yet another game into beta (a limited, one-market-only launch) in Canada and hoped that this time our perseverance would finally pay off. During development the game was codenamed *Soil*, but we launched as *Hay Day*, and it was an immediate success on a level we had never before experienced. We launched it globally on June 21, 2012, and the rest of the world began to love it as much as Canada did. Within months it became one of the highest-grossing games in the world.

Just before the start of summer vacation in Finland in July of that year we released another new game to beta in Canada. During development its codename was *Magic*, but today everyone knows it as *Clash of Clans*. It soon became very popular and we launched it globally in August. One of the most satisfying aspects of this was that it was not the first project we had codenamed

Magic, the original had been one of the projects we abandoned with the move to mobile-first. In fact it had been the most difficult game to kill, as the team was so passionate and pretty much everyone else in the company loved it. But the team did decide to kill it and then went on to build *Clash of Clans.*

Now four years later, both *Hay Day* and *Clash of Clans* remain global hits with millions of players every single day. It took *Clash* three months to become the top-grossing game in the U.S. and it hasn't left the top five globally ever since. It has become our biggest hit game so far, reaching number one in more than 150 countries, and holding on to that position for years, something that no game on mobile has been able to achieve. This is testament to the approach we took and to the Sisu that kept us focused on our ultimate goal.

That's not to say that these two games meant that our goals were accomplished or that it was time to change our approach. Having released two globally successful games in quick succession, there was mounting pressure over the coming months to repeat the process and deliver something new. Beta releases could no longer be quietly released and then killed if the team wasn't happy. Instead they'd be scrutinized and speculated upon in the media. We also began to experience external pressures to expand the company quickly; to port our games to PC or home consoles, to expand into merchandise such as toys and t-shirts, to develop movies and other distractions.

One of the things that I am most proud of is that through all of this we had the courage to stay focused. We said "no" to all of the things that we considered distractions. Despite the fact that all of a sudden we had the financial resources to hire a huge number of new people quickly, we instead stayed true to our roots and continued to hire very slowly. We remained true to our unique culture and committed to our founding goal: enabling the best people (and teams) to make the best games.

It would be almost two years before we released another game globally, *Boom Beach,* in March 2014, and then another two before our latest, *Clash Royale,* in March 2016. During that time our games teams killed many, many other games in the development stage; some were never seen by anyone outside the team and others were played, discussed and picked apart by hundreds and thousands of gamers and journalists in beta launches. But what's important is that every one of those decisions was made by the team making that game, not by anyone else and certainly not by "upper management" (to the extent we even have one). This is how we think about "responsibility" and this value is at the very core of Supercell.

They made those decisions simply because they did not believe those games would be true to our vision of "games that people play for years." To make these hard decisions at least a tiny bit easier we have tried to create a culture of embracing failure and seeing the opportunity for growth it presents. We like to think that every failure is a unique opportunity to learn and every lesson will ultimately make us better at what we do. That's why we have a tradition of celebrating these lessons by drinking champagne every time we have a major failure. Don't get me wrong; we are not trying to pretend failing is fun. It is definitely not, especially when you need to kill a game you've worked day and night for months. It is something you don't celebrate. But what is worth celebrating, are all of those valuable lessons that come from the experience of developing a failed game. (By the way, some time back, someone pointed out to me that not only do we learn from failures, we learn from successes as well … so these days we have started to celebrate our successes with champagne too.)

But to get back to failures, one of my proudest days at Supercell was when we held two post-mortems in a single all-company meeting (we have one every Friday). One of the post-mortems was on the decision to kill a game called *Smash Land* during its beta period and the other on a major marketing campaign that had resulted in a significant financial loss. I can't say I know of any other company where senior team members would be so open and honest about such major failures, and I couldn't be more proud of that.

For us, it's clear that releasing hit games means having to take risks. By definition, taking risks means that you'll fail more often than you'll succeed. So whenever we realize that we haven't failed in a while, it's a sign that we haven't taken enough risks; that we haven't been brave enough, that we haven't been sufficiently focused on reaching our goals. Basically, that we haven't been showing Sisu.

And that is the worst thing we could possibly do because I believe that every business, organization and individual, no matter where they come from, could use a bit of Sisu.

Trust and Growth

Kristin Skogen Lund

"In Norway, everyone knows someone who knows somebody who knows the Prime Minister."

Nordahl Grieg's "17th May 1940" is a poem about Norway's national day during the German occupation. Grieg states:

"So few we are in our country,
We are kin with all in our slain"

In Norway, everyone knows someone who knows somebody who knows the Prime Minister. We are a country with 5 million inhabitants. That explains much, but not all.

Because Grieg also writes:

"Our lands, our seas, with their harvests,
Were won through a long drawn strife,
And the labour has bred affection,
And a weakness for growing life"

Nordahl Grieg was not just a national poet; he was also an ardent communist. There is no class hatred on display here, however. Rather, he paints a picture of a population held together by a shared struggle against the harsh forces of nature in the far north.

History provides some strong evidence for his arguments: Norway has had little in the way of nobility or wealthy landowners, and slavery disappeared a thousand years ago. The Reformation brought the sacrament of confirmation, and with confirmation came schools. From 1739, every child in Norway was taught to read.

Trust is the Foundation

Combined with political stability and relatively little war and unrest, this formed the foundation for a high degree of trust among Norway's citizens. In communities where this sort of trust exists, it is easier to create strong public institutions, not least a good and sustainable welfare system.

One might expect that this correlation would run in the other direction; the welfare state creates trust. However, studies show that the descendants of Scandinavians who immigrated to the United States in the 1800s—long before the welfare state came into being—enjoy higher levels of trust than the majority of Americans. Trust came first.

If we examine how the Norwegian working environment is organized, that trust can be found in the close cooperation between employers, employees and authorities, from a national level right down to individual workplaces. A high degree of organization and centrally coordinated wage settlements ensure a steady wage growth, based on competitive industries' need for sustainable wage levels. Close cooperation between the authorities and the social partners contributes to a welfare system that offers safety and protection against the sudden loss of income. This, in turn, allows for flexible employment.

Equality Leads to Growth – or Is it the Other Way Around?

Things have gone well, so far. The Nordic countries are generally characterized by high and evenly distributed levels of wealth and welfare. They top all the international comparisons one could wish to top.

However, it would seem that this way of organizing a society primarily benefits employees who work little and earn a lot, and the ones supported by a wealthy state. What about production and productivity, what about the welfare of businesses?

Most companies in Norway are private enterprises. Many of the largest companies have some degree of state ownership, but by and large they are subject by legislation to the same conditions and limitations that apply to private companies in any other country. Anything else would be difficult, not to say impossible, in a global market.

The results are not bad from a business standpoint. Even if we ignore the revenues generated by the petroleum industry, Norwegian businesses generally show high levels of productivity and profitability.

In international comparisons, Norway scores low on indicators for innovation, but does well on productivity indicators, even without considering oil and gas. We are effective in the workplace, but we struggle to identify the reasons why. And this is where we may have to revisit the trust mentioned above.

Internationally, Norway, Sweden, Denmark and the Netherlands lie at the very top of what is called discretionary learning. With little hierarchy and flat organizational structures, work life in these countries is dominated by employees themselves taking initiative in problem solving. It is far from unthinkable that this sort of innovation and learning goes unregistered and is therefore underreported in innovation statistics.

The special model for wage determination, with centralized tariff agreements and high levels of income equality, may also have contributed to a positive development for businesses. The Swedish Trade Union Confederation (LO) introduced the theory behind this: The idea that centralized and solidarity-based wage agreements bring about increases in productivity by pushing up the costs associated with low-productivity labor, while costs associated with high-productivity labor are pushed down. This reduces income inequality and, moreover, increases productivity because high wage levels make productivity enhancing automation much more profitable. At the same time, generous social benefits ensure an acceptable level of income even for those who lose their jobs.

The connections between equality and growth are controversial. Statistically speaking, we can see that rich countries have the lowest levels of inequality, with the U.S. as the major exception. Many believe that this proves equality promotes growth. That may be an interesting discussion, but we can also look at it from a slightly different angle. When we have enough wealth to afford it, we can treat ourselves to equality as a social good. This good benefits us all, not just the ones in the direst need. First, it increases the purchasing power of the least wealthy; a group likely to spend any new income on consumption, which in turn, is good for businesses. Second, equality benefits everyone because equality contributes to security and stability for all of society.

Challenges for the Nordic Model

Equality has its price, however, and we can see disturbing signs. Norway owns the world record when it comes to the percentage of adults who are outside the workforce receiving health-related benefits. Since there is nothing especially wrong with public health in Norway, it is tempting to search elsewhere for an explanation. Of course, the generous benefits are an explanation in and of themselves. More importantly, however, the explanation is competence. Ultimately it is those lacking the competence to find a place in the highly paid Norwegian workforce who depend on these benefits.

Of course the problem is that these benefits cost the State money, a lot of money. In Norway, workforce participation is decreasing, with the greatest decrease among the young. The older members of society are actually working more now than in the past.

Two strong factors indicate that this is probably not just an expression of economic cycles and conditions:

Technological development steadily calls for higher skill levels in all areas of employment, especially in countries where wages are high and automation is relatively profitable. There are fewer and fewer jobs for people with little or no education. The relatively generous social benefit levels ensure that no new low-income jobs are appearing either.

A strong and sustained flow of immigrants with consistently low skill levels increases competition for the jobs at the bottom of the hierarchy. Relatively high wages for low-skilled work makes Norway an attractive country for low-skilled immigrants, and net immigration to Norway in the last decade is equal to 8 percent of the total population.

An answer to these challenges is education and considerable efforts are devoted to education in Norway at all levels. It seems apparent, however, that not everyone is capable of raising their skills to the level needed to enter the labor market.

It has been suggested that the authorities could establish subsidized jobs for people whose skill levels are so low that they are unable to enter the labor market in any other way. This is a possibility, but one that would come at great expense in terms of subsidies and administration. And the risk of subsidized employment crowding out regular employment would be considerable.

Increased taxes on the most productive citizens could pay for the social benefits, as long as they do not move out of the country. But they do of course, when taxes get too high. The youth of today are born globals.

It seems that greater inequality will inevitably emerge if we fail to resolve these challenges in one way or another. In practice, social benefit levels would go down, which would allow for the growth of new low-income jobs. However, greater economic inequality will also result in social unrest, with everything that could entail in terms of reduced security and ultimately the crumbling bonds of societal trust.

The question is whether we can still maintain a society with high levels of equality and trust even if market forces are pulling in the opposite direction. My answer is yes we can, but it will come at a cost; even more of the nation's value creation must be used to buy equality.

However, affording this presupposes a business sector that is a world leader in technology, productivity and profitability. Highly productive, profit-maximizing firms that are competitive on a global scale are a prerequisite for, and a consequence of the Nordic Model at its best.

Nordic Cooperation and the New Geopolitics

Ulf Sverdrup

"Closer Nordic cooperation on issues of strategic importance could enable the Nordic countries to better secure their own interests, and ensure that they can play a larger role in influencing global developments in directions so that it fits with their own interests."

We have recently seen an increased interest in the Nordic region and new attempts at strengthening Nordic cooperation. In mid-May 2016 President Barack Obama convened a special Nordic summit at the White House, where Nordic Prime Ministers and the Finnish President met. The high profile gathering in Washington was not unique. During the last few years we have observed similar developments in Europe and Asia. For instance, the UK Prime Minister recently hosted workshops with his Nordic colleagues and initiatives have been put forward to explore the possibility of establishing a Sino-Nordic political consultation forum.

Since attention and time are scarce resources, many of the larger states prefer to meet the Nordic governments simultaneously rather than one by one in order to save time. However, there are also other political factors that contribute to increased interest in the Nordic region.

First, the changing security situation has made this region much more important and valuable. The Nordic Countries enjoy close proximity to Russia, and they are closely linked to the Baltic States and Baltic Sea region, an area that has gained increased strategic importance in the aftermath of Crimea. The Nordic countries are also key actors in influencing the dynamics in the Arctic and the High North, an area of growing strategic importance as the ice cap shrinks due to climate change.

Second, the concerns with the risk of disintegration or further fragmentation in the EU, the rise of Euroscepticism and the risk of other countries following the decision by the UK to leave the EU represent a considerable challenge to the post war European political order. In this shifting environment the Nordic countries remain a relatively stable region and they can and should contribute positively and actively to European unity and leadership.

Third, the Nordic countries, with their open and globalized economies, are good and solid performers in the global economy. All of the Nordic countries score well in international rankings on topics such as global competitiveness, transparency, innovation and the UN Human Development Index. Many are therefore interested to learn how the Nordic countries have been able to successfully harvest the benefits of globalization, while at the same time able to develop targeted and well-functioning measures to prevent inequality, ensure taxation and develop compensatory mechanisms for those groups who lose out or risk marginalization as a result of globalization.

Finally, these small Nordic countries play a significant role in providing global public goods. The Nordics are constructive players, both directly and indirectly, in developing and maintaining the international order. They provide resources and funding for UN institutions, are strongly committed to preventing climate change, addressing poverty, promoting gender equality, disarmament and peace. And their policy style is usually quite sober, pragmatic and solution oriented, which in itself might have appeal for others. In the much cited interview with President Obama in the "The Atlantic," Obama said that he sometimes tell his staff that, "if only everyone could be like the Scandinavians, this would all be easy."

These factors suggest that there can be several benefits of more intense and systematic Nordic cooperation in an age of global shifts. Closer Nordic cooperation on issues of strategic importance could enable the Nordic countries to better secure their own interests, and ensure that they can play a larger role in influencing global developments in directions so that it fits with their own interests.

Separately, the Nordic countries are small and lack major significance on the global scene. However, when taken as a whole, the Nordic region is not insignificant. It has almost 26 million inhabitants and while only 0.3 percent of the world population lives in the Nordic countries, their economies represent almost 2 percent of the world GDP. In fact, the Nordic economies together constitute the 12th biggest economy in the world, placed just behind India and Russia, but ahead of South Korea and Spain. The Nordic region represents a considerable economic force, a sizeable market and an attractive region for foreign investment.

Nordic cooperation also benefits from considerable legitimacy and popular support deriving from its citizens. The informal nature of Nordic cooperation is often perceived as being natural, and it is often regarded as less controversial than the more formal and legally oriented European cooperation in the EU. In some of the Nordic countries, like Sweden and Finland, Nordic cooperation has traditionally also been seen as less politically sensitive than transatlantic cooperation.

In many areas Nordic cooperation has certainly been successful, but there are still some key obstacles to truly comprehensive and effective Nordic cooperation, not least in the field of foreign and security policy.

First, some have traditionally viewed Nordic cooperation primarily as an alternative pathway, separate from European cooperation and distinct from the transatlantic framework. Historically, most attempts at developing such a genuine third-way approach have failed, particularly in the areas of economic integration and security cooperation. In fact, modern history has demonstrated that Nordic cooperation has been most successful when it has developed within, and not outside, of European and transatlantic cooperative structures. As such, European and transatlantic cooperation should not be regarded as alternatives to Nordic cooperation; they should instead be seen as prerequisites for effective Nordic cooperation.

Secondly, it follows from the above that the differences in the way the Nordics are integrated with the EU and NATO serve as an obstacle for genuine and deep Nordic cooperation. Sweden and Finland are not members of NATO, while Denmark, Norway and Iceland are. Similar differences exist in relation to the EU, where Norway and Iceland are non-members, while the other Nordics are full-fledged EU members. All the Nordic countries have, in different ways, made attempts to overcome these institutional hindrances. Norway and Iceland have for example developed dense cooperation with the EU, through the European Economic Area and numerous other agreements. As a result they have become deeply integrated with the EU. In the case of Norway, an extensive government commissioned report estimated that Norway was integrated into about three-quarters of the EU and that it was more inside than outside. In a similar way, Sweden and Finland have over time pursued a policy of gradually strengthening their cooperation with NATO, and both countries have become important strategic partners of the Alliance. Nordic countries have also developed intensive internal consultative mechanisms resulting in comprehensive information sharing on issues related to European and NATO cooperation.

However, in spite of these "near membership" ties, all parties are well aware that at the end of the day it is only formal membership that matters. It is only formal membership in the EU that will give a country a vote in decision making and it is only full membership in NATO that can ensure full security guarantees. Truly powerful and encompassing Nordic cooperation can probably only happen if Sweden and Finland seek membership in NATO, and Norway and Iceland seek EU membership.

For some time these options have been considered politically unlikely due to domestic politics. Iceland has frozen its bid for EU membership, and there is little popular support in Norway for joining the EU. However, when it comes to the NATO debate in Sweden and Finland there have been some noteworthy developments of late. Some in the political and military establishments in Sweden and Finland have grown increasingly positive to the idea of NATO membership, despite the reluctance of the general public in both countries.

A third hurdle for Nordic cooperation has been that it is associated with little interest and status. Many Nordic political leaders considered it more exciting to seek cooperation with countries in remote areas, rather than with their stable neighbors. Moreover a generation of politicians and experts who have advocated for and identified with Nordic cooperation are now leaving politics; this while a new generation of younger experts has yet to step forward. In addition, we cannot ignore that in some areas there are significant conflicts of interest between the Nordic countries that might prevent effective cooperation, as recently seen with migration and border policies.

As I have highlighted in this essay, some of the external factors are clearly pointing in the direction of a Nordic renaissance. In this new geopolitical world, the geography and the strategic location of the Nordic region will likely result in an even greater role for these countries, and should create momentum for improved cooperation. External actors, such as the United States, Germany, China, the United Kingdom and others, can play a role in encouraging closer Nordic cooperation and might stimulate the Nordics to take a leadership role in reforming Europe.

Economic restructuring and increased pressure on public budgets might also make Nordic cooperation even more relevant in the field of defense and security policy. However, it is ultimately the domestic developments within the Nordic countries that will determine the direction and aspirations of the future of Nordic cooperation. We see some signs that leaders in politics, culture and economics are now engaged in a process of rethinking the future of Nordic cooperation. Do they dare to develop genuine and encompassing Nordic cooperation fit for the challenges of the 21st century?

6.

Energy and Environment as an Existential Concept— The Responsibility of Being Arctic Nations

Energy security and sound environmental policies are partners in this Nordic model. How do Nordic countries ensure that growth and prosperity are achieved through sustainable and resilient practices, such as the livable cities concept, and through architecture that is integral to these same ideals? What approaches can succeed to ensure a bright future for the Arctic region?

The Nordic Recipe for Growth is Green

Connie Hedegaard

"The saying goes that, you cannot win elections on environment, but you can lose them."

"Remember," my American counterparts often said in the international climate talks, when Europeans blamed them for dragging their feet "Remember that we have a different culture. In the U.S. people do not want to pay taxes…" These statements always annoyed me a bit.

How come that Americans think that Europeans including citizens living in the Nordic countries like taxes any better than Americans?

Often we have learned how "difficult" Congress is when it comes to getting environmental and climate policies adopted: Climate targets, pricing pollution, CAFÉ standards for cars, regulation of power plants and more. But how come our American friends seem to think that it is just a walk in the park to get the European policies, targets and regulations through our Parliaments?

The truth is it is not always politically uncontroversial and uncontested to move on with ambitious forward looking policies. Either the timing is wrong or the ambitions are too high or the design should be different. At the end, however, things move forward in the right direction. So what is the difference?

To say it is about culture would be too easy. Take a President like Theodore Roosevelt who 100-years ago took nature and environment so seriously that he laid the foundation for the unique system of American National Parks and Forests, arguing that we (America) cannot allow the destruction of natural capital. At that time America was a leader in the environmental field. Something got lost in recent decades, but in the Nordics the moral obligation to preserve nature for future generations and maintain it in as good condition as we found it, is still an oft-used argument.

One of the big differences between the Nordics and the U.S. today is that in Nordic countries environment and climate is an important issue right, left and center. Yes, there are nuances and discussions about the speed in which to move forward and differences over the right balance between market and state lies. But broadly speaking, in Norway, Sweden and Denmark even the right of center political parties put emphasis on environment and the green transition toward a low carbon economy. Only the extreme fringe seriously questions the science behind climate change.

There is simply a long and strong tradition for fact based politics. NOT to be fact based is somehow embarrassing. Moreover there is a Parliamentary tradition in all these countries for collaboration across the aisle, because this is a prerequisite for getting anything done in political systems with multiple political parties. The combination of small countries and many parties have led to a specific political culture. Indeed, there is a modus operandi where in order to create certainty for investment, parties have to find common solutions and compromise, and must stick with them when the color of the government changes. In other words, stop and go politics are avoided.

Take Denmark as an example. Going back to the 1973 oil crisis when Denmark almost overnight lost imports from Saudi Arabia, which created an energy situation so dire that driving your own car on Sundays was prohibited, key parties had to work together to develop an alternative energy system. Denmark exploited its own North Sea gas and oil, created a new infrastructure and energy saving approaches which later led to developing and supporting wind as an energy source. Today wind provides more than half of the country's electricity. It was only through a thorough and consistent cooperative approach, across all political blocks, that long-term certainty could be given to investors thereby ensuring this entire transformation. And today, renewable technology is a major Danish export.

Similarly, there was strong bipartisan support for developing hydro power in Norway, and while Sweden and Finland had significant internal debate about nuclear power (which led to the birth of green political parties), in general environmental matters have strong bipartisan support in all Nordic countries. In Sweden and Finland the green parties established in the 1980s have worked very closely with both right and left of center governments. Interestingly, Norway and Denmark have no tradition of green parties as so-called green issues have been incorporated in the agendas of traditional parties. In Denmark it was a leading Conservative politician who in the late 1960s said, "Smoke, Noise and Dirt" are the big future challenges; challenges for the states to handle.

An even greater fundamental difference between Nordic and U.S. traditions is that in Nordic countries there is an acceptance of strong state involvement when it comes to tackling common challenges. As a Nordic citizen one would normally not only expect, but demand that elected representatives present strategies and policies for handling common challenges. Citizens would very much be inclined to take responsibility for themselves on the small scale issues, but would expect government and parliament to defend you and your children against pollution, chemicals, bad air quality and the like. And in the case of such "worthy causes," regulation is generally accepted. There is a strong sense of a "we," of being part of a national community. In short, for these kinds of issues, you are not on your own.

There is also a tradition for involving the business community in big societal challenges which creates a collective sense of direction. This has been the approach toward climate change in all Nordic countries. Of course it also helps that there is a tradition of accepting taxation for the common good. In the Nordics there is a long tradition for applying the polluter's pay principle. Taxing waste, energy and fuel to create an incentive to save resources will normally be politically acceptable, just like putting a price on clean water so that authorities can reinvest in water treatment. There is extensive cooperation and interaction between the public sector and the private sector, where traditionally the public sector - nationally and not the least locally - has had a big say over utilities. In recent years this sector has seen increased privatization, but done in such a way to maintain a key role for public authorities to ensure continued modernization.

The same approach goes for energy infrastructure where the integrated Nordic energy system sets an example for the rest of Europe; this largely because individual Nordic countries did not stop energy planning at national borders. It has been in the common Nordic interest to enhance energy security and cost efficiency through extended cooperation and coordinated expansion of the grid. Thus, for example, hydro-generated electricity from Norway, or nuclear energy from Sweden, is sent to Denmark when the wind is not blowing. At other times surplus wind-generated electricity goes the other way.

Additional regulatory requirements exist for emissions, recycled waste material, building codes for new and refurbished structures and their components. Within the EU, where environmental policies saw a surge after establishment of the single European market in the 80s Nordic countries have also benefited. As frontrunners on environmental issues they have inspired the EU to implement legislation to, "lift the bottom and minimize the risk of outliers." Because the EU had high standards in Europe, it was in its interest to have others, their competitors, apply high standards as well. In a world of increased global competition it is important to avoid the free riders.

As part of Nordic values and self-perception, the environment is one of the important areas where the Nordic countries can exert soft-power in the world. So it is extremely important that political parties and governments not fail; it can cost them an election. While many Nordic citizens will not necessarily list the environment as a key political priority, government neglect can trigger an unwanted outcome. The saying goes that, "you cannot win elections on environment, but you can lose them."

It is often debated whether it is too costly to care seriously about the environment, climate and the transition to a low carbon, resource-efficient society. Has the balance between economic growth and the ecological footprint come at a too high price? In this context it is interesting to note the number of jobs and export opportunities created in the environmental sector. Equally thought provoking is that while the Nordics have pursued ambitious environmental policies for 40 years, they have simultaneously moved to the top of all sorts of global wealth and competitiveness indexes, investment attractiveness and even the global index of happiness.

Perhaps the value of being good environmental stewards is not a contradiction to being a wealthy, competitive and happy nation. The Nordic example shows it is possible; perhaps ambitious climate, resource and environmental policies in the 21st Century are the prerequisites for true wealth and sustainable growth.

In Our Nature:
The Case for the Future of
Sustainable Transport

Emmi Itäranta

"Affordable public transportation makes resources like fuel, energy and raw materials required to construct, maintain and eventually dispose of vehicles available to everyone, whereas focusing on private cars makes them primarily the realm of car owners."

Ancient Finns believed that human beings have several souls. While lore was mainly passed on orally, through song, tale and verse, and written record only goes back a couple of centuries, the surviving knowledge suggests that old Finnish faith held the soul to be threefold. In this pre-Christian world view, the human soul consisted of "henki," which could be translated as "spirit;" "itse," which translates as "self;" and "haltija," or "luonto." Haltija has several meanings that are slightly more difficult to convey. It could stand for "elf," which was also a name for guardian spirits of houses and places in Finnish folklore, or "keeper." The latter name, luonto, however, is straightforward in its meaning: the word stands for nothing less than "nature," thus highlighting the role of humans as part of their environment.

Each of these three dimensions of the soul was attributed slightly different qualities. Henki, or spirit, was loosely understood as the physical life force that made humans breathe, that which made their hearts beat blood through their veins. Itse, or self, was what gave individuals their personality, the distinctive characteristics that separated them from everyone else. The third dimension of the soul, luonto, or nature, was responsible for protection, well-being and good fortune. It could manifest as an animal or a person, something akin to spirit animals of many indigenous cultures, or guardian angels of Christianity. Sometimes it might take the shape of a doppelgänger of the physical body it was connected to in order to cross distances and bear messages. If this aspect was weak, it could be strengthened through magic; indeed, people with strong luonto were often held in high esteem, regarded as shamans or magicians who had special powers.

Losing this protective part of the soul was considered a serious ailment. It meant the person became unhappy, weak and depressed. Being disconnected from your own nature usually also meant being disconnected from the community. The word luonto persists in the Finnish language even today and, besides nature, is used to refer to character or personality. A similar meaning exists in English. We talk about good-natured people, for instance, or say, "It's in my nature."

We do not know to what extent ancient Finns thought about the future, or if they ever tried to imagine what life would be like dozens of generations on. In all likelihood, their main concerns were finding food for themselves and their families, staying away from the path of dangerous beasts and sheltering themselves from the harsh climate as best they could. In their time, the society changed at a much slower pace than in ours; it is not impossible that they believed their way of life would remain much the same forever. If some among them sat down to sing of a world far beyond their own, no record of it has survived, written or oral.

This much we can speculate, however: ancient Finns transported to the present day by the means of time travel or magic would probably be shocked at the ease of crossing distances that modern technology has made possible. For them, traveling was a primitive, time-consuming and unsafe pursuit. It meant long journeys on skis across snow-covered plains, in horse-drawn carriages through dark forests or on rowboats along icy lakes. Weather conditions were frequently less than ideal. Forest was not a friend, but a dangerous wilderness where you might be attacked by beasts or be lured into the woods by malevolent spirits. Trips were rarely taken for pleasure, but out of necessity, and at your peril. The fact that people now dart around in metal boxes with engines, capable of great speed and safety, might seem to them out of this world – and once the initial shock wore off, a source of comfort, security and convenience. Which is, of course, not far from how we see modern travel.

But where convenience has replaced danger, other challenges have risen. Finland is sparsely populated, which translates to long distances for freight, commuters and leisure travel. As a result, Finland has relatively high car ownership numbers—in 2015, over 93 percent of Finns lived in households with at least one car—and the near-highest traffic CO_2 emissions in Europe, second only to Norway. At the same time, public transportation has long been seen as a worthy investment, particularly in cities. The earliest horse-drawn trams appeared in Helsinki in the 1890s, when Finland was still part of Russia. Tram, train and bus networks were popular enough that cars took over in Finland later than in many other industrialized countries—in the 1960s and 1970s, as opposed to the 1940s and 1950s in the U.S. This development was also partly due to the fact that with life focused around smaller rural communities prior to the mass movement to cities that took place around this time, there was less need to move around. Furthermore, Finns were used to walking long distances, both in the country and in cities.

Against this backdrop, it may not come as a surprise that Helsinki wishes to be at the forefront of creating sustainable transport solutions for the digital age. In 2014, a news item made something of a splash around the world about the ambitious plan of the Finnish capital to get rid of car ownership altogether by 2025. The headline on Smithsonian Magazine ran, "Helsinki Has a Plan to Get People to Stop Owning Cars." The technology news website Zdnet went a step further with its version: "Death of the car: The tech behind Helsinki's ambitious plan to kill off private vehicles."

While it turns out that these reports of the private car's death in Helsinki were greatly exaggerated, there is a real story behind them. The Finnish capital is seeking to shape its urban planning towards a direction that takes the challenges of sustainability and possibilities offered by new technologies, such as smartphones, as one of its main points. A city official I contacted denied that Helsinki was trying to get rid of private cars, but emphasized that the city is committed to developing other means of transport, including cycling and pedestrian traffic, and bringing their viability, convenience and attractiveness to the same level as private car use – to the extent that private car ownership could eventually become unnecessary. In other words, instead of planning the city primarily around private vehicles, the intention is to spread it more evenly around several methods of transport, making space for many equal alternatives instead of favoring just one.

One example of a pilot project mapping the possibilities of new kinds of flexible transportation was called Kutsuplus. Ran by the Helsinki Regional Transport Authority (HSL), it was an innovative Uber-style minibus service that allowed users to choose their route, book a ride and pay for it on their smartphones. The service functioned for 18 months and was closed down in late 2015 due to a lack of funding; despite high user satisfaction, in an uncertain economic climate the Finnish government was unwilling to make a long-term investment in Kutsuplus required to make it profitable. However, the experience gained from the trial was valuable for future planning, and Helsinki is looking into creating another comparable service. It also speaks for the viability of the concept that Ajelo, the Finnish tech start-up that was involved in developing Kutsuplus, now operates in Washington D.C. as part of the car-pooling service Split, which uses a similar technology.

Why, then, do such plans, pilot projects and trials matter? The proximity of Finland to the Arctic sets special requirements in many areas of the society, including housing, heating, road maintenance and energy production that must meet the demands of cold weather and changing seasons. One of the biggest future challenges is the impact of climate change. Studies suggest that this is most keenly felt in territories near the poles, and the effects in Finland are tangible. Statistics released in 2015 by the Finnish Meteorological Institute show that annual average temperatures in Finland have already risen by 2°C (approx. 3.6°F), a significantly higher rise than the estimated global 0.9°C. December temperatures have at times been as much as 10°C above average. Since car emissions are one of the biggest culprits in contributing to man-made climate change, it would be irresponsible not to take them into account when considering the future of transport, both public and private.

The most obvious pragmatic reasons for favoring public transport, cycling and pedestrianism include the much-needed reduction in CO_2 emissions, saving of energy resources—which are put to use more efficiently in mass transit than in private car ownership—and safety; car accidents claim far more victims than accidents in public transport. But the case for public transport also deserves a deeper look into the core values behind it, something that the Finnish example may illustrate. I will look into three of them below: freedom, democracy and community.

Private car ownership is often associated with freedom and individuality. In many cultures, a car is not only a status symbol, but also a symbol of personal independence. It embodies a freedom from timetables, routes and connections; the ultimate comfort of getting from point A to point B at one's own convenience, or simply being able to take to the road without a need to determine point B beforehand. So deep-rooted is this idea that we often ignore the reality of car-ownership that has little to do with freedom at all: the considerable cost and commitment of buying and maintaining a vehicle, the congested traffic and the time and cost invested in parking. In early 2016, I spent two months in Silicon Valley. One of the things that struck me the most about the area was that every household seemed to have at least one car. Having grown up in a country and city where public transport was both frequent and reliable, and having never owned a car myself, this came as something of a cultural shock. Instead of a sense of freedom, I felt a sense of entrapment: endless second-guessing of traffic, parking and complete dependency on cars. Public transport can easily offer the same amount of freedom and flexibility as cars, and with a little help from smart technologies, more.

Another core value of public transport that often gets overlooked is its inherent democracy. This could be further divided into democracy of space, movement and resources. Cities have a limited amount of space, and the means of moving around this space is also limited. How the space and movement are distributed among the people of the city cannot be overlooked. Limiting urban planning around private car use places space, movement and resources primarily in the hands of car owners, whereas planning around a wider variety of transport methods distributes all three more evenly. We could also talk about equality here: the post-war Finnish welfare society, including its infrastructure, was built around the ideal of egalitarianism. While a car will be recognized as a status symbol, there is no stigma in Finland in using public transport, and there is very little connection between the social or financial status of a particular method of transport and its user. Due to investment placed in them, buses and trains tend to be safe, clean and comfortable, and people from all walks of life use them.

I would argue that the democracy of resources is even more important than the democracy of space and movement. Affordable public transportation makes resources like fuel, energy and raw materials required to construct, maintain and eventually dispose of vehicles available to everyone, whereas focusing on private cars makes them—again—primarily the realm of car own-ers. Furthermore, the environmental burden is not only reduced, but also shared between more people. This is a significant consideration in a world where the availability of natural resources is limited and the need for action to prevent extreme effects of climate change is acute.

The value of community is also closely connected with the means of transport we choose. It could be argued that public transport highlights community over individuality and ego. It connects its users with others and brings to the fore the collective responsibility—and enjoyment—of using the resources available to us, as well as an awareness of the mark these actions leave on our shared world. In short, it makes us a part of something larger beyond ourselves, a part of continuity between the past and future.

Our ancestors lived by the changing cycles of seasons. The harsh climate shaped their everyday activities, their culture and their very consciousness. Our lives still shift and find their patterns in the shadow of seasons, now more changeable and unpredictable than ever, as we grapple with the new reality of transforming temperatures and precipitation, extreme weather phenomena like floods, wildfires and hurricanes, melting glaciers and rising seas. And here the soul-view of ancient Finns may have something to teach to our era. What-ever the shortcomings in their knowledge, whatever the differences in their circumstances compared to ours, Finns of yesteryear bore at least one wisdom that is still true.

Luonto, the third dimension of the soul they believed in, was what pri-marily connected people to the community. It was known by the same name as nature around us, hence also connecting people with the rhythm of day and night and seasons, and with plant and animal life. Losing this part of one's soul was an ailment, an illness that affected the wellbeing—because to lose connection with nature was to lose connection with part of your own self. Ancient Finns did not see themselves as detached from nature, or above it. They could not function outside it, because they were dependent on it, part of it, and nature was part of them. They understood that to protect and strengthen our luonto, our nature, is to protect and strengthen ourselves—indeed, our very souls.

If this sounds like whimsical tree-hugger talk, it is worth remembering that modern science, while admittedly undecided on the existence of soul, backs up this view. Many studies have shown that a connection with nature increases wellbeing. Spending time in a forest, or near bodies of water, or in a garden or a park, all these things relax and revitalize us, restore our spirit and our self. They make us feel physically and mentally better; the henki and itse of our soul are strengthened, but most of all, so is our luonto, nature. That which we are, and which is vaster than ourselves. As we plan a way forward to the future, towards a world that may look as strange to us as ours would to our ancestors, it is our responsibility to come up with solutions that intensify this connection, rather than gnaw away at it. Any use and distribution of resources should come with an awareness of humanity as part of nature, rather than separate from it. Otherwise we are gnawing away at our own wellbeing.

Public transport was once upon a time seen as a lucrative business opportunity and a wonder of new, cutting-edge high technology: when the first trains arrived in Finland in the 1860s, people would travel long distances just to marvel at them simply because nothing of the kind had ever been seen before. With smart and green industries combining forces in the transforming landscape of climate challenges, perhaps we are on the doorstep of an era when mass transit has the chance to regain the aura of a sense of wonder once again through the opportunities provided by new technologies and planning based on the values of democracy, freedom and community.

We stand always in the present, the now-already-gone-as-it-arrives. We stand at the forever-crossroads of past and future, ourselves a bridge between them, as fragile and short as our human lives. Yet it is a responsibility we cannot give up, because it can only be ours; no one else is around to take it, not those gone before us, not those yet born or grown. We can draw from what the people of the past knew – or did not know – and do our best to leave something worthwhile to the people of the future, a connection that makes us part of the world instead of separating us from it.

It is in our nature.

I would like to thank Transport Planner Mette Granberg from HSL Helsinki Region Transport and Transportation and Traffic Planning Division Director Reetta Putkonen from City of Helsinki for answering my questions and providing helpful information for this essay.

Greenland— An Up and Coming Arctic Island Country[1]

Mininnguaq Kleist

"For a number of years now Greenland has been the showcase for global warming."

Introduction

Greenland is a vast Arctic island with a small population of only approximately 56,000 people spread all over the coasts of the island, but mainly along the West Coast facing Canada. Greenland is a self-governing part of the Kingdom of Denmark, with a mostly Inuit population. It is a former colony, which through its ties with Denmark also has been influenced very much by Nordic values and cultures, while the people very much stay true to their Inuit heritage.

The Arctic is an underdeveloped, but peaceful region, with tremendous industrial potential. It is a region which slowly but surely has crawled higher up on the international political agenda—due to global warming, where the effects of the rising temperatures are most visible in the Arctic, but also because of the industrial and investment potentials of the region. And Greenland sits right in the middle of it. Greenland's geopolitical importance has for

1. I would like to thank my colleague and friend, Mr. Innuteq Holm Olsen, for commenting on an earlier draft of this essay. This essay has borrowed but re-written sections from an article I wrote in the Polar Law Textbook from 2010, edited by Natalia Loukacheva and sponsored by the Nordic Council of Ministers, Copenhagen. That article's title is: "Greenland's Self-Government."

a long time been recognized, the U.S. has had a presence on the island since the Second World War—today mostly through the U.S. Thule Air Base with its potent surveillance radar in the far North of Greenland which is part of the missile defense system. This makes Greenland valuable to the U.S. military and to NATO of which Denmark is a member. Geographically being part of the North American continent and ethnically and linguistically part of the Inuit peoples who live in Canada, Alaska and Siberia, while politically and economically closer to the Nordic countries, makes Greenland a natural bridge between North America and Europe.

For a number of years now Greenland has been the showcase for global warming. High-ranking officials, including German Chancellor Angela Merkel, former Korean President Lee Myung-bak, former President of the EU Commission José Manuel Barroso, UN Secretary General Ban Ki-moon, French Foreign Affairs Minister Laurent Fabius, President of the European Council Donald Tusk, Senator John McCain (R), Secretary of State John Kerry (D) and many others from all over the World have travelled to Greenland in order to witness the dramatic effects of global-warming. Nowhere else can it be seen as visibly as in Greenland and some sceptics are even converted. What also meets visitors to Greenland are clean air, breath-taking views and scenery that make a trip to the island even more unforgettable.

Having an Arctic and sub-Arctic climate and a long stretching geography creates challenges to infrastructure and economic development. This is a major factor in the quest to further develop Greenland's public and private sectors. On the one hand, ongoing climate change is presenting challenges but also creating new opportunities in agriculture across Southern Greenland. Inuit from other parts of the Arctic are often surprised to find Inuit farmers in Greenland. Inuit are people that from time immemorial have been known as hunters and fishermen who have specialized under harsh Arctic conditions.

To counteract the infrastructure challenges, the political system in Greenland, including the parliament and government, decided upon an airport package in 2015, including five projects to extend and build new airports in order to make it easier to travel within and to Greenland. Some of these projects are potentially open to foreign investors.

The airports will improve the transport sector considerably. The development of tourism will be enhanced, and industry, including the mineral resources sector and the country as a whole, will benefit from this strengthening of infrastructure facilities. The airport projects will join the Sikuki Nuuk Harbour[2] construction project planned to be completed by the end of 2016, and will thus enlarge the capital's port facilities—with options to enlarge it even further. If the North-West Passage in the future ever develops into commercial usage, this port might become a relevant player in that scenario.

Greenland's economic foundation is comprised of few but significant building blocks. Greenland receives a major share of its income from the substantial annual Danish block-grant subsidies that are guaranteed through the Self-Government Act. Greenland also has a large fishing industry, cold-water shrimp, Greenland halibut, cod and other fish species generate income through exports. EU funds also support the Greenland economy through the partnership agreement (which focuses on education) and the fishing agreement between the two parties. Greenland is not a member of the EU, even though Denmark is, but has an Overseas Country and Territory (OCT) status.

The tourism sector of Greenland still makes up only a small part of the economy.

There is, however, a concrete tourism strategy plan and efforts are being made to develop the sector.[3] And there is real hope that the tourism boom in neighboring Iceland will have ripple effects for Greenland tourism, especially once access becomes more convenient with increased, better and larger airports.

Greenland has vast mineral wealth potential with numerous minerals, precious gems and metals such as gold, platinum, diamond, rubies, pink sapphire, zinc, lead, iron, rare earth elements, uranium, anorthosite, molybde-

---

2. www.sikuki.com

3. The national tourism company's website: www.greenland.com

num and oil and gas potential.[4] This sector is a growing industry. There is long-term potential for this industry, and future exploitation may contribute to a more self-sustaining economy, but it is currently only a small fraction of the economy.

Water export projects might also develop into interesting income sources for Greenland depending on investment. Greenland could conceivably use its immense water resources as exports to regions with water shortages through bottled and bulk water.

Renewable energy in the form of hydropower is a major part of Greenland's energy consumption. Approximately 65 percent of the electricity produced in Greenland is from hydropower and extensive testing of hydro and other renewable energy sources in the Arctic climate are routinely conducted. The potential for expanding the use of these renewable sources is significant and could be used to supply energy intensive industries with green electricity—such as mineral smelters/refineries, it-server parks, etc. in Greenland, and as cable technology is developing, Greenland has a potential for exporting renewable clean and green energy. Renewable energy for Greenland is good for the economy and leaves Greenland less dependent on oil and its price fluctuations.

History in Short

More than 4,000 years ago the first people arrived in Greenland. Throughout history different pre-Inuit and Inuit peoples and cultures have inhabited Greenland. Today Greenland's Inuit people are descending from the people who came to Greenland roughly a thousand years ago. The Norse first came to Greenland just before the dawn of the first millennium AD, and disappeared after about 500 years. The Norse could thus be said to be the first European colonizers of Greenland.

Modern colonization began in 1721 with the Norwegian-Danish missionary Hans Egede, who went to re-Christianize the Norse in Greenland, but found "only" the Inuit, whom he then Christianized. Hans Egede travelled

---

4. A good overview of what have been found so far and the activities can be made on the government website: www.govmin.gl

on behalf of the Danish Crown. Greenland thus effectively became a Danish colony in modern time.

From 1945 to 1954 Greenland was on the UN-list of non-self-governing territories in accordance with the stipulation of UN-Charter chapter XI. Greenland was taken off the UN-list in 1954 after Greenland integrated into Denmark through the constitution of Denmark, and through which Greenland got two members in the Danish parliament–Folketinget.

In 1972–73 Greenland became a member of the European Economic Community (EEC) together with Denmark, even though the large majority of people in Greenland voted against membership in the 1972 referendum. Denmark with its much larger population pulled Greenland into the EEC when it joined. However by the beginning of the 1980s and after the introduction of Home Rule in Greenland, a new referendum on the island resulted in a "no vote" and finally in 1985 Greenland left the EEC and attained the status of an OCT to the EEC, now the EU.

On June 21, 2009 Self-Government became a reality in Greenland. This was the outcome of a thorough process of deliberation, debate and negotiations between Greenland and Denmark which produced recommendations that led to the popular referendum[5] in Greenland (November 2008), which endorsed Self-Government. Self-Government replaced Home Rule, which had been in place since 1979. Home Rule introduced the first Greenlandic parliament and government in 1979, and Self-Government is a further extension of this.

Through the enactment of the Self-Government Act, the Greenlandic people are recognized in their own right under international law and have the right to self-determination. Among other rights, Greenland has the right to secede from Denmark and become an independent state if so decided by the people of Greenland. The Greenlandic language has also become the official language of Greenland, but Danish can still be used in official matters, and English is taught in schools. The Self-Government Act also stipulates that

---

5. On the 25th of November 2008 the referendum took place on whether or not the Draft Act on Greenland Self-Government should re-place the Home Rule Act of 1978. The result was 75.54% in favour of the introduction of Self-Government, and 23.57% against. 71.96% showed up to cast their vote.

Greenland can take control over more than 30 other areas of competence including the judiciary and its mineral resources. And in 2010, after decades of trying, Greenland did assume control of its mineral resources.

Greenland has also under the Home Rule-period assumed control over social affairs, the health-system, education, environment, housing, infrastructure, energy, finance, taxation, fisheries, industry, the labor market, commerce, trade, mineral resources (both on land and offshore) municipalities, culture, the church, amongst others. Within the Kingdom of Denmark Greenland cannot take over the competence of foreign affairs, but can enter into international negotiations and agreements with other states and organizations in areas in which Greenland has assumed control from Denmark, and which deal with the geographic territory of Greenland. Thus Greenland has its own foreign affairs service and safeguards its own interests, in cooperation with the Danish Ministry of Foreign Affairs.

Conclusion

Greenland is a former colony that keeps developing its self-governing capacities and competences through constructive talks with Denmark. This also indicates that the self-government system is an ongoing growing process with regard to Greenland's competences. It also includes a high focus on educational efforts in Greenland's development, something that further characterizes Greenland's cooperation with the EU.

With its breath taking views and scenery, clean air and water, there are high hopes for tourism to blossom in the years to come which will be helped by a vastly improved transport sector. Greenland does not yet have a self-sustaining economy, but the potential for economic growth and investment in industrial projects are definitely part of the future landscape. The world is beginning to take notice of Greenland's economic potential, as witnessed by a substantially growing number of visits from international delegations from both the public and private sector. Everyone is aware that climate change is happening fast in Greenland which brings both challenges and opportunities. And Greenland wants to explore these opportunities in a sustainable manner consistent with its Inuit heritage and Nordic values.

The Nordic Urban Design Model

Jeff Risom

"By bringing the project to people, decision makers meet the general population wherever they are in the city as part of their everyday routine as opposed to inviting people to a church basement or community center to hear presentations and view boards of illustrations that are difficult to understand."

Our world is becoming decidedly more urban (over 75 percent of the population will live in cities in 2050), but in the United State the urban future is more uncertain than ever. This uncertainty centers among numerous inter-related factors. While some cities struggle through gentrification, others suffer from a lack of investment. Cities in the rust belt and the south are especially susceptible to depopulation sparked by the change from manufacturing to the technology and service economy. Nationally, four million more people live in urban poverty in 2010 than they did in 1970. With voter turnout in some local municipal elections barely in the teens, there must be ways to increase civic engagement in U.S. cities.

Even within some of the same cities the quality of life is uneven with adjacent neighborhoods displaying radically different indicators of life expectancy and income mobility. Climate change induced sea-level changes threatens to alter the landscape of cities effecting where we can build and the ecosystem of our shorelines. Our ability to re-design cities impacted by this change, and to adapt them to accommodate increased population of people displaced from affected areas, threatens the very balance between nature and humanity.

The city can be a platform for creative collaboration to address many issues simultaneously. The public realm – civic institutions but also streets, parks and squares can be the conversion point where differences interact, solutions can be found and, most importantly, empathy between people who are different from one another can be cultivated. It is these streets and spaces, the connective tissue of our society, that not only represent a plentiful civic asset (streets are typically 30–35 percent of all urban areas), but one that is undervalued. It is the life between buildings cultivated in these spaces that Jan Gehl has been studying and writing about for 50 years. It is the love of people that drove Jan's work, and inspires mine.

This love of people is born in a Danish context and cultivated out of a Nordic humanistic tradition. How can the public realm be a tool to combat violence and inequality in our cities? Can promoting enhanced quality of life help combat the largest problems facing society today? What type of urban design will invite all those who live in these cities to meet and interact in the public realm, both in times of protest but also as part of everyday public life?

The Role of the Built Environment

For years, vast majorities of urban populations have been excluded from positively contributing to their city. Ironically, excluding human capital while naively exploiting natural resources has robbed our cities of an opportunity. In 2016, by engaging and empowering a greater segment of our population we can invert that paradigm. It is this notion of investing our collective resources into the individual capabilities of all human beings that represents the greatest change of mindset.

Recent studies indicate that place matters; a need for humans to flourish. Raj Chetty, and The Equality of Opportunity Project document how the physical and social composition of cities ranging from commuting times, to two-parent households contribute to economic mobility. The chances of achieving the American Dream, of improving one's economic lot, seem to vary widely from neighborhood to neighborhood. Physical inactivity accounts for five million deaths globally and new studies published in the British Medical Journal, Lancet show that urban design, density of residences and interconnectedness of streets can mean that people are active for up to 90 minutes more than in less well-designed areas. These studies and others are proving that accessible public space, attractive parks, safe streets and vibrant public life are not just nice to have, but are vital to how well or how badly we live. The quality of the urban future is intertwined with the quality of the built environment in which one lives and the type of public life with its routines and activities.

Keys of the Nordic Urban Design Model

The Nordic countries are characterized by a large middle class and a low Gini Coefficient (a numerical statistic used to measure income inequality). From pre-school on, the notion of "our" is ingrained through education and cultural norms. This culture is one where the collective quality of "our" environment is more important than the individual one. Citizens in Nordic countries pay the highest taxes in the world, but do so understanding that those taxes are put to good use, ensuring all Nordic citizens have access to resources as well as basic dignity represented in the quality of cities. With a high percentage of these taxes dedicated to local authorities (upwards of 30 percent in Denmark) and services ranging from trash collection, to child-care and basic medical services, citizens can see their tax dollars put to good work. On the national scale, these services: universal health care; free education including college; and subsidies to the unemployed, students, young families and the elderly provide a sense security throughout life.

This all leads to a strong notion of trust between citizens and decision-makers, and between citizens themselves. Importantly, this ethos manifests itself in the "Human Scale" physical environment of Nordic cities. The dignified quality of public realm—from sidewalks to civic service halls and community cultural centers—this investment in public spaces, makes it possible for all people to be treated as worthy human beings.

Design, Outreach, Engagement, Policy and Governance

This concept is about how observational studies that literally "count people," but also "make everyday behavior of people count." Edward Glaeser, the Harvard economist and author of Triumph in the City, states that,

"Remember that the real city is made of flesh, not concrete." Human behavior, people's preferences, local culture and other types of "software" can vary widely, making performance difficult to predict. As a result, many design professionals, and the local authorities or companies that employ them, typically shift their attention to "hardware" such as technology and infrastructure, which they can control and measure.

Jan Gehl influenced the City of Copenhagen to begin measuring this "software," including how pedestrians and cyclists move from A to B, when they do so (time of day/week/seasons) and who is walking (age and gender). These studies also focus on where people spend time, in what activities they are engaged and who is participating. Often times those not present (age, race and gender) is as enlightening as those who are.

Facilitating a change in mindset (software) is as important as implementing high-quality cycling and public transit infrastructure (hardware). This change of mindset is embodied in the perception of safety, accessibility for everyone, inclusion of young and old, the fit and the unfit and men and women. We must purposely create "invitations" for these various groups to feel welcome based on understanding people's behavior and their specific reasons for transit integration, rather than trying to design and build our way blindly out of a problem.

This approach can be applied to quality of place as well as mobility. Every two years Copenhagen, Denmark, carries out a survey of cyclists to assess the quality of its cycling facilities and to understand direct benefits to cyclists. Over the years, this survey—the Copenhagen Bicycle Account (CBA)—has become more comprehensive and sophisticated. It now questions non-cyclists on why they choose to ride (or not) and aims to assess their perceived level of safety while cycling. The CBA is a brilliant tool that has helped optimize municipal investments in cycling infrastructure and ensure that campaigns are successful.

Integrating the views and patterns of behavior of people in these studies has been a consistent ingredient to making Copenhagen more Livable. Since the 90s elected officials, city staffs and most importantly citizens themselves, are demanding more from their streets and spaces. In 2010, the City created a "Metropolis for People" guide modeled to unify city policy around people-first and public life-driven success criteria. It is centered on encouraging more people to walk (20 percent increase) inviting more people to spend time (20 percent more staying activity) and measuring general satisfaction (80 percent of people should be satisfied with the quality of the public realm).

As stated so clearly by Bente Frost, Mayor of Buildings and the Environment in Copenhagen from 1994–97, "Without Public Life surveys from the Royal Academy of Architecture we as politicians wouldn't have had the courage to implement the many projects we have that increase the City's attractiveness." Tina Saaby, the City Architect of Copenhagen in 2013 said, "More important than any individual work, Gehl (the people-first approach) helped to change the planning and design culture of the City. From politicians to department heads, project managers and citizens—the notion of people first and Life, Space, Buildings has infiltrated all aspects of making Copenhagen what it is today." In short, we require a shift in focus from objects to people: from concrete to flesh, as Glaeser would have it. Only then will we be able to address the all-too-common error of confusing mobility with the infrastructure that supports it.

Enable Shared Experiences

This Copenhagen People First Approach works great in a largely economically and racially homogenous society. But can it be translated effectively to other places and more multi-cultural societies with greater inequality between rich and poor. The key is to create opportunities to celebrate what we all have in common as Homo sapiens and what is different based on race, age, ethnicity and culture. An effective way to accomplish this is through demonstration or pilot projects. Small scale urban interventions—recently coined as tactical urbanism—grew out of our work with New York City's Department of Transportation in the transformation of Broadway in Manhattan.

This approach of using real life projects as a platform for civic engagement could increase the number of contributing stakeholders. By bringing the project to people, decision makers meet the general population wherever they are in the city as part of their everyday routine as opposed to inviting people to a church basement or community center to hear presentations and view boards of illustrations that are difficult to understand. With a chance to touch, see and experience a project first-hand, citizens regardless of personal experience and education, are better equipped to engage in a constructive dialogue with experts and decision makers. This approach leads to a more authentic form of city development made possible through inclusive empowerment; thus allowing a broader segment of community to express what is most vitally needed in community development.

Today, citizen involvement is strongest when opposing change; citizen groups are most fervently engaged when saying "no." In addition to serving as a more inclusive form of empowerment, pilot projects can become a platform for a more positive use of citizen energy aimed at saying "yes" to particular interventions. The New York City Plaza Program and San Francisco Prototyping Festival are two examples of projects Gehl helped to spearhead that invert the typical antagonistic relationship between the established community and city agencies.

Building upon the successful "World Class Streets" transformation of high profile public spaces along Broadway in Manhattan, the New York City Department of Transportation created the NYC Plaza program. Using a simple, but robust spatial model we helped to create, carefully selected access road space (often in the form of right-hand turn lanes) could be reclaimed as public plazas. Sites were identified based on their ability to connect active ground floor functions (like hair salons, cafés, laundromats, kiosks) and adjacent traffic islands. The new coherent public space would be paid for by city funds, but only if local community groups established broad support and could prove they had the means to operate and maintain the new plaza after the original city investment.

The city put forth a rigorous and simple set of criteria and indicated that city investment would be limited; the city could only pay for three to five plazas per year, so if a community wanted one, it would need to compete with other communities to capture vital but scarce city support. This brilliant approach inverted typical reasons for citizens to become active. Rather than fighting against change, the loudest voices were now positive ones, competing for city investment. So far, over 70 new plazas have been created in all five boroughs of Manhattan.

In San Francisco, we worked for three-years to create a new vision for a vital downtown corridor. "The Better Market Street" project would transform the City's most important transit thoroughfare while connecting vital civic assets from the Embarcadero waterfront to City Hall. Yet when the project hit budgeting snags, Gehl along with the Yerba Buena Center for the Arts and the Department of City Planning, conceived of a way to re-imagine the street while waiting for funding to be secured.

The "Living Innovation Zone" concept identified ten zones along the two-mile street that could be turned over to various citizen groups or cultural institutions with interest drive and hunger to positively contribute to the vitality of the street. The Exploratorium Science Museum built the first installation with the help of citizen volunteers and was financed through the crowd funding platform "In Our Back Yard." The first zone, opened in 2012, has since been scaled up to five buoyed by the advent of the Market Street Prototyping Festival. The three-day festival launched in 2014 will open again in fall 2016 and will leverage philanthropic funding to catalyze 80 citizen-led and built "prototype installations" conceived and built with broad community input. Both of these innovative approaches to activating citizen and community group talent, entrepreneurship and creativity are examples of a Nordic-inspired approach that builds upon the broad capabilities of a diverse cross section of civil society.

Inspired by these examples, Denver is currently applying a holistic new approach to major projects. The approach, best described as "Action Oriented Planning," breaks the entire long-term planning, engagement and design process for re-imagining the 16th Street Mall into a series of small incremental actions and activities. The city is partnering with the private sector to host a series of events aimed at radically re-thinking the role of the Transit Corridor in downtown. Utilizing the Gehl method for measuring behavior and use, city bus routes were altered during summer weekends. What began as a special event on two Sundays in 2014, has grown to five consecutive weekends of authentic Denver culture expressed in a space usually dominated by bus traffic. The Downtown Denver Partnership partnered with numerous community, cultural and civic groups—providing them with space and money to empower citizens to contribute to public life. From typical street festival activities to live music, climbing walls and park games to more innovative evens like interactive art, cultural performances by ethnic minority groups and multiple forms of sports and recreation, the transportation corridor has been transformed into a vibrant expression of diversity, culture and lifestyle of a city in transition.

What to Do in the Future—How to Apply the Nordic Model in the U.S. Context

I find solace and inspiration in knowing that the best way to tackle the overwhelming, complex problems facing our cities is by equipping more people with the ability to work toward dealing with them in their own ways. Our collective future as a species can only be ensured by empowering all segments of our global population to address the issue in their own ways.

This approach, described in a different context of the global urban poor by Nobel Prize winner Amartya Sen, is one where we measure the advancement of civilization not by GDP growth, but by the development of the human species. Sen's notion can also be captured by the idea of a common places civilization. Olmstead wrote of it almost two-hundred years ago, but rather than focusing on the grand utopian dream, I prefer to focus on small incremental changes made possible through policies like Copenhagen's Metropolis for People, the incremental but steady reclamation of space in New York or the empowerment of citizens through prototyping in San Francisco. These are examples where citizens of all races, genders and orientations are able to collectively contribute to a brighter urban future; when a greater percentage of people feel like stewards of shared public and civic assets like our public spaces.

Reflection and Limitations of the Nordic Model

It is our streets and spaces in which we meet to show our collective outrage and our common hope for solidarity and change. In July 2016, people protested the tragic shootings of unarmed black men and the murder of police officers. From San Francisco's Market Street, to City Hall Plaza in Philadelphia, citizens organized marches and rallies, while other protestors blocked

Hwy 40 in Memphis and I-94 in St. Paul. The streets and spaces, the public realm of our cities, are the platforms for demonstration and protest. But these same streets and spaces of cities are rarely seen as a tool to realize the change to which protestors aspire.

In 2016, the majority of the people who plan, design and build our communities and cities still lack the diversity and perspective of those same communities and cities. As Columbia University Professor Justin Moore said in a recent FastCoDesign article, "It will only be after we have more informed and empowered communities comprised of engaged citizens can we hope to achieve our full potential as a human race. It is the power of seeing the 'other' an alternative reality between the polarized views of decaying and violent cities and flourishing and serene suburbs. This exposure to difference and the environments that invite it are vital."

That is why the Nordic tradition of urban design, and inviting people from all walks of life to experience this difference in comfort as part of their everyday routine provides an opportunity. It is this subtle exposure to difference one receives by occupying the same public realm and possibly participating in chance encounters with strangers that can accelerate the change that needs to happen in U.S. cities. Our urban future is indeed uncertain, but I'm comforted by the enormous potential inherent in a much greater share of the world's population possessing the agency to have control not only of their own destiny but also their trajectory as a meaningful contributor to a common places civilization. It will only be after we have more informed and empowered communities comprised of engaged citizens can we hope to achieve our full potential as a human race. This inclusive approach not only increases the likelihood of solving these interrelated complex issues, but also help ensure the U.S. moves beyond its history with a polarized view of urbanity stretching from decaying and violent cities to flourishing and serene suburbs.

Welcome to the Anthropocene!

Johan Rockström

"We continue to live in a world with islands of insight in an ocean of ignorance."

Human history on Earth is a remarkable journey where it is absolutely clear that modern societies as we know them have evolved and can with a very high degree of certainty only exist and flourish as long as Planet Earth remains in a stable and resilient state. Why? Because everything we do and everything we depend on emerges from the biosphere, i.e., from the thin layer of soil, water, minerals, biomass and living species, which in turn is a result of the state of the atmosphere, the cryosphere (permanent ice on Earth), the stratosphere (the thin protective layer of ozone in the higher atmosphere) and the oceans and hydrosphere (the conveyor belt of heat in oceans and the flow of water). In essence, humanity depends on Earth for everything we do and everything we wish for.

We, as humans, have not had to really worry about this fundamental dependence on Earth until recently, the last 30 years to be precise. The reason is that we have reached a critical juncture on a journey that accelerated in 1955, and which has culminated only in the last 30 years.

It all began in the 1750s, at the advent of the industrial revolution, which in essence was when the world took the step into the fossil-fuel driven mechanization of industrial processes that opened the door to a modern and rapidly globalized world. Interestingly and importantly, we as humanity, despite the rapid growth of environmental problems in the footsteps of the industrial revolution (millions of premature deaths due to air pollution following coal-burning and ecosystem degradation) and the subsequent industrial agricultural development (rapidly transforming over 40 percent of Earth's land area to agriculture), had very little, but not insignificant impacts on the planet as a whole.

We were a small world on a big planet. In fact, this is how the human journey on Earth has been from the advent of modern humans—some 100,000 years ago (when we see the first proof of modern Homo sapiens, giving us the same physical and intellectual capacity to develop modern societies as we know them today). We see local environmental problems and sometimes fatal, such as the fall of the Mayan, Incan and Mesopotamian irrigation societies, and impacts on the Roman and Egyptian empires, where local ecosystem degradation cannot be excluded as a key component behind societal downfall. But, humanity hitting Earth? No.

Then something dramatic happened. It is 1955, ten years after the Second World War. We are three and one-half billion co-citizens on Earth, and now, we embark on a remarkable acceleration of human pressures on Earth. Suddenly, essentially all curves of environmental processes that regulate how Earth operates shift from essentially flat (little or no change) to an exponential rise of human pressure. You pick any parameter that matters for human well-being and economic growth. This includes emissions of greenhouse gases to air pollution, nutrient overload, or loss of biodiversity. They look the same— a hockey stick of exponential rise in pressure starting 1955.

While this is extremely dramatic in itself, it is only a partial story. In the beginning of the great acceleration (1950s–1990) we see a remarkable exponential rise of human pressures on Earth, but we see very little dramatic consequences for human societies or humanity as a whole. The world generates wealth in an unprecedented way—delivering astonishing results, with a world population rising from three to over seven billion today living longer, eating better and accumulating more material wealth than ever before (at least for a rich minority while increasingly also reaching a poor majority)—but does so unsustainably. What does this mean? It means that Planet Earth subsidizes our wealth. We overfish, fill the atmosphere with greenhouse gases, cut forests, degrade soils, empty sources of rare Earth metals, pollute lakes and eradicate other species. In essence, operating through massive scale abuses against planet Earth; and what does Mother Earth do? She applies all her bio-geophysical capacities to buffer and wane, to dampen and adapt. To be, in simple terms, our best friend. Earth is incredibly resilient and has a remarkable, redundant space and ability to absorb our abuse, without sending any invoices back to societies. This is why our neo-Keynesian macroeconomics model has worked. We assume that we can consider only human and economic capital, while seeing natural capital largely as a global commons and externality. We allow ourselves to exploit nature at no cost, neither when we use nor when we are hit by impacts of overuses of natural capital.

This naïve "golden era" of unsustainable growth comes to an end by 1990 (that is what science shows, while there is a 25 year time lag as we still live in this unsustainable, planet undermining, growth paradigm...). It is by the end of the 1980s that we start seeing Earth's invoices piling up. From the sudden collapse of cod fisheries out of Newfoundland, to the myriad of lake collapses due to overfishing and eutrophication, the crossing of the 350 parts per million line for atmospheric concentration of greenhouse gases, the accelerated melting of Arctic ice, the accelerated loss of coral reef systems and mass-extinction of species affecting ecosystem stability. We start seeing from 1990 onwards, Earth starting to send invoices back to societies. We have reached a saturation point, where we, the world, are starting to hit the biophysical ceiling of planet Earth. And the response is also non-linear with abrupt and potentially irreversible impacts such as the loss of Arctic sea ice or triggering the ultimate collapse of coral reef systems.

In short this means that we have entered a new geological epoch (1950s onward), the Anthropocene, where we humans are the largest driver of change on planet Earth (exceeding the natural forces of change – such as Earth's position to the Sun—that explains the ins-and-out of ice ages in Earth's geological history). We have also entered a saturation point (from 1990s onward) where we (1) experience rising frequency of Earth invoices being sent to societies (droughts, floods, ecosystem collapse); and (2) can no longer exclude pressing on "buttons" for irreversible change, e.g., triggering a (long-term) but unstoppable melting of the Greenland ice-sheet (holding a seven meter sea-level rise), which may occur if we pass the global two-degree Celsius planetary limit.

Leaving Eden's Garden?

Even with the above planetary drama that we have now reached as a decisive point for the human future on Earth, we must address the core question of what has enabled us to develop modern societies as we know them.

Earth swings in and out of ice ages and warmer inter-glacials. It is during the last inter-glacial—the Holocene—that modern societies have evolved. We know today that the Holocene—the 12,000 years since the last Glacial period (of some 100,000 years) has been extraordinary, not to say miraculously stable with a climate system staying within an amazing sweet spot for us humans of approximately plus or minus one-degree Celsius! It is in this era of environmental stability that we invent agriculture and that we embark on the innovation and technological pathway that has built our modern world. The Holocene is our Eden's Garden, a prerequisite for the world as we know it.

This is what makes me really nervous. Science not only shows that we are rapidly pushing ourselves, as planetary agents of the Anthropocene, into danger zones in terms of triggering very dangerous changes in life-conditions on Earth. It also shows that the Holocene is our Garden of Eden, the sweet spot that has enabled us to thrive.

This is why we now urgently need a deep mind-shift, where we reconnect our modern world with our precious planet Earth. Where we once and for all recognize not only our dependence on the biosphere and Earth as a whole, but also that we are an imbedded part of the Earth system. We as humanity shape the planet and the planet shapes us.

Transformations to Global Sustainability

As robust as science is that we are in the midst of an unprecedented pace and scale of change, and the risks that follow for humanity in terms of potentially disastrous permanent outcomes for future generations. As convincing is the real world evidence that there is a little light of hope in the tunnel. Even though we will inevitably face social-ecological turbulence, in terms of unavoidable problems (tough adaptation needs) due to climate change and ecosystem degradation, we still—with the evidence we have today—stand a chance of leaving Earth in a manageable state for human development in the future.

In essence, this means transforming our human development paradigm into a world that evolves within the safe operating space of a stable and resilient planet that enables prosperity within planetary boundaries. This has fundamental implications for our relationship between humans and nature, shifting the rationale in economics, politics, legislation, institutions and human behavior.

This may sound—and rightly so—like a grand shift, not to say a revolution. However, it may be less dramatic than it appears at first sight as, at its core, it is about nurturing universal values that cut across religions, nations, business sectors and societies at large. It may sound naive, but just the core value shift of humans becoming wise stewards of the remaining beauty on Earth, what we love and depend on outside of our window—the oceans, rainforests and the sky—would be a transformation towards finding that light in the planetary tunnel.

And we see these values translated to efforts of global action. We have come quite far along the pathway towards a world where sustainable development is the path to human prosperity. In 2015 world nations adopted the UN (United Nations) Sustainable Development Goals (SDGs). Seventeen aspirational goals to be achieved by 2030 were adopted which at its heart sets out the ethical and moral "end game" for a desired world future with over 8 billion co-citizens by 2030 (food for all from healthy and sustainable food systems; no more poverty, gender equality, primary education for all, transparency and economic development). Moreover, this will be the first time it ever occurs as long as humans have walked on Earth. All these social and economic goals are to be achieved within global sustainability goals, in essence, within planetary boundaries. This is a grand paradigm shift. These seventeen goals, 169 targets and over 250 indicators, set out a roadmap for a transformation to an equitable, successful and sustainable future. As far as we know today, delivering on the SDGs—and the Paris Climate Agreement of staying as far below two-degrees Celsius and aiming for one and one-half degrees Celsius of global mean temperature rise due to Anthropogenic climate change, stands a good chance of enabling humanity to thrive on a stable planet that remains within a manageable Holocene-like inter-glacial state. No, not as miraculously stable as the Holocene, but yes, within the range of a manageable planet that does not, irreversibly, push us into a disastrous "hot state," of plus four-degrees Celsius or beyond.

The Nordic Way—How Sustainable Innovation and Biosphere Happiness Can Transform the World

We are at the tipping point. We have only a few years to bend the global curves of unsustainable human pressures from greenhouse gas emissions to loss of biodiversity, deforestation, overfishing, eutrophication, overuse of freshwater, soil degradation, in essence all planetary boundaries that regulate Earth's stability and thus, our future. In fact within four years we need to have permanently started bending the global curve of greenhouse gas emissions from burning fossil-fuels and from degradation of natural ecosystems to stand even just a two-thirds chance of meeting the Paris climate agreement. And still this requires racing downhill to reduce emissions by 6 or 7 percent per year in order to reach zero emissions by 2050, or soon thereafter. The same goes for loss of biodiversity, only we need to reach zero loss much sooner. We also need to realize that it is time to feed humanity through zero expansion of agricultural land – we have to safeguard the remaining natural ecosystems we have, in particular forests. Can this be done? Well, a look at the world today makes you wonder. We are still increasing coal mining and coal fire plants in Asia. We are still expanding the number of cars in Europe. We are still degrading ecosystems due to deforestation for palm oil in Indonesia and soya in Brazil. We are still loading the oceans with plastics and the biosphere with chemicals.

Today I can see a necessary troika of global disruptive actions that need to occur simultaneously to stand a chance of succeeding with a good future for humanity, and a transformation of the world within planetary boundaries.

First. We need planetary stewardship. Whether we like it, we now need to realize once and for all that we are no longer a small world on a big planet. We have shifted over to become a large world on a small planet. We, all seven and two-tenths billion of us in 196 nations, need to collectively start acting now in sustainable ways, from how we eat, to how we provide energy, shelter and "stuff." For this we need strengthened global governance. Today I can only see us succeeding in this state of planetary urgency with the UN Security Council taking up global sustainability as a top priority for human security, peace, equality and world development. I cannot see us succeeding without locking humanity to a finite, non-negotiable global carbon budget, a global nitrogen budget, a global forest budget and so on. We need to mentally reorganize the SDGs into a hierarchy where the four planetary SDGs (6, 13, 14 and 15 of water, climate, biodiversity and oceans) form non-negotiable boundaries for us to achieve all the social and economic goals. We can only succeed in attaining human well-being and long-term economic development within finite and scientifically defined planetary boundaries.

This will not, and I really want to emphasize this, NOT hinder economic growth and human wealth creation. Instead it raises the bar on innovation—it is not enough to "only" deliver novel breakthrough technologies and systems that make us more efficient and provide opportunities for better life, they must also meet global sustainability criteria—be 100 percent decarbonized, operate within a circular economy and provide for sharing within planetary boundaries. I call this double-innovation—better people solutions for a better planet—otherwise failure.

Second. A top down planetary stewardship revolution will not be enough. We also need a bottom up values mind-shift. We all need to change behavior, recalibrate values in life (consumption not being the ultimate indicator of happiness but rather experience, trust, health, social networks, culture, etc.) and in particular recognize that a big world on a small planet means sharing with all our co-citizens who have the same right to development within the remaining, finite and shrinking space on Earth.

And thirdly. This is an innovation and transformations journey into the future. It is the most challenging and most exciting we have ever undertaken. And most importantly, it is about the real future, about the most advanced technologies, frontier science and about adopting the most attractive and advanced solutions. Staying in our unsustainable Era—the great acceleration world from the 1950s onwards—is the back-water, a dead-end that means staying with yesterday's unhealthy, inefficient, planet damaging fossil-fuel technologies and linear production systems that exploit here and pollute there.

We face a real choice; either a dirty coal-future or a clean Tesla-future. The choice is ours. But how to make it? It is not very likely that sustainable technological solutions—from solar voltaics to fuel cells and biotech materials will be adopted by everyone all at once. Instead we should seek inspiration from the 19th century Italian economist Pareto who introduced the empirical 20/80 rule. Once 20 percent of a population, market or region adopts a new practice, solution or technology, this minority is large enough (within the market) to tip over the vast, indifferent and/or old practicing majority. This sustainable innovation David, tipping over a largely unsustainable Goliath may sound utopian, but follows the recent legacy of disruptive technologies, from mobile phones to internet, and soon, solar and wind power.

We have now come to a juncture where we need to expand the 20/80 rule to societies and nations. Recently an independent UN study (by the Sustainable Development Solutions Network, SDSN) concluded that Sweden is the country in the world best placed to implement the SDGs. The Nordic countries all fall within the top-10 list of countries. This provides evidence, together with indicators in HDI, GDP and the ability to create good quality life conditions, with cultures and values closely linked to nature, of a "David" region—the Nordic way—potentially with the ability of inspiring a world to transform to global sustainability.

No nations have come so far in proving that decoupling ecological degradation and climate change from economic growth is possible, yet still have good living conditions in advanced societies. And there are other "Nordic way" equivalents around the world, but we continue to live in a world with islands of insight in an ocean of ignorance. It is time for the Nordic countries to hold hands to jointly transform development within planetary boundaries, a transformation that can deliver on SDGs and Paris. We need to do this in an alliance with other nations and regions in the world. It is time to create a large enough minority alliance for global sustainability; to tip over our world Goliath to ensure a future where our only planet can continue to support us.

A New Utilization Movement

Thor Sigfusson

"From Maine lobster to Louisiana shrimp to Alaska salmon, the United States fishing industry could benefit economically and environmentally by applying the Icelandic model."

This is the story of how Iceland propelled a Nordic tradition to increase the utilization and value from seafood and by that create new job opportunities, especially for coastal dwellers. This essay outlines lessons for countries facing resource constraints and, perhaps unknowingly, resource underutilization.

History

Since the 9th century, Icelanders have derived vitality and stamina from fish. Seafarers, including women, dropped hand lines into the sea, caught fish, gutted and then hung them to dry on driftwood racks. Sea pants softened with fish oil allowed fishermen to stay warm and dry, and go out further away from the shore. Wooden rowboats led to sailing smacks and motor driven trawlers like *The Coot,* which reached even further into the North Atlantic swells. The fishing crafts may have changed, but the Icelandic determination to push the limits of what was possible remained constant.

Challenge

In recent history, fisheries and fish processing jobs have been on a declining slope in Iceland. Like many other countries, Iceland has faced reduced landings and been mindful not to overfish. With stock sustainability and the ecological effects of fishing and management systems as core concerns, how has Iceland become even more competitive in the global marketplace?

Solutions

The Iceland Ocean Cluster, a group of collaborating marine companies and experts, has traced the origin of Iceland's economic success. While Icelandic cod landings decreased from 460,000 tons to 180,000 tons between 1981 and 2011, the total export value of cod products actually rose from $340 million to $680 million (present value Figure 1). The number of fishermen and fish processing jobs decreased, but from a holistic perspective marine related jobs grew significantly in this period. The Iceland Ocean Cluster discovered and supported a network of 120 marine companies that have been instrumental to this success. This growth was in part due to two factors: a value-added approach and the strategy of 100 percent fish utilization, both of which, once again, pushed the limit of what was possible.

Company Spotlight: Codland was founded in 2012 by the Iceland Ocean Cluster and is owned by one of the biggest fishing companies in Iceland. Codland is a network of companies with a common goal of increasing the value of fish products and raising awareness of Icelandic fisheries. Codland specializes  in total utilization of fish products. One of Codland's new projects is Alda, a lemonade health drink that strengthens joints and prevents wrinkles with marine collagen.

The **value added approach** challenges the notion that a fish's primary purpose is a filet. The Icelandic industry has discovered and nurtured alternative applications for fish products through research and development in cosmetics, health food and pharmaceuticals (Image 1). This approach has benefited all levels of the supply chain, including fishermen in remote areas who have seen prices for cod liver triple in recent years due to increased interest in value added uses.

In Icelandic, *nýtin* is a positive word that describes a person who uses things to their fullest. **100 percent utilization** seeks to use every ounce of the fish. Iceland has moved to 80 percent utilization of cod while the average utilization around the North Atlantic is closer to 45 percent. By increasing the amount of each fish used, it becomes possible to create more value from fewer resources.

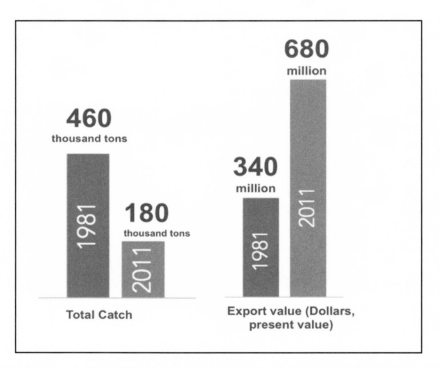

Figure 1. These charts show incredible value increase from fewer resources in the period from 1981 to 2011. These metrics demonstrate the potential of making more jobs and wealth with fewer resources.

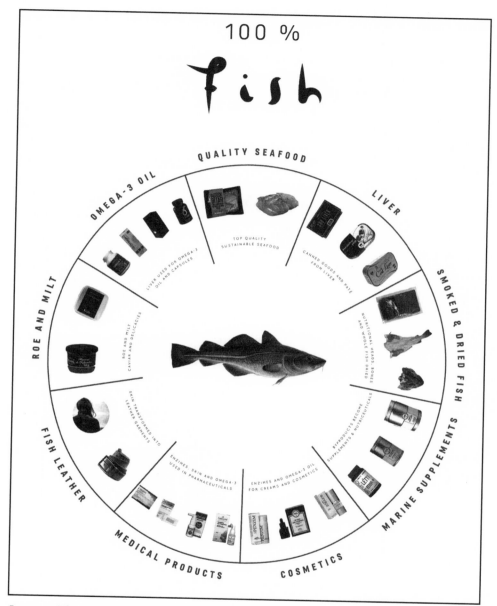

Image 1. This image shows the plethora of products that can be made from one cod. From enzyme-rich creams and cosmetics to fish skin leather garments, these products demonstrate that it is possible to move up the value chain from traditional fishing industry uses.

Implications for the Globe

Iceland has discovered one way of creating value and jobs, especially in remote and rural areas where opportunity is not taken for granted. With new partnerships and the sharing of best practices we may be on the cusp of a new utilization movement. Around the world 455 million tons of fish are wasted each year[1]. In the US for example, 40–47 percent (or 1 million metric tons) of edible seafood was wasted between 2009 and 2013[2]. From Maine lobster to Louisiana shrimp to Alaska salmon, the United States fishing industry could benefit economically and environmentally by applying the Icelandic model. U.S. seafood waste could be used for pharmaceuticals, health food, cosmetics, biodiesel, carbon blocks and even the cultivation of medicinal mushrooms. The Iceland Ocean Cluster has started dialogues with representatives around the world and from both coasts of the United States. There is an enormous interest in fully utilizing resources and now the question is how best to implement these strategies.

Scientists believe overfishing, unsustainable seafood farming practices, ocean pollution and acidification will threaten the future of seafood availability worldwide[3]. Icelandic companies have pioneered new ways to create jobs and value from fewer resources. Now it's up to the rest of the world to imagine, and then build, a value-added world with 100 percent utilization.

Credit: Jack Whitacre of The Fletcher School and The Institute for Global Leadership for research and writing assistance.

---

1. http://www.fao.org/save-food/resources/keyfindings/en/

2. www.sciencedirect.com/science/article/pii/S0959378015300340

3. www.sciencedirect.com/science/article/pii/S0959378015300340

7. The Nordic Identity and Diversity, Immigration and the Integration of Diverse Populations

How to cope with the pressure of migration from those without resources, and with little experience in a free and democratic society? How do you embrace diversity and still maintain the core characteristics of a liberal democracy among new populations? What are the challenges this brings to social cohesion in Nordic societies?

The Survival of the Nordic Welfare Model: The Migration Challenge

Grete Brochmann

"Today, globalization, individualization and pluralization, traits that have marked the past decades in Scandinavia, have reduced the public grip on people."

The welfare state was called "Scandinavia's holiest cow" by a Danish Weekly some time ago. "Islam has sharia. Scandinavia has the welfare state. It is not something that can be discussed among believers."

I am among the believers and have been studying the Nordic welfare model for quite a while. I have increasingly been occupied with the profound and systemic challenges (external and internal) the Nordic countries are facing today. I will come back to that, but first a few words about the model itself and its historical genesis.

As compared to the United States, Scandinavia is famous for its soft, value based economy in which the welfare system figures prominently. The welfare state or society represents the master-value, so to speak, of which most Scandinavians are genuinely proud. Scandinavia is the area where trust in political institutions and the state is the greatest in the world. Political actors in the three Scandinavian countries (Norway, Denmark and Sweden) now

---

1. An earlier version of this text was presented as a lecture at a New York Review of Books conference in NYC, March 2015 "What's wrong with the economy and with economics".

compete for the honor of having created and developed the welfare state. Institutionally embedded, equality, trust and social security are three essential parameters of the Northern political economy.

It is said in Scandinavia that it took 100 years to create the collectivist culture of the welfare state. In all three Scandinavian countries, this comprehensive framework emerged during a long process that accelerated after the Second World War. The income security system—protecting the citizens against the vagaries of the market—was based on a positive concept of freedom linked to public responsibility.

Security and equal opportunities enabled expansion of individual freedom, and it was basically this interaction that motivated the collective investments in the welfare state, constituting the basis for social integration via the allocation of rights. Much of the stock of ideas in the post-war states was inspired by the "productive social policy" concept of the Swedish economist Gunnar Myrdal. This legacy entailed the ethos of equal opportunity, and the redistribution and empowerment of the disadvantaged via public education, health and active labor market policies. The tax and transfers system were regarded as tools for *investment* in people and their productivity: What created equality and security also created growth. i.e., good social policy was also smart economics.

Apart from the social investment philosophy, Myrdal's concept of "social engineering" tolerated extensive public intervention in people's lives. "Bad habits must be put right," Myrdal stated in one of his writings, and guiding consumption, child rearing and decoration or renovation of homes was on the agenda.

The People's Home (*Folkhemmet*) became a central concept coined by the Swedish Social Democrats. A grand class alliance should replace the past class struggle to steer society towards a socialist goal. The integrative idea of the "folkhemmet," in which society was organized as a family, with the home as a metaphor, subordinated class struggle to national welfare. This compelling concept, which in fact was appropriated from the conservatives, was effectively used as an instrument for a comprehensive modernization process.

Standard solutions of high quality became a distinguishing characteristic of the Swedish welfare state, an approach which was possible in a country where the citizens gave massive support to centrally proscribed policies, relying on universal solutions financed by taxation.

Norway and Denmark were somewhat less ardent than Sweden, although guiding behavior through social policies was prominent in these countries too.

Today, globalization, individualization and pluralization, traits that have marked the past decades in Scandinavia, have reduced the public grip on people. The preconditions have changed and so has the legitimacy. But the social engineering still holds an essential position in Scandinavian policy making.

The most prominent institutional characteristics are still intact, and can be summed up as follows: Governance of the small, open Nordic market economies has relied on an interplay between stability oriented macro-economic policies, an organized working life with coordinated wage setting and a comprehensive public welfare system. Based on a regulated labor market governed by strong social partners its key traits are: Pooling of risks through extensive social insurance, public services, corporatist coordination and low inequality.

The Nordic countries have revealed a remarkable ability to adapt to external changes and crises, and have shown a capacity to invest in long term development of human resources, social security and arrangements that enhance trust and social capital. Social mobility is high in international comparison, which makes the American dream easier to realize in Scandinavia than in its mother country.

The Nordic model is in fact today seen more indisputably as a success than what was the case some decades ago.

During the crisis in the 1990s, the Swedish Conservative Prime Minister, Carl Bildt, claimed "that the time for the Nordic model had passed—as it created societies that were too monopolized, too expensive and did not give people the freedom of choice that they wanted—societies that lacked flexibility and dynamism."

Yet, The Nordics managed to work themselves out of that crisis without deconstructing the social model, and during the early 2000s they moved up to the top international rankings of economic efficiency, employment and equality. Even center-right parties in the EU are today praising the Nordics, which (except Finland) seem to have managed the financial crisis more smoothly than most of the EU countries. Indeed, the Economist magazine declared the countries the "new supermodels" in 2013. Best in everything.

Too Good to Be True? Yes and No

I recently came across an article written by the American editor and columnist Robert Kuttner from 2008, "The Copenhagen consensus. Reading Adam Smith in Denmark." This very valuable piece of "economic anthropology" is strikingly sharp and incisive in its take on a tangible duality of the current situation (it was written before the financial crisis, but the analysis still holds). He is struck by all the successes of what he calls "compassionate capitalism," yet he also tells the American audience that one "needs to recognize the Danish model not as a silver bullet of clever public policy-making, but as a product of a century of Danish political and cultural history." This benign path dependency is what he calls the "dead hand of prior learning as well as embedded economic and political power."

But the second half of his article deals with the question "can the Danish system survive?" We can add the Swedish and Norwegian ones as well.

The Scandinavian models are today confronted with the risk of being eroded by multiple forces, many of which are related to globalization. One central challenge is fiscal and demographic: the aging population makes it difficult to keep up high-quality benefits without raising taxes to levels that are bound to be contested. Yet the supposedly most serious challenge according to this external observer, is the one related to immigration.

Kuttner asserts that reconciling solidarity with diversity is a basic challenge. The Danish model is rooted in social norms that are enforced by subtle peer pressure according to the do your duty, claim your right-logic. Low skilled immigrants consume a disproportionate share of public services and the Danish middle class already feels overtaxed. There is not much margin for error, he says. Besides, immigration of low skilled migrants has implied low wage competition and social dumping.

Denmark's ability to adjust its social model in light of immigration will depend on the success of integration. "If immigrants remain an undigested lump of alien cultures in the midst of a generous welfare state, accepting benefits but rejecting its cultural norms, support for the social system will erode." Thus, he argues, migration undermines the social model in a number of mutually reinforcing ways, in which political sustainability is as important as the economic.

While financially the demographic changes may be the most significant worry, I also agree that large scale immigration is a challenge in the Scandinavian area, and the most serious challenge is systemic. The generous and well-functioning Nordic welfare states represent what has been called "bounded universalism" based on "obligatory solidarity within the nation-state," social democracy in one country, as it were.

The comprehensive and regulating state, economic transfers to exposed groups in society and the principle of equal treatment have had two key implications for immigration.

First, it has been vital to control immigration to the countries in the first place. The welfare model, all-embracing and generous in principle but undermined if exposed to too great a load, has to carry out selection and limitation of potential new members from the outside.

Second, it has been seen as necessary to integrate newcomers, especially in working life but also in society. If one is to maintain the societal framework, new residents must be made a part of it. Good welfare states cannot have large numbers of people or groups that fall through the net, disturb regulated working life, overload social budgets, or eventually undermine solidarity. It's a huge dilemma.

The Nordic welfare state is expensive so it cannot be for all. Yet it must at the same time be for all with legal residency, in order not to disturb the balance between a regulated labor market and a generous welfare state. The system depends on equal inclusion first and foremost in the labor market, but also in society more generally. Today the Scandinavian countries have among the highest employment rate in the world, but also the largest employment gap in Europe between the majority and the immigrant population.

In fact, the quality of the model and the compressed wage structure, is making the countries particularly attractive for the type of immigration that in the long term may come to challenge the basic structure of the model.

Before 2004 these challenges were associated with immigrants coming to the region from the global South, basically refugees and their family members. The systemic challenge with these groups was basically labor market inclusion. Lacking education, they had difficulties in the highly paid and skill-demanding labor market, and consequently the problem was persistent welfare dependence.

After 2004 a major change occurred, particularly in Norway. The EU extension eastward has resulted in the largest influx ever of semi-skilled and low skilled labor migrants taking advantage of the free labor market. As of now this EU mobility has served the economy well, yet it has called attention to some major challenges ahead: the EU system combines a transnational labor market with national welfare and labor institutions.

The EU's labor mobility disturbs the basic premises of the welfare state approach to immigration. All of a sudden a free market system is imposed from outside. In other words, receiving countries have renounced immigration control towards EU migrants. This unfettered and large influx of workers has resulted in low wage competition, which contributes to   dualization and erosion of collective institutions in the labor market.

What's at stake is general social protection via the balancing mechanisms of the welfare model. To have work pay is a pillar of the expensive, tax based system. If the wage level is pressured downwards through low wage competition, the level of welfare benefits will also come under pressure to maintain the incentives to work. In practice now, this means playing weak groups off against each other.

But the Scandinavian countries are also challenged emotionally, so to speak, as the high numbers of labor immigrants are supposed to be left alone until they can support themselves through paid work, according to EU regulations.

Visitors to Oslo are now struck by the sight of brute poverty on nearly every street corner: Romanian beggars have entered the city legally through the EU's free movement clause, are somewhat self-supporting by collecting money from pedestrians, but live in appalling conditions outside in the cold, and understandably with very little pride in cleaning up when leaving. Parts of the public are instinctively calling for state intervention to give these new migrants shelter and food, whereas the authorities are having a hard time practicing their newly adopted free market philosophy to avoid kindism (which it is called) becoming a magnet for even more beggars. This phenomenon is disturbing on many levels (as it would be in many places), yet in the Norwegian context it highlights the human challenges revealed when a free market system meets the social model of one of the richest oil-economies in the world.

After the summer of 2015, the refugee crisis in the wake of the Syrian civil war posed another emotional and systemic challenge to the Nordic welfare states. The humanitarian responsibilities as stated in the UN Refugee Convention have been a pillar in Nordic policies since its initiation, although with a different impact on the realpolitik of the Scandinavian countries. Sweden has been the "humanitarian superpower" for decades, attracting a significantly higher number of asylum seekers than Norway and particularly Denmark, which after the turn of the century has tried to signal a more restrictive stand. After an extraordinary inflow of asylum seekers during the summer and fall of 2015, the receptions system in Sweden was close to a collapse, and the authorities reintroduced border controls to stem the flow. Denmark and Norway followed suit before the numbers were even close to the ones in Sweden, in order to avoid becoming the new "magnets" of the region. The impact of the refugee crisis on both humanitarian policy approaches and the public discourse in Scandinavia, has been vast, the full bearing of which is difficult to assess for the time being. It is the first time since the Second World War that systemic challenges from the outside are on the agenda, and this time largely through the movement of people in a desperate situation, with legitimate claims for protection.

The beginning of 2016 came with some breathing space for the Nordics after the crisis management in late fall of 2015, yet the conflict in the Middle East lingers, and the needs of the affected populations have not disappeared.

The systemic necessities of the Nordic Welfare Models, a productive balance between an orderly labor market and redistributive welfare state, are still there. The substantial inflow of people with a strong need for higher qualifications or basic education to match the demand side of the labor market will definitely influence future policy-making in Scandinavia. The extraordinary situation comes on top of the already existing challenges being discussed in this article and may trigger reforms in the basic social rights approach of the welfare systems. The endeavor of getting people productively absorbed in work as soon as possible will be the public task ahead.

The Scandinavian welfare model has had, as an underlying assumption, that social rights contribute to societal integration and to economic growth. Only in recent years have we seen a competing thesis stating that such rights to welfare benefits are an impediment, at least an impediment to getting low skilled people into productive employment.

"Subsidized isolation" is increasingly viewed as an unforeseen consequence of a too-lenient rights policy. Yet, the populations are still strong defenders of The Nordic Model, and have stakes in its preservation. In all three countries social model transformation is politically risky. Even conservative parties favor the welfare state in Scandinavia, especially the new populist right. And these parties today have a significant following in all three countries.

What may happen in the near future is retrenchment at the margins, possibly moving towards a more contribution based welfare system, leading to a more layered multi-tiered social model. In such a scenario the core majority will basically maintain their welfare, but we'll find increasing divisions between insiders and outsiders as we have seen in other places in Europe.

I am nevertheless modestly optimistic.

Social models have important tools for cushioning effects of external and internal pressure. Still the state represents a very visible hand in the economy through evolving social engineering. The welfare model itself appears to be both part of the problem and the solution in the current situation. The universalistic model is systemically vulnerable to pressures from inside and outside, yet the central mechanisms of the model are indispensable in order to meet the inclusion challenges.

Broad investment in people is still one of the essential instruments in order to rescue the future of the Nordic Model. Yet, reading Gunnar Myrdal in the U.S., or in the Scandinavian capitals for that matter, is most likely not sufficient in today's political economy.

The Nordic populations will probably have to face some significant adjustments of the universalistic model too, in order to retain its robustness.

The Danish Model:
Excellent, but Under Pressure

Naser Khader

> *"So there I was. A young boy with a Palestinian father and a Syrian mother, about to face the challenge of becoming a Dane."*

When I came to Denmark in 1974 at the age of 11, I had already lived in several other countries: Palestine, Jordan and Syria. However, this time my new home was in Western Europe. The weather was different. The people were different. The language was different. The religion was different. Above all, the customs and norms of this new country were nothing like those with which I had grown up. This essay examines "the Danish model," my own experience with it and its current challenges.

Moving to Denmark was not that new for my father. He had worked his way around Europe since the end of the 60s. First in Germany then Denmark. At that time there was plenty to do for willing, unskilled workers, regardless of where they came from.

So there I was. A young boy with a Palestinian father and a Syrian mother, about to face the challenge of "becoming a Dane."

Our first home was on Istedgade, the red light district of Copenhagen where I spent the first seven years of my life in Denmark. We did not feel threatened. The "working girls" were nice to us and gave us sweets (candy) and my father used to comment that it was the safest place to live. The police constantly patrolled it, and so the Denmark I first got to know was rather unusual for the average Dane.

Naturally, I was homesick at first, but after 6 months in a reception class together with my two older brothers, I started in a Danish school with Danish classmates, though I still had a couple of hours of practice in my mother-tongue each week.

To my mind, it was going to school, playing with other boys, trying their food and learning their ways that paved my way to integration in Denmark. In those days integration was not something that was planned or organized, it just happened. We immigrants were unusual, slightly exotic and not many demands were placed upon us. Yes, we were Muslims, but there was not a huge interest in our religion. Nobody insisted that we learn Danish. Many of us did not expect to stay either. A lot of people thought that they would make some money and then go home. For most of them this never happened.

I suppose you could say that my integration was a success. I graduated from high school and studied at university, finally achieving a degree in political science. I even became a Member of the Danish Parliament.

Those early days of the 70s and 80s are now a thing of the past. Times have changed. Danes usually take their holidays in other countries and try other foods. Turkey and Egypt, for example, became regular travel destinations. And the focus has changed from migrant workers to refugees. Danes are far more used to seeing "foreign faces" and know about different religions. There are far more people from a greater number of countries. Unfortunately, many of them live in ethnic enclaves, sometimes having little contact with Danish society.

The "live and let live" attitude has also changed. Now immigrants are expected to learn Danish and, if they do not, they cannot become Danish citizens. There is a greater focus on getting people to be active in the labor market. Not only does this make them self-supporting, it also encourages integration.

Sweden has been slow with "enforcing" integration. Many Swedes feel that they cannot criticize government policy. The Swedish "open door" policy has created problems for its own population. Many feel that their voices are not heard and believe, wrongly, that protest and violence are the only ways to make politicians listen. Indeed this rise in nationalism is not only a Swedish phenomenon. The financial crisis, years of austerity budgets, followed by the latest surge in refugees, has opened the door to a feeling of helplessness among many European populations. As it is, the Swedish government has realized that it cannot save the world and has now started to change its policies and guard its borders.

Denmark could see at an early stage, that there had to be some limitation on the number of immigrants and refugees. If you take in so many that the entire welfare system breaks down, nobody ends up having his or her needs met. And if you take them in, they must become part of the general population and not an isolated group.

The only way to become truly integrated is to work alongside each other. Danes and migrants alike must have a common shared language. In this case Danish. They need to understand and learn each other's humor, and for the immigrant, that elusive task of learning how to be a Dane. This means learning what you cannot find in books, to observe, to talk and to mix with others. Even if you don't think their jokes are funny—learn to laugh at the right moments.

Denmark has recently been heavily criticized in regards to new legislation in response to the European refugee crisis. I strongly question the picture that has been painted of Denmark in this case. In comparative measures, Denmark takes on vastly more responsibilities in regards to refugees and migrants than the majority of countries now furiously attacking Denmark. The critique comparing Denmark to Nazi-Germany is especially far-fetched and out of order. This essay seeks to unveil the facts about Denmark in this context, which hopefully will bring some food for thought to those who have jumped right into ripping Denmark apart for its "inhumane" handling of refugees.

First of all, last year Denmark had almost 20,000 asylum seekers, of which 86 percent were granted asylum. Denmark is a country of 5.5 million people. The U.S. has taken less than 2,000 refugees, and thus it is quite remarkable that numerous U.S. media outlets have attacked Denmark on its refugee policies. Both in comparative and absolute numbers, Denmark provides help to more refugees. Furthermore, Japan has taken less than 100 and the rich Gulf States have taken none. Examining these figures in a vacuum, it is highly questionable why Denmark of all the countries in the world should have something to be ashamed of.

Additionally, last year Denmark spent 0.47 percent of its GDP on refugees. The UK spent 0.02 percent, and yet it was the leading British newspaper, The Guardian, that portrayed the Danish Prime Minister as a Nazi recently. This exemplifies how the criticism of Denmark is completely blown out of proportion and not rooted in reality.

Another aspect is foreign aid. Denmark has always been in the absolute top of aid providers, and continues to be. The United Nations (UN) has set a target of 0.7 percent of gross national income (GNI), which only a handful of countries globally have prioritized to meet; yes Denmark is one of that handfull. It is true that Denmark has recently cut the percentage from 0.87 to 0.71 because of the need to reallocate funds to accommodate the rising levels of refugees in Denmark. Despite this, Denmark's foreign aid still is among the global top five. On the other end of the spectrum, we see countries such as the U.S., Japan, and Australia, which all provide less than 0.3 percent in foreign aid. Is Denmark really that inhumane?

Much of the controversy about Denmark was sparked from one out of more than ten new legislative pieces regarding refugees—the one about refugees' valuables. This specific piece of legislation states that if a refugee possesses valuables of more than 10,000 Danish kroner (DKK) when entering Denmark, these must be used initially to help fund the stay. Now, what has been severely twisted, misunderstood and miscommunicated is the aspect of sentimental value. *Of course*, no valuables with any kind of sentimental value or personal affection will be seized from refugees (regardless of its financial value). Of course not. These valuables are completely exempt from the legislation. Various media stories have portrayed how Denmark planned to confiscate wedding rings and other jewelry, which is of course complete nonsense.

However, I have to clearly say that the Danish government has not done a good enough job of making this crystal clear from the very beginning in mid-December 2015. On the other hand, even some Danish politicians and others from the opposition have a responsibility in this context because they have likewise played into this misunderstood agenda of portraying Denmark as a country that turns refugees' upside down at the border and strips them of all their valuables. Quite frankly, the number of people who have tried their best to spin these misunderstandings and miscommunications about Denmark internationally appalls me. Their content has simply not been based on reality.

Denmark has passed this 10,000 DKK limit because it is the *exact* equivalent to what Danish citizens on benefits must contribute, if financially able. I think it is fair that if you have the financial resources, you contribute to help fund your own stay.

This leads me to how refugees and immigrants are treated in Denmark. I believe it is important to illustrate how Denmark is very focused on creating a safe environment for these very vulnerable people. Everyone is entitled to free medical attention. Everyone. Denmark is a welfare state, and hence the medical attention and availability of care for refugees are of the highest standards. Access to the universal education system is another highly important aspect. Refugees receive benefits which increase when learning the Danish language, and meeting other goals. These are all examples of how Denmark truly takes care of incoming refugees and does its best to integrate them into the Danish society.

It has to be said that Denmark is a relatively small country, and thus we cannot operate with entirely open borders. We simply would not be able to cope with the amount of people coming to Denmark in that scenario. However as the recently passed legislation seeks to communicate, Denmark would much rather take a specific number of refugees and make sure they have reasonable living standards, instead of accepting a much larger number which would result in a significant decrease in the quality of care Denmark could offer refugees. In other words: we want to take as many as possible, but our welfare state needs to be able to cope with the pressure. This is not only in the interest of Denmark, but also the refugees.

While many have been busy criticizing Denmark, I believe we forget the most vulnerable people in this situation: the people who are not able to flee to a country like Denmark, the people who are stuck in Syria or neighboring countries facing life threatening conditions. In some ways I believe the asylum system lacks solidarity, because the millions of these people far exceed the one's who have been able to flee to Europe. They lack food, medicine, security and those basic necessities that we take for granted. I therefore suggest that a person should be able to apply for asylum in Denmark (for example), while still living as a refugee or internally displaced person in Syria's border regions, instead of physically having to go to Denmark to apply for asylum. This also ties into another demon we must not forget in this spectacle: the human trafficker, who each and every day makes a fortune from enticing refugees with the prospect of going to Europe, usually via extremely high-risk water crossings. We have to dis-incentivize the need for human traffickers, because the most vulnerable and poorest people are those left behind.

We need to focus on how we ensure successful integration of refugees in society as well. Sometimes I encounter a massive lack of flexibility. For example, in Denmark the minimum pay is around 110 DKK an hour (almost 17 U.S. dollars), which is a level that can hinder the job opportunities for many refugees. However, if we lowered this level a bit, we would see more refugees able to work, which is often the best way to foster successful integration.

Another rather bizarre example was a refugee from Iraq who had worked as a translator. He was provided with temporary accommodation, which is great, but regulation stated that he must be driven by taxi to his new residence. The cost was 1,500 DKK (roughly 230 U.S. dollars). In other words, we have a system where a man can manage to flee all the way from Iran to Denmark, yet we do not believe he is able to find his provided accommodation a few miles away from his location. This is just an everyday example of how we can increase our efficiency in our refugee efforts.

Let me get back to the international outrage over Denmark's new legislation regarding refugees. Besides the massive misunderstanding in context to the legislation piece on valuables, there has likewise been a massive misunderstanding on the piece regarding family reunification. Many international media outlets described how Denmark had increased the option of family reunification from one to three years. It is true that it has increased from one to three years, but *only* for non-convention status refugees. 90 percent of all refugees receive the so-called convention status, and hence this legislation does not apply for the vast majority. To receive convention status one must be personally persecuted. This example shows very clearly that by refusing to examine nuance and detail, a far too simplistic picture is painted, which simply does not reflect reality. I am always open to criticism, but it bothers me when the critique is not researched even remotely adequately.

To make it absolutely clear, Denmark will not take away wedding rings, watches, necklaces, mobile phones, etc. from refugees. Valuables with sentimental value (affection) should naturally be left untouched, which has always been the goal of the new legislation. The Danish government has not been good enough at communicating this and its general handling of the misunderstood outrage has generally been catastrophic. Another point we must remember is that refugees able to flee all the way to Denmark have typically paid between 10,000–20,000 U.S. dollars per person, thus it is the most vulnerable and poor left behind in and around Syria.

Rather than criticizing Denmark, we should be discussing how we could protect civilians in and around Syria, who die each and every day from the atrocities committed by ISIS and Assad. Talking about refugees in Europe is certainly important, but this solely discusses the symptom, not the treatment. The influx of refugees into Denmark, the rest of Europe and the rest of the world will only increase until the day we manage to end the madness in Syria.

We need to establish safe human corridors out of Syria, which would allow some of the most vulnerable civilians in Syria to leave. We tend to forget that around 10 million people are internally displaced in Syria. Additionally, safe-zones within Syria must be established (most likely in and around border areas), in order to protect the large part of internally displaced Syrians who are not able to flee. By establishing safe-zones guarded by the international community, we provide help to many of the vulnerable civilians (including many elderly and children) whose voices we never hear.

Furthermore, it is absolutely essential to create no-fly zones. This was one of the most effective initiatives to stop Saddam Hussein's aerial attacks on the Kurdish population in 1988. Likewise today, no-fly zones will create a comparatively safer environment for civilians. Let's not forget that Assad has previously used chemical weapons on his own population. This is a horrific war crime and the international community is not doing a good enough job of holding Assad accountable. ISIS must be eliminated to end this crisis and so must Assad's regime as well.

Domestically, Denmark needs to focus on improving our Danish model, because the entire system is currently under severe pressure. We have had a tendency to apply a model, where both the borders and economic benefits have been "open." I have already mentioned the majority of these, and while this model has been created with all the best intentions, we have to challenge whether the provided economic resources given to the newly arrived pose challenges to the Danish welfare society as a whole. I believe they do. And I say this while still being very positively disposed towards the Danish model in general.

What I challenge is that newly arrived people are provided with certain benefits from day one. It is of utmost importance that newly arrived people are helped and warmly welcomed, but it is a misunderstood "favor" to think that large economic benefits are the way forward. There are many other much more crucial ways to help people integrate. In Denmark we unfortunately have very high rates of unemployment and people still on benefits who immigrated to Denmark in the 1980s, this likely due to the very generous economic benefits they received from day one. There was barely an incentive to get a job as the benefits provided almost the same income. This has isolated a lot of these people in Danish society which obviously is not in anyone's interest. I believe that by providing a lower economic benefit package for the newly arrived (to the benefit level of all students in Denmark), the odds of successful integration will increase.

Some Danes are provoked by the high economic benefits the newly arrived can obtain, and in some contexts this thought resonates with me. The general tax level in Denmark is one of the highest in the world and we often say this with a sense of pride because it creates the foundation for the universal Danish welfare system. We know that regardless of social and economic status, one will always have access to free health care, education, etc. This has created a unique bond of trust between citizens and the state in Denmark. I believe this trust is what the Danish model is all about. However we must acknowledge that it is currently under pressure and this is also the reason why some aspects of the Danish immigration policies have been slightly tightened over the past months. As stated previously, this has very much been rooted in a responsibility to be able to provide adequately for those taken in, instead of being unable to provide the same standards for a larger number. If we chose the latter solution, the economic and social security net that lays the foundation for the Danish welfare society would be at risk for disappearing.

This brings me to the need for a global solution I mentioned earlier in this essay. In the 80s, the world efficiently allocated Vietnamese refugees so that all countries took responsibility. The UN also acted strongly. Today, the UN has not been nearly as politically decisive and the fact that we still do not have a global, coordinated plan is disappointing.

To sum up, I do not believe Denmark has anything to be ashamed of in regard to how refugees and immigrants are treated. In comparative terms, Denmark takes on much responsibility, and we provide refugees with a safe environment, food, clothes, medicine, shelter, education and other necessities. Denmark certainly treats refugees with the needed respect and dignity with which vulnerable people should be treated. The recent criticism of Denmark has not been rooted in reality, but rather in headlines without nuance and context. This crisis demands nuance and context. Political correctness has prevented certain important things from changing in the right time – for many years laissez-faire has dominated our integration approach. The Danish model is excellent compared to many others, but it is vulnerable and under pressure.

Equality Brings People Together

Nasima Razmyar

"I do not foresee that natural curiosity of humans would be diminished into fear of new things or people, if they have a way to give room for others."

Equality brings people together.

I have heard many times that I can never be, nor become a Finn. I have been in Finland since the age of nine. I have gone to school here. Graduated first from high school and then later received my bachelor's degree. I have worked here my whole life and paid my taxes. I have been elected by Finnish voters first to the Helsinki City Council and then to the Finnish Parliament. Even that is not enough; after I was elected I heard this more often than before. I can never become a Finn. My blood is not Finnish. This view; these lines that are drawn, remain a part of Nordic and Finnish culture. They are something we have struggled against and maybe always will to some degree. Fortunately these harsh words are uttered by fewer people these days and no longer form the opinion of most in Finland.

Change has been and always will be difficult, even more so in countries which are just opening their doors to the rest of the world. Today Europeans to include the Nordics are on the move going from one country to another like never before. The reasons for this "voluntary mobility" vary: Work, education, family connections, love and the desire for new experiences to name but a few. But at the same time, too many other people are being forced into an "involuntary mobility," having to find a new place to live because of war, political instability, persecution or natural disasters.

In this world we need even more cooperation and a greater understanding towards each other. We need to believe in people, recognize that most of us are good at heart and that there will always be a prospect for a better tomorrow. It might sound a bit "cheesy" or even trite, but I still believe this is the key to the success we see in the Nordic countries, and will continue to be key to how we will manage in a more diverse society.

These precepts have also guided me in the pursuit of successful integration. My family came to Finland in the early 1990s when the number of refugees was still quite small. We were given a chance to stay together and to keep many aspects of our culture. But we were also openly welcomed in Finnish society. There was school for children, a possibility of an apartment and a clear way forward to a normal life. Learning the language was an important part of being integrated into daily Finnish life. And in the end we were able to merge our two cultures together in a way that worked for us. Indeed, success rises from possibilities not from hopeless struggle or force.

I would never be where I am without my family, nor would I ever be where I am today without the Finnish welfare system. Without societal support of services and structures we could not have climbed this high. And we know that today, with so many people in need, we cannot take this support for granted. Immigration policies have come under intense scrutiny because of the rising number of people. It has become popular to say that we can no longer afford paying for this anymore.

But what Finnish society can actually not afford is leaving people behind. Inequality, lack of skilled workers and having people doing nothing is expensive and a very unsustainable way to build a society. At its worst, it creates unsafe societies for us all. We have an obligation to make certain that these people have possibilities and a way forward, especially when they have come here with so little.

We whom have received help are always willing to give back if given a chance. That is also something essential to being a Finn and a Nordic. Our identities are built on the willingness to be part of what our societies are and can be. This means making decisions that take everyone into account, and carrying the responsibility of our country together. No Nordic person has every fit in a single role. We all come from different backgrounds and cultures. It may well be that there is more variety than ever, and the tasks more difficult, but we will build a new Finland together day by day. We will do this because Nordic society is based on trust and solutions, not through fights or behaving superior to others.

Some might say that I am giving an unrealistic picture of the Nordics and that reality cannot possibly live up to these ideals. It is true that when talking about immigration or the inclusion of people we have much to solve. What we need to keep in mind is that these are challenges to be solved, not problems in which to wallow. This is one of the main reasons why I chose to run for parliament; to first and foremost try and find solutions.

We are quite proud of our successful school systems in the Nordic countries, are ranked highest in learning results and considered among the best educated countries. One reason for this is equality. All our citizens have access to education beginning with primary school through university, including doctorates. And within the past few decades we have begun to take this for granted. But lately the level of education correlates more with the background of the parents and their income. Our youth are being divided into those who are able to take additional courses outside of the regular schools, and those who cannot afford books for their secondary school, let alone if they also had to pay tuition fees. They are further divided into those who are pushed to succeed at home and read books, and those who lack a similar environment. These divisions are not yet very wide, but we should not simply give up and look the other way.

All of these things become even more important as we face large scale immigration. How can we ensure that our citizens still get the best possible education? The Social democrats tried to push forward legislation that would diminish the differences between schools. It is not possible to achieve good results if only students with similar backgrounds are put in the same classes. Variety and equality brings better results, but it does not come naturally. It needs active policy-making and responsibility from politicians. And this approach must apply equally to all levels of education. This is the way to give hope and possibility to everyone, especially in a world where basic education is no longer enough. We need to guarantee that as many people as possible have at least a secondary school degree either from high school or a vocational school. In this regard we launched the legally binding "youth guarantee" which makes certain that every young person has a place to study, or a place to work.

Another critical value that is very much related to immigration is gender equality. Sustainable societies can only be built upon equality between people and genders. Both genders must have the possibility to work and build careers; to be represented in parliaments and city councils; and in leading positions in all Nordic countries.

Despite what some may say equality will not be attained just by kind words. Our societies are filled with decades-old structures that prevent equality. Nordic countries have established mechanisms that push away those obstacles to true equality. We have made political decisions so that parental leave can be applied equally and that men have an opportunity to stay home with their children. This together with a widely available and affordable child care system has enabled women to work. A country that only enables half its population to enter the workforce cannot succeed. Politically we have quotas in city councils requiring that there must be at least 40 percent of both genders represented. In some Nordic countries quotas are implemented in the corporate world to show that women are able to lead large companies.

Equality is one of those core values raised when explaining to others, and the people who come to live in Nordic countries, what is meant by Nordic values. Explaining what equality means in our culture and how it is an integral part of our daily lives is often far different than what new residents know or understand. There are obvious clashes between cultures when people are told that they need to adapt their way of life to a society far different from the one they just left. But understanding these differences are key because their children will face this in school every day and they will have to adapt to these values in the work force.

I have been part of the Finnish Multicultural Association "Monika" for years. The Association develops and offers social services especially to immigrant women. There are several good examples of women getting jobs and families happily integrating in this new society. But there are still way too many cases of domestic violence, ethnic discrimination and "honor violence." The need for education and knowledge among these men and women is huge. I have had too many discussions where everyone is blaming the other for these problems. Instead of leaving people behind, we need to offer support and find solutions to stop violence against women, not only among immigrants but in Finnish society as a whole.

Equality and education are just few critical examples of how people can achieve a better future. And they are difficult to defend as essential in today's world of austerity and pessimism. While the speeches we give say the right thing and almost everyone agrees with what is said, political decisions are lagging behind. We are facing an increasing amount of populism, hate speech and racism and it is difficult to fight against easily spread lies or the type of language that flows from prejudice and ignorance. But we must continue this fight.

We can only move forward with a vision of equal and sustainable societies. People want to live peaceful lives and make their dreams come true. The natural curiosity of humanity would not be diminished into fear of new things or people if they have a way to make room for others. We need to learn to share what is ours if we want to achieve something more and something bigger.

Between Two Models of Solidarity: Sweden the Welfare State and Globalization

Lars Trägårdh

"The nation-state refuses to disappear in spite of all rhetoric about globalization."

One of the great puzzles of the great refugee crisis during the fall of 2015 was the abrupt reversal of Sweden's policy from an initial embrace of open borders to the resurrection of border controls in early January of 2016. Only months separated a brave and morally charged claim by Prime Minister Stefan Löfven that, "my Europe does not build walls," and a tearful press conference during which the government was forced to back down in the face of chaotic conditions and increasing popular resistance expressed not least in rising support for the anti-immigration party, the Sweden Democrats.

How are we to understand this turn of events? One simple explanation is that the number of asylum applicants—162,877 in total, 2 percent of the total population and the equivalent of five million arriving in the United States during one year—simply overwhelmed the capacity of the local and national government to handle in an orderly fashion the needs for housing, schooling and social services. However while this may indeed help us understand why the governing alliance, including the Green Party and many pro-immigration Social Democrats, chose to reluctantly pull the breaks and declare the boat full, it explains neither the deep divisions nor the confusion that characterized both the political debate and the response by citizens acting in civil society. The crisis was about more than numbers of refuges and the cost of handling them; it struck at the very heart of Swedish national identity.

To grasp this crisis it is useful to underline that Sweden has long been known for both for its domestic welfare state and its embrace of international, humanitarian ideals. For many years expansive social investments in Sweden and ambitious development projects across the globe seemed to be part and parcel of a unified commitment to solidarity and equality at home and human rights and development aid abroad. However, what the refugee crisis of 2015 has exposed in dramatic fashion are the tensions and contradictions that exist between these two commitments. Indeed, Sweden is today a country that is torn between two competing and conflicting solidarity ideals.

The first ideal is based on the idea of citizenship and national community. The Swedish social contract is in this sense rather straight-forward: an alliance between state and citizens, whereby citizens work, pay taxes and earn their fundamental social rights. It is a combination of a national solidarity project, an egalitarian social investment scheme, and a giant insurance company. In this guise Sweden became famous as the quintessential welfare state; as early as the 1930s both Swedish politicians and foreign journalists began to promote Sweden as a "model" with global, universal claims. To this day Swedish politicians from the left to the right remain eager to claim ownership of "the Swedish model." It is also a social contract that enjoys great popularity and legitimacy among the citizens of Sweden.

The second ideal is the notion of human rights (HR), an idea that historically shares roots with citizenship and can be traced back to the founding documents of the American and French Revolutions. After the Second World War, HR and UN (United Nations) inspired internationalism became increasingly important to Swedish international politics and national identity. Not least Dag Hammarskjöld, the second Secretary-General of the UN, and the prominent Social Democratic Prime Minister Olof Palme, came to symbolize Sweden´s special role in this regard. As the commitment to foreign aid and the political support of "third world" countries grew, the idea emerged that Sweden was a country especially devoted to peace and international solidarity. If the United States was the ultimate military power, Sweden was the "moral superpower." The headquarters of SIDA—the Swedish Development Agency—was Sweden's answer to the Pentagon.

In other words, there are not one, but two Swedish models, both with strong historical roots and popular legitimacy. It is my contention that while these two models have peacefully co-existed for a long time—thought of not only as compatible but even conceived of as synonymous—they are in fact based on fundamentally divergent solidarity ideals and "rights logics."

One model gives primacy to the nation-state and citizenship and pre-supposes borders and differences. Social rights are limited to those who are citizens or enjoy legal residence in the country. Furthermore, many of those rights are tied to work, income, taxes and national budget. The primary rights logic is *conditional reciprocity* tied to earned income (pensions, unemployment insurance, parental insurance, and sick-insurance); the secondary rights logic is *solidarity within the nation-state* covering the young, the elderly, the infirm, and the disabled (healthcare, schools, elderly care and disability rights).

The other model—HR—invokes a borderless universalism; human rights are unconditional and are derived from quasi-religious ethics with roots in natural law ideals. The primary rights logic is *altruism and compassion*. Rights are intrinsic to every human being, not earned through work or con-tributions, nor limited by citizenship. Indeed modern human rights doctrine developed as a reaction to the atrocities and discriminatory policies carried out in the name of the nation before and during the Second World War.

Furthermore, the two models differ in another crucial regard. The social rights that constitute central parts of the Swedish welfare state are ultimately products of national, democratic, political processes characterized by a rather crass and cold-hearted concern for money and keeping within budget. Even though one often talks of "rights", these are not rights in a strict legal sense, i.e., rights that are claimable in a court of law. Rather they take the form of legislation through which the state takes a broad but unspecified responsibil-ity for providing certain collective goods, such as healthcare, on equal terms for all citizens and legal residents. These rights are at heart political and collec-tive rights, rather than juridical and individual rights.

Human rights, on the other hand, are fundamentally different in this regard. Indeed, they are meant to serve as trump cards that protect individu-als and minorities from abuse and arbitrary decisions made by politicians, not just in authoritarian regimes but also in majoritarian democracies. Thus both constitutional amendments detailing individual and minority rights at the national level, as well as in international conventions that seek to protect human rights globally, express attempts to nudge governments to respect universal human rights and to counteract discrimination against minorities. International conventions establishing human rights catalogues are thus examples of the juridification of politics and the challenge by lawyers, judges and courts to the primacy of politicians, parliaments and the sovereignty of the nation-states. HR is, to summarize, a juridified secular religion, decoupled from both nation-state and from the mundane concerns with budgets and popular legitimacy that characterize democratic politics.

In other words, global human rights ideals stand as a matter of both legal principle and moral logic in conflict with the idea of national citizenship. For a long time this tension between human rights and citizenship has been largely invisible. Indeed, to many people in Sweden and abroad these two ideals seemed closely linked, even synonymous. However, with the great refugee crisis of 2015 the latent conflict was suddenly exposed with brutal clarity, expressed in a confused official Swedish policy characterized by sudden shifts between open and closed borders; between high-strung HR rhetoric and defensive references to the primacy of citizenship; between national sovereignty and the international conventions that challenge that sovereignty. These contradictions were apparent also in civil society: even as thousands of citizens volunteered to welcome and assist refugees, an increasing number of (other) citizens joined or otherwise supported the anti-immigration Sweden Democrats in their critique of Swedish immigration policy.

Enthusiasm for post-national visions can be found across the political spectrum in Sweden, among politicians, journalists and academics as well as among ordinary citizens. In fact, HR-ideals have become trump-cards in the political debate, played against those who are accused of being "nationalists," a label that often is associated with other pejoratives such as "xenophobic" or "racist." The HR-left and the liberal right are united in their abhorrence of borders and "excluding" nation-states that embrace what is sometimes called "welfare chauvinism."

The critique of the nation-state is directed at both components: the state as well as the nation. But notably the *nation* is primarily the target of the post-national left, which sees it as excluding and xenophobic, whereas the *state* is more likely the bête-noir for the liberal right, which sees the state as an obstacle for free enterprise. In the one case a vision of a solidaristic and equal world without borders beckons at the horizon; in the other a global market society without annoying politically motivated regulations and taxes. Together these anti-nationalists and anti-statists constitute an unholy but very powerful alliance: a perfect storm that from two directions undermine the legitimacy of the nation-state.

The allure of post-national utopias creates problems for both the Swedish center-right and the Social Democrats. The vision of a global market society, in which we ride an "urban express" towards an exciting future designed by destructively creative entrepreneurs, is not always shared by the center-right's voters—who at times take a rather skeptical view of their leaders' enthusiasm for free trade and immigration. In this regard Sweden is by no means unique. On both sides of the Atlantic the political debate is currently dominated by anxiety and anger. To some extent this is a consequence of the fact that the current economic order has posited the winners of globalization against the loser. While economists in general insist that immigration and free trade in the long-term have positive, aggregate effects, many citizens experience—in an era of increasing inequality and declining social mobility—which these rather abstract advantages by no means compensate for their own immediate and highly concrete losses and sufferings. This angry gap between elites and people characterize politics throughout the West; from the debate over "Brexit" in the UK, to the US presidential campaign where politicians like Donald Trump try to channel popular revolt while casting the opponents as beholden to urban, cosmopolitan elite interest.

But cosmopolitan internationalism is above all a challenge for the parties to the left, not least the Social Democrats whose ideals and historical legacy is so intimately tied to the idea of the "people's home"—folkhemmet. Indeed, the democratic welfare state has been the chief instrument for the political left in their mission to tame capitalism and create a balance between politics and market. This project, anchored in the nation-state's promise of a civic social contract through with citizens pay taxes in exchange for social rights, is now challenged not only by neo-liberal globalization at the material level, but also ideologically by a cosmopolitan internationalism in which the figure of human rights have come to be pitted against citizenship and national belonging.

This turn towards internationalism is directly linked to the decline of the old socialist left after the fall of the Berlin wall. With the collapse of communism and socialism as a serious alternative to liberal democracy, a political vacuum developed on the left that was filled by HR-idealism, attracting young people and finding expression both in academic programs and in a variety of political initiatives spearheaded by organizations like the Ford Foundation, Amnesty International, and Human Rights Watch, as well as by environmental organizations with global ambitions, such as Greenpeace. Common to these professional, elite-driven, organizations was a post-national and even post-democratic stance that tended to stress the role of global civil society, international conventions, and juridified rights rather than that of the democratic nation-state.

In this perspective, the current crisis in Europe and the West more broadly is primarily a crisis of social democracy. The post-national turn of the left has to grapple with the fact that the nation-state refuses to disappear in spite of all rhetoric about globalization. Indeed, while economic globalization continues to make headway, political globalization seems to be stuck or even in retreat, as the current crisis of the EU shows. Thus all democratic politics remains national at a time of a growing gap between elites who more easily can imagine being or becoming world-citizens and those who continue to live local, national lives. And this dangerous tension characterizes the left as much as the right. For each Donald Trump, there is a Bernie Sanders; both criticize free trade and defend the primacy of the nation-state and its borders.

In spite of these similarities, the undermining of the nation-state is uneven in its effects. For the winners in the global market economy denationalization and post-democratic tendencies result in more freedom from troublesome politicians and social movements that demand tax-based social investments; that the liberal right has a critical perspective on the classical nation-state makes sense. But for those who have historically fought for equality, solidarity and an extensive welfare state, the demise of moral logic of the nation-state would appear far more problematic.

Of particular concern is the tendency to reduce all resistance to post-national visions to xenophobia, ethnic nationalism and racism. Equally or quite possible far more important is what we can call "civic statism," that is a preference for the nation-state rooted in an enduring commitment to the traditional social contract that allies citizen and state through the elaborate system of taxes paid and social rights earned. For this reason a key challenge for Sweden in years ahead will be how to balance its dual commitments to the national welfare state and to international solidarity and, thus, to reconcile the growing tensions between the two Swedish models.

8. Gender Equality, Individual Freedoms and LGBT Rights— A Mainstay of the Nordic Agenda

Why are all the Nordic countries leaders in closing the Gender Equality Gap? Nordic countries have embraced LGBT rights. How have these values shaped social thinking, equality and competitiveness now and in the future?

Dreaming North

Anne Sofie Allarp

"These narratives cloud the fact that wealth is the prerequisite of wealth in most societies. The Nordic countries were and are no exception."

The essence of a state is community, something that lies beyond families, beyond individuals.

Communities offer possibility. A good society provides a sphere to prosper within, a sphere that is greater and holds a greater potential than your immediate environment. Great civilizations aim at lifting you up and unlocking your potential, not holding you back.

In the future, if humanity does not falter and our common effort turns into full-on dystopian brutality, civilization will likely turn its focus onto people with the aim of developing the best and most superior qualities in each individual. Empathy, interest and tolerance could replace imposed acceptance of human suffering and pride as a main human driver.

The Nordic countries could hold inspiration for such a future. Strong communities and social mobility is the essence of the Nordic welfare states. But we seem to have hit a crossroads.

Early on, the people of the North dreamed of a population that felt safe enough to reach for the dark-blue night skies. This area, with its strong winds, inhospitable conditions, wild, rugged and bear-filled landscapes, wet and freezing climates and excruciating winter darkness did not provide the ideal backdrop for dreaming big, but we were not deterred. We dreamed of prosperity and freedom, and we came a long way as Nordics.

A century ago, the average Nordic family worked as farmers, factory workers or fishermen.

Industrialization, urbanization, democratization and mass emigration coincided during those years. In many Northern communities, a substantial part of the population had left, or was about to leave. In Sweden 1.3 million people emigrated between 1850 and the 1920s, many propelled by famine as several harvests failed in the 1870s. Most ended up in the United States, whereas the less fortunate ones became farm workers in Denmark or Germany. 600,000 Norwegians left during the same period.

Through democratization, industrialization and urbanization, Nordic Labor movements were gathering momentum in the cities. Inspiration came from Germany and by the early 20th century social democracy was becoming a strong force politically with strong ties and frequent communication between the Nordic countries.

The Social Democratic Labor movement was to become the dominating force in creating the welfare state in the Nordic countries. The aim was to eradicate poverty, enable social mobility and the liberation of the individual. However, both labor movements and other strong political movements in the Nordic countries were built on centuries of community education, conflict resolution and local dialogue.

The populations were ethnically homogenous and small, but unequal. Much activity throughout history has aimed at promoting social acceptance of inequality and injustice; an acceptance that likely runs counter to human instincts. Inequality has been justified through race, civilization, gender, caste and class and later sold as rationality through near mythical narratives of differences in talent and ability. These narratives cloud the fact that wealth is the prerequisite of wealth in most societies. The Nordic countries were and are no exception.

But during the early decades of the 20th century Nordic leaders were dreaming big: How best to provide a framework to unlock the potential in each citizen became a common quest. How could the servitude in the footsteps of past generations and senseless wars be replaced by optimism for the betterment of society through prosperity among its citizens?

Embarking on the task, one of the great thinkers of the social democratic Swedish movement was Per Albin Hansson (1885–1946). During the 1920s he started to ponder how to furnish a good common home for all Swedes. He also found a name. After considering home to the citizenry, a phrase that felt good to a social democrat, but sounded pretty awful, he settled on the folk-home Folkhemmet. The Swedish Folkhemmet was to become a key term in the development of the Swedish welfare state.

Per Albin Hansson spoke of Folkhemmet as a place where unity and community dominated, a home in which people were not divided into those privileged and those left behind. No favorites and no step children, he said. Here, we do not look down upon each other. The architects of the Nordic welfare models were dreamers, but also tenacious implementers. They identified their objectives and grabbed opportunity, power and economic up-turns to realize their dreams.

Those dreams, and steady growth during most of the decades after World War II, enabled a social revolution and turned the Nordic countries into social mobility heaven. Forget the American dream. Dreaming North became the thing to do. The Nordic countries realized intergenerational mobility to a greater degree than any other region. We did it through free education, though a relatively small degree of social segregation, through valuing equal opportunity, through active communities and an active civil society and through welfare and social intervention. Economic safety meant freedom and the possibility to break family traditions.

Today, as a group, the five Nordic countries are unrivalled when it comes to intergenerational social mobility. The same goes for income equality. Social mobility and income inequality have become worldwide hot topics. Our achievements have inspired the rest of the world towards an ideological shift in the way inequality is viewed.

French economist Thomas Pikettys is poised to become a modern day Keynes after the publication of his bestseller, Capital in the 21st Century. In the book, he showed how wealth generated income is greater than labor generated income, which is why increasing inequality is to be viewed as a norm rooted in our economic model. The only exception to this rule is bouts of excessive economic growth.

The International Monetary Fund has pointed to the fact that great inequality can deter economic growth. The UN has addressed this directly in its sustainable development goals; number 10 is to reduce inequality within and among countries by the year 2030.

The level of income redistribution and equality is being debated intensely within the Nordic countries. We seem to have fallen somewhat out of love with our own achievements. Where other countries are increasingly addressing their inequality, the Nordic countries are becoming more critical of their welfare states.

Both Sweden and Denmark have lowered income taxes to promote a greater degree of income inequality with an aim to make it more attractive to work, and Finland is bravely studying ways of replacing a social security system based on control and mistrust with a Universal Basic Income model.

For all their success, the Nordic welfare states seem to be unable to unlock the potential of a substantial and stable minority who are stuck on welfare. That lower rung of the ladder and the presence of 10–15 percent immigrants, challenge the cohesion and solidarity that is the prerequisite of the Nordic redistribution model.

From the 1930s and onwards, the Nordic countries have created elaborate systems of redistribution, education and varying forms of safety nets, where children of factory workers and craftsmen became professors and prime ministers. But Nordic politicians seem to be losing the ability to dream and to invent the new bolts and screws needed to build new structures in which to prosper. Imagination has disintegrated into the administration of increasingly both starved and cavernous welfare models.

That is a shame, because as Swedish social democrat Ernst Wigforss (1881-1977) put it: Welfare is not socialism, but a reason for further conquests.

Our project and purpose lie ahead of us Nordics, not in the past.

A Human Agreement

Gertrud Åström

"We know that patriarchal societies that subordinate half of humanity are not only unjust, they are also unable to create sustainable, good living conditions."

Is a woman-friendly state possible? That startling question was formulated by Norwegian political scientist Helga Hernes in the 1980s, but the question is still relevant today. Within feminist, Anglo-American research, the standard assumption was (and often still is) that the state and its private institution, the family, form a patriarchal axis that maintains the subordination of women. This subordination centers on how reproduction is organized, both in society and in the family. Specifically, it is about how the complex regeneration of the human species—through political legislation, reforms, and the allocation of resources, as well as traditions and cultural norms—leads to (different) conditions for women and men. Hernes poses the question of whether the Nordic welfare models, through their policies, have in fact severed the usual patriarchal partnership between the state and the family and brought about a new woman-friendly and inviting human agreement.

Through my many years of working with gender equality and women's issues as a government analyst, businesswoman, and leader within the women's movement, I have met thousands upon thousands of people all over Sweden who support and accept this equal footing. Of course, not all are enthusiastic supporters, but the vocal opponents are few. At lectures I have sometimes almost physically felt how people abandon their opposition and lower the shield they have held up for protection from all talk of change. Instead, they become involved in the discussion on how to move forward. The world will not end. We can do better than this.

Gender Equality and Favorable Development

In international surveys that measure equality, human development, and good living conditions in the broad layers of the population, the Nordic countries always end up on top. Why is this? Is it perhaps because we are so few? Because we are few. The total population of the Nordic countries represents only about 0.5 percent of humanity. The idea would then be that it is easier to achieve gender equality in smaller groups. Is this true? No. In every survey there are countries with very small populations that have glaring inequality and hugely diverse living conditions for its citizens. Some tend to offer peace as a crucial factor. This seems to be true for Sweden. We have had peace for 200 years. But it is not true of Norway and Denmark, and certainly not for Finland. Others usually suggest the cold climate. It is an old idea that climate explains much of the structure and culture of societies, but then shouldn't other cold areas of the planet report the same results? They don't. And another question that undoubtedly also arises is how much colder does it perhaps have to be for people to be treated equally? Are we approaching absolute zero? All attempts to explain why the Nordic societies are as equal as they are tend to allege a few principles: democratic governance, secular constitution, and individual human rights. This is true for all Nordic countries, but it is also true for many other countries that aren't especially equal. These principles seem to be a necessary foundation, but they don't suffice to explain the degree of equality.

A common view, which I think is very central, albeit incorrect, is that the Nordic countries became equal because we are rich. But that is not how it is. It is rather the opposite. The wealth we have is due to the level of equality we have. Today, organizations like the World Bank, World Economic Forum, OECD, McKinsey, and others assert that equality between women and men is a prerequisite for and an effective gauge of favorable development. Even at the local level in Sweden we say that gender equality is smart economics and businesses fumble about for a way to express gender equality in their business models.

That equality is openly fostered in this broad manner is something that has grown over the past ten years. It can thus be seen as a consequence of, or even a victory for, the societies and the people in the Nordic countries and elsewhere who have led the way. We know that patriarchal societies that subordinate half of humanity are not only unjust, they are also unable to create sustainable, good living conditions.

Wanting Equality

The national goal of Swedish gender equality policy is that women and men should have equal power to shape society and their own lives. When people are asked what they think of this goal the most common response is that it goes without saying. How else should it be? When the question however is how we got where we are, why our social model is the way it is, and what we can learn from it, the answers are often tentative. So, why is it the way it is and how did it get that way?

Former Prime Minister Olof Palme said that politics is to want something. That is also how it is with equality. Equality is about wanting. It is something we can have if we decide that we want it. Equality is not something we have, it is a normative for how we want it to be, and that requires change through decision and action.

Swedish gender equality policy was formed in the early 1970s when the Delegation for Equality Between Men and Women was set up. Palme was then quite new as prime minister and wrote in the directive to the delegation that "the quest for equality between women and men has growing public support." According to Palme, the aim of the policy was to support these efforts and to implement measures that would lead to greater equality between women and men in all walks of life. The directive states: "Targeted and coordinated initiatives are required, shaped by a comprehensive approach. Gender equality cannot be established in isolation."

The big problem in Swedish society in the early 1970s was the labor shortage. If this could not be resolved, all social progress would come to a halt. Structural change had been rapid and required a larger workforce with new skills. Education policy was therefore reformed from the ground up in the 1960s with a new nine-year compulsory school, new high school (both types of schools with equality included in their respective curricula 1968 and 1969), and major reforms to higher education and adult education. Sweden's population was not highly educated at the time. Of the adult population, only

2 percent of women and 5 percent of men had the equivalent of a high school diploma in the mid-1960s.

In addition to education policies, old-fashioned family policies were highlighted as an obstacle to the creation of a modern society. The political parties' women's organizations and to a wider extent the women's movement made demands concerning working and earning their own money. The policies were to include reforms that made it possible to combine marriage, children, and a paying job. Demonstration chants included cries for "daycare for all." Cleaning women and seamstresses went on strike for better conditions and became visible in the public debate. The proportion of women among students increased.

It was these efforts that Palme wished to support. The first half of the 1970s was characterized by major reforms that arose from the gender equality policy, but were implemented in other policy areas such as family policy, tax policy, and social policy. First was the separate taxation of married women and men in 1971. It was a fundamental reform in which women and men became autonomous economic individuals relative to the state and was a base on which the other reforms could be built.

One of these reforms was the internationally acclaimed parental insurance that was introduced in 1974, replacing the maternity allowance. The fact that for the first time in history fathers became parents in the same way as mothers with basic individual rights and compensation was discussed widely. The reform's transformative power lay not in this, since few men suddenly changed their life choices, but in the powerful financial incentive it gave to women to have an income of their own before they had children. Parental insurance originally covered only six months, so the demand for public child care was a necessity if women were to seriously become part of the workforce. A decision in principle on the expansion of public child care was therefore made in 1976.

The effect of these reforms was reflected in the rapid growth of the female workforce. From the mid-1970s to the early 1990s, the relative workforce participation rates for women went from 60 percent to nearly 90 percent. That is an unprecedentedly rapid development with a huge impact on the economy.

The 1980s were characterized not by grandiose reforms as in the 1970s, but as a decade of expansion for parental insurance, child care, and new issues. Men and gender equality as well as domestic violence were placed on the political agenda. At the United Nations (UN), The Convention on the Elimination of all Forms of Discrimination Against Women (CEDAW) was adopted in 1979, and for the third UN World Conference on Women's Rights in Nairobi in 1985, Sweden presented separate gender statistics for the first time in a collective publication. In order to know what to do, you have to know how things stand, was the Swedish message. Societal research from a gender perspective also grew, as well as the issue of division of power. In a democracy, women and men should each have 50 percent of the power; that was the message launched in 1987 in the report "Varannan Damernas" (approx. Every Other Lady).

Sweden underwent a deep economic crisis in the 1990s that affected the entire society. Unemployment rose, job security decreased, cuts in public spending swept through the economy. Without a doubt this affected women as well as men, in both similar and different ways, but looking back now it is interesting to note that the equality model stood the test of time. And perhaps it is precisely here that the importance of gender equality principles is most apparent. Parental insurance was expanded and now covers 480 days. Legislation that gives everyone the right to child care once the child is a year old was introduced in 1995. A maximum fee was introduced in the early 2000s, making child care available and affordable, which means the most to those with low incomes, such as single mothers. The principle of "varannan damernas" was not only implemented on state agency boards, it also had an impact on directly elected assemblies. The first government cabinet with 50 percent women and 50 percent men was appointed in 1994.

The oft-cited threat that women who work and have their own money choose to not have children, such as in Susan Faludis' well-known book *Backlash*, has been proven wrong by the Swedish example. At the lowest point of the 1990s crisis the birth rate declined, particularly among unemployed women, but has now recovered. Despite all the flaws in the model and all that remains to do, women demonstrate through their actions that they deem it possible to have children in Sweden. 86 percent of Swedish women have children, nearly two on average, and 82 percent are in the workforce.

In the 1990s, The Act on Prohibiting the Purchase of Sexual Services was introduced, which criminalizes purchasing sex. Buying sex is seen as violence against women. The focus is thus on the buyer who can choose not to buy a person, while the one being bought is seen as a victim. When the law was introduced, it was the first time across the globe that the buyer was the only one criminalized. Today there are several countries that follow the Swedish model.

In the 2000s, reforms like childcare allowances were introduced and revoked. The requirements for employers to do salary surveys have been weakened and tightened again. A Ministry of Gender Equality was founded, soon to be discontinued. Issues regarding family honor culture and crimes have shown up in a new way. Child marriage, forced marriage, and genital mutilation have been banned for a long time, but it is only now that the large flows of refugees and migrants have brought these issues to the forefront. Women who come from countries with family honor cultures are especially keen to be fully included in this society of gender equality.

New technological and medical possibilities have also helped to focus on the issue of how the principle of women's dignity and the absolute prohibition of buying and selling people should be handled. Using surrogates to have children is not allowed in Sweden, but an inquiry was launched to investigate how so-called altruistic surrogate motherhood could be introduced. The conclusion was that such arrangements can never be allowed.

As leader of the Swedish Women's Lobby, I have argued the importance of a strong and independent women's movement that can analyze society and make political demands. It is my firm belief that gender equality continues to be part of the solution to the problems facing society.

Not subordinating women, but rather building all aspects of society on the equal power and pro-active citizenship of both women and men. Starting with equal rights and creating real opportunities for education and paid work that provides lifelong economic independence. Organizing child care so that women and men can give and receive care on equal terms and without subordination. Pronouncing that men's violence against women must stop. Asserting the principle that a person should never be used as a means to satisfy someone else's needs; that is equality.

Equality is hard work but well worth it.

To Come Out is to Come Home

Jonas Gardell

"A man at the store was so provoked to see two guys together that he decided we had to die and started chasing us with a knife. The police are summoned, get there—and defend the man."

2013. The final of the annual Gay Gala at Stockholm's biggest theater was approaching. One more award to hand out.

The one for Homo of the Year.

Without much fanfare at all the Master of Ceremonies said: "It is my pleasure to present the evening's final award presenter, her Royal Highness, Crown Princess Victoria."

There was no immediate reaction.

Most of us in the audience probably thought at first that it would be Christer Lindarw or one of our drag show artists dressed up as the princess.

Then, it was like an electric shock went through the whole room.

Because it was her.

For real.

The *real* Crown Princess Victoria had come to us. It was no joke. It was not pretend.

And seconds later, our jubilation knew no bounds. We stood up and screamed and applauded like mad, and never wanted to stop.

Why, an outsider might ask with surprise, why this deafening cheering? It may seem incomprehensible that a representative of the royal family should cause such a stir by their mere presence.

Let me explain why.

Today, Sweden and the Scandinavian countries are at the forefront of LGBT rights worldwide. Nordic embassies have been the mainstay of the nascent LGBT movements, especially in Eastern Europe. We can get married, we can adopt, at least on paper, and our rights are protected by law and public authorities.

Of course, this is something I am both happy and proud of, but it really has not always been this way.

I'm homosexual. In the country I live in, homosexuality was classified as a sickness until 1979. I was 15 then. The reason why the sickness stamp was removed was not that the Swedish authorities suddenly saw an injustice and righted it. Certainly not.

Freedom is not something you get for nothing. Freedom is something you conquer.

Gay men and women occupied (a sit-in) the authority for the classification.

You've taken yourself to where you stand today!

Without political struggle and personal courage, nothing happens.

The same year that Crown Princess Victoria came to the Gay Awards to hand out the award for Homo of the Year, I became an honorary doctor of medicine at the University of Linköping.

A university, which 25 years earlier had doctors associated with it who advocated concentration camps for those who were HIV-positive. Every person who tested positive for HIV was to be immediately separated from their families, their children, their loved ones and be taken to special so-called AIDS communities where they would remain until they died.

It's hard to imagine that it was actually like this in Sweden not so long ago.

It's easy to forget that it wasn't always like it is today, in the liberal, so tolerant Scandinavia.

When I published my first novel *Passion Play* in 1985, *Expressen*, Sweden's largest newspaper, printed in their review that "disgust and loathing wash over the reader."

And no one reacts to it. It's a perfectly natural and accepted way to address homosexuals.

Or when my husband Mark and I go to Ikea to buy a Billy bookshelf and a man at the store was so provoked to see two guys together that he decided we had to die and started chasing us with a knife. The police are summoned, get there—and defend the man.

"You have to try and understand, boys, how unpleasant it is for this guy to have to see you."

The police refuse to charge him.

Or when Mark and I renovate our apartment and when we come back home we see that the workers wrote "FUCKING FAGS" over the whole bedroom wall.

And we don't say anything, because we've never been addressed any other way.

This is Sweden not that long ago, a few measly years.

When I was about 18, when Swedish gays for the first time in history dared to grab hold of their freedom—the emancipation demonstrations at this time still consisted of just a few hundred brave souls—the most beautiful of us suddenly began to take ill, lose weight, fade away and die from a disease that the newspapers in Sweden called the gay plague.

We're told that it's God's punishment. That we have ourselves to blame. They say that gays are killers who spread AIDS!

And we don't say anything, because we've never been treated any other way.

When the suite of novels I'd written on homosexuality in Sweden, *Never Wipe Away Tears Without Gloves*, begins in 1982, it's been only three years since society still officially classified homosexuality as an illness. The country's leading psychiatrists still described homosexuality as a defect.

As a teenager, I sneak into the library, and with a pounding heart I look for a book on homosexuality in the "medicine" section, and on the back cover I read that its main emphasis is on "possibilities for preventing development of homosexuality." I read on about what a Danish zoologist has to say about "perverted urges in the animal world."

A teenage boy tries to find himself and learns that he's got perverted urges. That should be prevented.

That's how it is.

In the Sweden I grew up in, I'm an illness, I'm a blurb in the school biology book about degenerates, I'm a deviant that can possibly be cured by electroshock, I'm abnormal, unnatural and feminized.

And above all, I'm invisible. An early term for homosexuality is the "unspeakable sin."

I don't exist.

With the advent of AIDS, homosexuals in Sweden are noticed for the first time in decades. The last time was in the 1950s when the papers spread scandals about a homosexual mafia, cliques that were said to reach all the way up into the Swedish government.

All the attention when AIDS came in the 1980s was not about how to help us, but rather how to protect yourself from us. We're described as plague rats: if we're allowed to run free, we'll soon infect the whole society.

And we are not to be trusted. "Why do we need to isolate all 5,000 virus carriers?" as a Swedish commentator rhetorically asks. "Well, because we can't trust that people refrain from new sexual contacts and not spread the infection. ... It's likely that homosexuals are driven by a dependence that's far more difficult to manage than that of heterosexuals. It would be difficult to be convinced that there is some kind of "love" that drives the sexual activity of homosexuals, given that the average homosexual has dozens of partners every year."

There are guilty and innocent infected persons.

There are the infected and the infectors.

The newspaper *Aftonbladet* interviews policeman Hans Strindlund at the Norrmalm Police Station regarding a campaign to close the sauna clubs. The headline is unambiguous: "Those who spread AIDS are murderers."

So we homosexuals who are infected are not victims.

We're murderers.

One doctor goes so far as to seriously suggest that anyone infected should be marked with a tattoo so they can't hide their disgrace, like the Jews in Hitler's Nazi Germany.

These are unfortunately not solitary voices in an otherwise tolerant society.

Even the newspapers *Expressen* and *Dagens Nyheter*, which both consider themselves liberal, run regular campaigns for tougher measures against "the homosexuals."

An editorial in *Dagens Nyheter* in 1985 said "The homosexuals must now be forced to take responsibility." That same year on August 17, just after the first Swede died from the disease, the headlines screamed: ALL GAYS TO BE EXAMINED IN HUNT FOR AIDS.

This was supposed to reassure a terrified public. A public who needed to know that vigorous efforts were being made to protect against infection—and The Gays.

It's hard to believe. But it's true.

And it happened in my country. In tolerant Sweden.

It's not true that the Nordic countries in their broadmindedness threw rights and freedom at homosexuals.

Freedom is not something you get for nothing. Freedom is something you conquer.

Swedish society with its foundation in social engineering was, on the contrary, one of the countries that responded most repressively against homosexuals during the AIDS catastrophe in the 1980s. There was talk of registration, mass testing, isolating the infected, banning sauna clubs, etc.

But at the same time that there is demand for concentration camps for the HIV-positive, there are government officials who understand that you can't simply threaten. If you want to achieve the main objective, preventing the spread of the disease to the heterosexual majority, you have to find ways to reach the gay community and win their trust, get them to cooperate—the only problem is that the gay community never had any reason to trust any government agencies.

Sweden is a country with a long tradition of popular movements and associations. Homosexuals are no exception, being represented by the organization RIKSFÖRBUNDET FÖR SEXUELLT LIKABERÄTTIGANDE LIT (The National Confederation for Sexual Equality-RFSL).

By accepting RFSL as a "negotiating partner," the authorities could reach the LGBT community. This led to the association receiving a huge increase in financial support and gay activists in RFSL were slowly turned into a sort of semi-official authority.

The authorities then continue to give and take, threaten and reward.

So, in the same year that they prohibit the sauna clubs they introduce the so-called cohabitation law. For the first time, the legal rights of gay couples are regulated. It's not a sure thing anymore, for example, that surviving partners will be ejected from their homes by the deceased partner's family.

While they prohibit homosexuals from donating blood, they introduce an anti-discrimination law.

With the new cohabitation and anti-discrimination legislation and in combination with the visibility of openly public LGBT persons, public attitudes also begin changing for the better, and it happens extremely fast.

Today, an overwhelming majority of Swedes have no problem with homosexuality.

When Mark and I got together, society wasn't really agreeable to two guys being together at all. Every time we were in contact with the authorities, we were classified as single even though we obviously lived together. And then the law changed and we could cohabitate, and a few years went by and the law changed again and we got to register as partners, and then the law was changed again and we were able to get married.

Our children are now growing up in a society where same-sex marriage is a matter of course. But none of this would have happened if those of us who went first had not gone first.

Homosexuals were made visible in Sweden through political struggle, we were made visible by the disease (society could no longer afford to not see us), and we were made visible because a host of public figures, some of our most famous and beloved writers, actors, singers, politicians and athletes, came out as openly gay.

If you get to know someone you can no longer be afraid of them.

With the 1990s came a new generation of politicians, including the future leader of the Social Democratic Party, Mona Sahlin, and the future moderate Prime Minister, Fredrik Reinfeldt, who "grew up" with more and more open LGBT persons and a more modern view of homosexuality, politicians who saw it as an important rights and freedoms issue. With the engagement of the moderate Reinfeldt, the LGBT issue tipped over from having been considered a "left" issue to becoming more neutral on a left-right scale, and with the general attitude change, politicians would eventually no longer have anything to gain by being reactionary when it came to LGBT rights.

But it sat deep. For a long time, it was difficult for any representative of an official Swedish high office to even utter the word homosexual.

When Prime Minister Göran Persson was going to speak at the opening of Stockholm's conference for Human Rights on the Holocaust at City Hall in 2000, he was lobbied intensively to persuade him to do the obvious, to be historically accurate by including homosexuals as one of the groups persecuted by the Nazis. The Prime Minister did not want to utter the words.

It's that unmentionable thing again. To speak something has always been tantamount to invoking it. That which is spoken exists. It has been so ever since God in the beginning did not create through action, but through words. Says: Let there be light! And there is light.

It is in that context that the Crown Princess' participation in the Gay Gala is so interesting.

In itself it's a historical event. No such eminent royal has anywhere in the world previously participated like this in an LGBT context. Somewhat solemnly one can say that by coming to a room full of the traditionally invisible and say the simple sentence: "It is a great pleasure for me to be here tonight, to feel your strength, your joy, your community," the HBTQ community in Sweden as a group is finally made visible. Unlike the Prime Minister 12 years earlier, by uttering the word "homosexual," she named us—and that which is named exists and cannot cease to exist.

In the same way, just a few weeks earlier, President Obama made the LGBT community visible in the United States.

When he was sworn in for his second term, he mentioned the 1969 Stonewall Rebellion—the symbol and the start of gay liberation—as an important part of the American struggle for freedom on a par with other freedom fights.

"We, the people, declare today that the most evident of truths—that all of us are created equal—is the star that guides us still, just as it guided our forebears through Seneca Falls, and Selma and Stonewall…"

The struggle for LGBT rights is thus mentioned on a par with the fight for women's rights and the fight against racial segregation.

And then Obama added: "Our journey is not complete until our gay brothers and sisters are treated like anyone else under the law. For if we are truly created equal then surely the love we commit to one another must be equal as well."

That which is spoken exists and cannot cease to exist.

Nine days before the gala in Stockholm, Russia passed a ban on spreading "homosexual propaganda." If Victoria had done the same thing in Russia, she would have been sentenced to prison.

I think that I and many LGBT persons perceive both the U.S. President's and the Swedish Crown Princess' inclusivity as a necessary, belated and long-awaited, "Welcome!"

And Obama is right. It is a journey.

You know, we've journeyed so far to get to where we are today.

We've journeyed so far to get here.

When I was born, I was an illness. Then I became a ruthless killer.

The society I lived in threatened forced registration and isolation, my friends who were infected with AIDS received the wrong treatment from doctors, were denied dental care, shunned at their workplaces and disowned by their families, and when they were dead, were dumped into black plastic bags and buried in silence.

If you understand where we came from and how far we had to go, perhaps you can imagine why it was so childishly huge for us on that Monday in February when the Crown Princess came to us at our own crazy gala. We were finally a welcomed part of Sweden.

Gender Equality—
A Democratic and Cooperative Issue

Ingólfur
Gíslason

Johanna
Lammi-Taskula

Øystein
Gullvåg Holter

"Much earlier than in other countries, the Nordic region was characterized by a growing realization that gender equality was an issue for all going beyond the older notion of gender inequality as a women's issue."

The Nordic countries have a reputation for being committed to advancing gender equality. They also seem to have been fairly successful in that aspect. Most or all international comparisons place the Nordic countries within the top ten on gender equality. The Gender Gap Index (by the World Economic Forum) is one example. Looking at general parameters such as health, participation in the labor market, education and political participation all give similar results. The Nordic countries are fairly gender equal and they have been moving towards a closing of the still existing gap in the last decades.

Over the past few decades most or all the major political parties have been committed to gender equality, as have trade unions and employers associations, and the educational system has been used to also promote equality. Different women's organizations have promoted gender equality as a whole, or elements of it. Many still believe that not enough has been done and that some of the main actors play the game half-heartedly. But on the whole, there has been little or no organized opposition.

The general idea behind the work for gender equality is that it be seen as part of the process of democratization. If a society is to be truly democratic with citizens as active participants in decision making on all levels, it cannot tolerate discrimination, overt or covert, of any groups of the population. And since discrimination on gender grounds has been obvious in many spheres, it has to be addressed and rectified in order to further democracy.

The promotion of gender equality really took off in the sixties and seventies particularly because married women began to enter the labor market in high numbers. There were many reasons behind this, amongst them economic needs and a labor force shortage, but also many women found the role of a housewife far from fulfilling. They found it intellectually and emotionally stifling and wanted more out of life. Women poured into the universities and began to organize emancipatory movements and even political parties. At the same time, and partly out of necessity, day care for children was greatly expanded and transitioned from being a sort of last resort for very poor single mothers to being regarded as something good for children, even a right. Parental leave was also expanded. This obviously eased the plight of the mothers and made it easier for them to pursue a career in the labor market and in universities.

What grew out of these turbulent times was a new model or gender contract where the countries moved from the ideal of a male "provider" and a female housewife, towards the idea of "dual earners and dual careers." The degree to which this ideal was realized differed between the Nordic countries, but all embarked on this similar road in the 1970s. The goal was that partners would both be active in the labor market where they would earn their independent living and experience the joys and hardships of daily working and daily interaction with colleagues. This was aimed primarily at changing the role of women and later geared toward changing the role of men. The idea was similar; both parents would participate on equal grounds in the care taking of their children, thereby sharing the experience of the joys and burdens of raising their offspring.

This was also seen as a part of a democratic process. By sharing these aspects of life, men and women would gain a greater understanding of both working outside the home, and raising children, and thus have a better perspective of what had characterized the life of the other gender. Men experienced that taking care of children and other aspects of unpaid care and housework was a job in itself, but they could now also experience the joys of having a close relationship with someone completely devoted to them and trusting them with everything. Women experienced what was like to only see their children for a few hours every day and not being the primary parent. But they would also experience the intellectual and emotional stimulation of interacting with colleagues on a daily basis and the satisfaction of doing a good job.

Much earlier than in other countries, the Nordic region was characterized by a growing realization that gender equality was an issue for all going beyond the older notion of gender inequality as a women's issue. This twist from a sole focus about the situation of women to a realization that a change in their social situation also necessitated a change in the social situation of men, really took off in the 1980s and 1990s, even though academic radicals had begun discussing it in the late sixties. While this change encompassed different aspects in individual countries, the focus was primarily on giving fathers a real opportunity to take parental leave. Men became engaged as part of solidarity with women, as helpers for women's new work roles, and as fathers who now could spend more time with their children; this was a central element.

The Nordic countries have taken somewhat different roads in this area and it is fair to say that some aspects of paternity leave are still contested. However, most social actors agree that fathers need to be more active in the caretaking of their small children. Individualization of the right to parental leave has been a road that all the Nordic countries have tried to varying degrees, stretching from the social democratic "father quota" to more liberal "premiums" and "bonuses" that promote a more equal sharing of leave between parents. Research confirms that this cross-political approach is successful: the proportion of fathers taking parental leave has increased.

One of the authors of this essay (Ingólfur) had his first two children in the eighties while living in Sweden, though he is Icelandic. Sweden was then far ahead of Iceland in parental leave policies and promoting more involved fatherhood. All of a sudden, there was the possibility to reverse traditional roles. This didn't really have a big effect on the first child as both parents were studying and could pretty much use the hours as they thought best. But for the second child, he was at home alone with the child for two months. It was a revelation. All of a sudden he had to interact alone with someone unable to talk and try to interpret the different moods and expressions. There was also the aspect of sticking to a routine alien to him but necessary for the child. No reward can be greater than the smile of a happy baby when you know it is because of you that the child is happy.

Of course there was a downside. He missed interacting with other grownups and there was much less time to work on his thesis than he had expected. Still, every day brought new insight and an increased ability of the child to communicate and to explore this amazing world. The girl began to walk while in his care; that day still stands out both for him and his partner. He experienced the immense joy of being the first to see this new development and the mother had the not so enjoyable experience of being the second. For many fathers who have been home alone with their child or children, a similarly unforgettable experience is when the child prefers him to the mother when there is time to hug and comfort.

Another of the authors (Holter) remembers how the paternity leave, called "the daddy's month" or "the father quota," often met mixed reactions from men when it was introduced in 1993 in Norway. It was seen as somewhat "unmanly." However, the debate turned more positive as men related experiences for this "new" role. The popular columnist Andreas Hompland wrote in the national newspaper Dagbladet 1996 (our translation): "To care for and take responsibility for a small child continuously is different from helping the child's mother and take a part of the puzzle of everyday organization. It is labor of a different kind, requiring surrender. It follows a different rationality and cannot be isolated. If you believe you can plan your own day and your own night, you will be frustrated. The child occupies you and demands your care without consideration of your agenda." Such statements helped change the perception. By the end of the 1990s, most fathers in Norway used the father's quota of parental leave and in the 2000s, the leave period was extended "step-wise" to 12 weeks, with most fathers using the new extended period, step by step (in 2015, the period was unfortunately reduced to 10 weeks).

We have seen in studies both in the Nordic countries and elsewhere that fathers enjoy the experience of being at home with their children and want to do it again. We have also seen that those fathers, who start caring early, continue to be active caretakers and are more active later in their children's lives than those who have not made use of parental leave. Interestingly we have also seen studies showing that fathers taking long parental leave are punished more harshly in the labor market than mothers in a similar situation, both in terms of career possibilities and wage development. This indicates two things. The labor market is still hostile to parenthood and it is still (to a degree) stuck in traditional gender roles, deeming women the primary parent while fathers who prioritize parenthood are seen as deviant in some ways. This is one of the main explanations for the still existing gender pay gap in the Nordic countries.

The "dual earner/dual career gender model" generally being promoted in Nordic countries seems to be a very promising one from most perspectives. From the male perspective: he does not need to be a sole provider for his family as the economic burdens and responsibilities are shared as employment of mothers of young children is accepted and encouraged. He also is expected to participate in the care of his children in everyday life activities and as such gets to spend a great deal of time with them. Because he can have as close a relationship as the mother with the children, if the parents separate he has a better chance of maintaining a close relationship with his children. Indeed, the more active the sharing in unpaid childcare work, the lesser the risk of separation as equal sharing of family responsibilities increases marital satisfaction.

From a female perspective we see a similar scenario: She is not alone in caring for children and family, as fathers are accepted and encouraged to be active in childcare and housework. Getting an education and participating in the labor market is expected which is fundamental to economic independence. And the fact that her children have a close relationship with their father does not mean they love her any less.

From the child's perspective: the child is far more likely to receive care and have its basic needs met when care responsibility is shared by the parents. The risk that a parent cannot cope with everyday burdens is smaller, so the child is more likely to experience security and well-being while it grows. And because the child sees its father and mother partaking in all kinds of activities unstifled by gender traditions, means that it will grow up with a broader view of what it can do or become regardless of gender. According to data from a recent international survey study, gender equality among the parents or primary caretakers is a key element for the well-being of children. Gender equality strongly lowers the chance of violence against children. Violence against women is similarly reduced. Gender equality also means a better chance that conflicts are resolved non-violently.

Nordic research indicates that the cost of caring has been reduced over the last decades—although it still exists. The EU report "The Role of Men in Gender Equality" (2012) shows that increasing the role of men in caregiving, at home and in the workplace, is a central matter for the development of gender equality. This is confirmed by new studies. Men's share of care is closely linked to the degree of gender equality.

Perhaps the fact that Iceland has the longest parental leave for fathers has had an impact on the relationship between fathers and their children. The latest report from the study "The Health Behavior of School-aged Children," shows Iceland at the top of 42 countries when 11, 13 and 15 year-old children are asked how easy they find it to talk to their fathers. These are the first cohorts to experience the full effect of the three-month long parental leave reserved for Icelandic fathers.

Society as a whole also benefits as humans are increasingly judged on the basis of what they know and are able to do rather than on the basis of their gender. When the father's leave quota was introduced in Iceland, few people expected fathers to generally make use of it; they were expected to be afraid of compromising their "masculinity." Today 80–90 percent of fathers make use the leave and nobody makes fun of these fathers or thinks that what they are doing is something "unmanly." But, it hasn't always been like that in the Nordic countries. Holter remembers gender myths circulating in the 1980s and 90s. Norway was called a "nanny state." Men who supported gender equality were not "real men." There was something amiss, an extra debt to be paid. Like a two time blush: first, for taking up such a "soft" issue of gender and gender equality, next, for bringing men into the scene.

These myths had, and have, a certain logic of development: Beyond the "not real men" stage comes the "we all support gender equality BUT" stage. For example, it is fine with men on paternity leave, but they mainly use the leave for other things than care for children (like holidays, or even elk hunting to mention a few myths).

We have seen an educational revolution among Nordic women who are now active in all areas of higher education. They have also made serious inroads in political life and are close to 50 percent in government, municipal councils and legislative assemblies. Though the development has been slower in companies, more and more women are taking seats on the boards of major companies, in some countries helped by laws setting gender quotes on representation. We have also seen more and more Nordic fathers becoming increasingly active in caring for their children. In general, the policies of gender equality have been a success, helping to create better, more democratic societies. The success has been based on broad social support and the general experience of the public that this is a better way than the earlier gender separation approach.

Nobody makes the claim that "we are there"—the Nordic countries are definitely not gender equal or a "feminist paradise" as one over-enthusiastic journalist stated a few years ago. The failure to reach reasonable gender balance, even as gender equality goals are advanced, can be seen as a main challenge of the Nordic model of gender equality.

Although the Nordic efforts regarding paternity leave and the father's quota of parental leave have been strong, they have not been followed up in other areas. For example, the Nordic educational system needs further reform to undo segregation and ensure gender equality. Male domination at the top university levels, females at mid-levels and boys dropping out of school at lower levels, are parts of the same picture. Similar patterns appear in other areas, like gender-based violence.

According to a recent analysis of Europe and the United States, the level of gender equality is positively related to men's well-being and health, as well as women's health. Earlier research has shown stronger evidence for women than men, but it now appears this is true for mean as well. Gender equality is an independent factor for a better quality of life (controlling for other variables like income level and distribution). Men's happiness is generally greater in gender-equal countries, compared to more gender unequal countries. Depression levels are lower, and the tendency of men to commit suicide more often than women is also less.

With this background is should not be a surprise that gender equality is key for explaining the persistent global success of the Nordic model in today's global competition. Despite somewhat higher labor costs, tax levels and some misguided bureaucratization (as seen by conservatives), and despite shifting economic adaptations, the Nordic region has remained in the top group of economically prosperous countries.

In conclusion, the effort made in the Nordic countries to first increase women's possibilities in traditional male spheres and, later, to increase men's social possibilities to shoulder intimate care of their own children and partake to a greater degree than before in housework, has in general been success-ful. The guiding principles have been increased democratization of the Nor-dic societies and gender cooperation rather than juxtaposition. Historically speaking men and women have cooperated in many spheres. Prior to indus-trialization they worked together on farms where there was often little room for separating tasks by gender. Everyone who could work did so, whatever the task. This is not to claim any gender equality at that time but just to point out that cooperation in many fields, something we are increasingly witnessing in the Nordic countries, is not brand new and unheard of, on the contrary, it is a reinvention of a very old principle.

Sex, Work, Gender Equality— And a Prosperous Welfare State

Katja Iversen

"In short, when you invest in girls and women, everybody wins."

Women deliver, and so much more than babies. When you invest in gender equality and in the health, rights and well-being of girls and women, evidence shows that there is a ripple effect that goes way beyond the individual. It benefits families, communities and nations. In short, when you invest in girls and women, everybody wins.

The Nordic countries have proven this beyond a doubt. It is no coincidence that Denmark is named the happiest country on earth, the best place to be a woman, and the best place to raise a family. It boils down to equality and investing systematically in girls and women. It wasn't always like this and to get where we are today has required hard won victories, social mobility and deliberate policies and investments. But before getting deeper into that, let me tell you about my grandma.

Valborg Jonasen was born in Denmark in 1914, the year before Danish women won their fight for the right to vote and during a time where the first heated debates about sexual liberation, reproductive health and access to contraception took place in Copenhagen. But that was in so many ways very far away from the poor, rural family into which my grandma was born as the second of five kids. Her mother was frail; her dad was a dreamer, so from a very young age grandma took care of the home and worked their small plot of land to help feed the family. She had the brains. But after some years of sporadic schooling she was sent to serve as a maid and the little money the family made went for the education of her older brother.

In the 1930s she left home on her bicycle, traveling some 200 miles to Copenhagen, met my grandpa and was working seven days a week as a home care assistant to get him through teachers' college. The agreement was that when he was done it would be her turn. She wanted to become a carpenter, or a nurse, which was a more achievable goal for women at that time! As you can imagine, this was not the right time for her to become pregnant. More about that later.

A Little Bit of History

The 1930s were the years where the debates of what is today known as the Nordic Model—defined by free market capitalism in combination with a comprehensive welfare state – started to manifest itself and where some of the first real laws were put in place. Against a backdrop of growing urbanization, economic crisis and more women in the workforce "Crisis in the Population Question," (Kris i befolkningsfrågan, 1934, Alva and Gunnar Myrdal) was published, a book focused on population and social policies. It opens with the provocative statement:

"The question of reproduction has come fully under the control of reason."

One of the basic ideas of the book, which inspired the subsequent social reforms throughout the Nordic countries, was that since people were having fewer children the state should put in place reforms and conditions that would encourage people to choose to become parents and have healthier children and wealthier families. It was a loud call for: free healthcare for all; better living conditions; minimum wage; child support; social security etc. It also suggested conditions like affordable day care, which would make it possible for both parents to work outside the home. It called for gender equality that addressed both public structures and intimate reproductive choices; imperative to driving both economic and societal progress.

I am sure Alva and Gunnar Myrdal, who both went on to win Nobel Prizes, would have rejoiced had they seen how their ideas have been taken to heart, grown and today embedded deep in Nordic societies that all champion a well-established welfare system with a market economy.

Not a single country in the world has yet to achieve gender equality, but some are closer than others and the Nordic countries are in the lead (Gender Gap Report 2015, World Economic Forum). So let me hone in on three themes inspired by the Myrdals' study and the others who have come before and after them. These themes form the foundation of (gender) equality, and some would say, prosperity in the Nordics particularly in Denmark today: girls and women's sexual and reproductive health and rights; women in the workplace; and the re-defining of the family.

But first let me get back to my grandma. Not because she is my grand-mother, but because looking at her life is a great reminder that gender equality is not a given, but something that requires frontrunners, choices and breaking with individual and societal norms.

Sex Is Here to Stay

My grandparents lived together for some years before getting married in 1938. They lived in a small room in a flat they shared with five other young people. While living together either unmarried or in a collective was not as common as it is today, it did not raise many eyebrows in Copenhagen. It was practical, fun and cost-effective.

Grandma and grandpa had their lives planned. He was a gardener, but work was scarce and he wanted to study to become a teacher. For five years, grandma was the sole breadwinner and with no other means of economic sup-port, they could barely make ends meet. Getting pregnant was not an option.

Contraception was available but not in common use. Hence, grandma went to Dr. Jonathan Leunbach, a co-founder of the World League for Sexual Reform, and a progressive doctor known for his open-minded views on sex education, abortion and for providing contraception to poor and unmarried women.

Dr. Leunbach, together with some of the feminists from the workers' movement, engaged in a significant social effort between the first and second world wars to change the norms surrounding the role of women. They opened the first 'Prevention of Pregnancy' clinics and provided the first sex education courses which were at the forefront of sex education that continues to be taught in every school in Denmark today. Despite having to go to prison for three months for his work, most of what Dr. Leunbach and his feminist partners originally fought for is nowadays regarded as self-evident and right.

In general, sex is considered natural and not taboo in Denmark today. The Danes speak rather openly about sex and sexuality and it is not uncommon that sexual "debuts" happen at home, with mom and dad watching TV next door.

Unlike in the U.S., sex education in Denmark is mandatory, comprehensive and more holistic. Overall the goal is for the child/young person to be able to make good choices regarding their sexual health and well-being. Sex education starts at the age of six. In the first years the discussions are about feelings, family, the body and accepting people for what and who they are. Later discussions are about puberty, falling in love, social media conduct, equality and boundaries. When the children are around 14-15 years old the curriculum delves into sex, sexuality, stigma, contraception, sexually transmitted infections (STIs), abortion and pregnancy.

One of the concrete results of comprehensive sexuality education is a very low number of adolescent pregnancies and births in Denmark and the Nordic countries in general. According to the latest statistics, only 0.2 percent of 15–19 year old girls in Denmark have had a baby (State of the World Population, 2015, UNFPA). In the United States the rate is ten times higher.

Sexual and reproductive health and rights are not a political battlefield in most of the Nordic countries. With full support from all parties in the Danish Parliament, contraception is readily available and abortion is free and available until the end of the 12th week of pregnancy. A woman's right to choose if, when, how often and with whom to become pregnant and have a child, is considered a cornerstone in achieving gender equality and societal prosperity.

Equality, sexual and reproductive health and rights are priorities for Denmark's extensive overseas development aid and in international negotiations where the government often joins forces with the other Nordic countries to highlight these values. In addition, both the Danish Crown Princess Mary and the Norwegian Crown Princess Mette Marit are active, global advocates for gender equality and women's sexual and reproductive health and rights.

The strong societal support for these issues is one of the reasons why the global advocacy organization, Women Deliver, chose to hold the world's largest conference on the health, rights and the well-being of girls and women for more than a decade—the Women Deliver 2016 Conference—in Copenhagen, May 2016.

The ripple effect of good reproductive health policies and comprehensive sexuality education is visible both in the number of Danish girls who get an education and women who can support themselves financially and socially, backed by a labor market that promotes gender equality.

Women at Work

Denmark was in 2016 named the world's best country for women in which to live. The country also performs very well on the OECD's Better Life Index, topping the list regarding work life balance and overall life satisfaction. To a large extent this is because of women, family friendly work place policies, which are supported across the political spectrum.

A quick portrait of the 2016 labor market in Denmark includes: An instituted 37 hour work week; a minimum wage around $20 an hour; the right to at least 25 paid annual leave days (for all employees); benefits for the first two years of unemployment; good and affordable day care; and parental leave (on the books since 1939) entitling couples to 52 weeks of paid parental leave to share between them. Moreover house chores are almost equally shared between women and men (OECD), and in general it is socially acceptable for parents to leave work mid-afternoon to pick up children from daycare.

These family and employee friendly policies almost sound too good to be true. And yes, there is a bill to be paid through taxes, of which the upper and middle classes pay the lion's share (OECD). But at the same time, Denmark tops Forbes' Best Countries for Business and one of the top five best places to start a business according to the Global Entrepreneurship Index. These benefits do not seem to harm the business environment which is also fueled by a well-educated workforce, a product of free education for all at every level.

In general, the Nordic countries are in the top of the World Economic Forum Gender Gap Index 2015, though Denmark is trailing slightly behind at number 14, but ahead of both the UK (18) and the U.S. (28).

Evidence has shown that investments in gender parity in the work place, not only improve women's economic security, but also contribute to economic growth at large (The Power of Parity: How advancing women's equality can add $12 trillion to global growth, 2015, McKinsey). It is also globally recognized that for women to be able to live to their full potential, a solid level of economic empowerment and independence is needed.

In Denmark today almost as many women as men are working, and more women than men earn higher education degrees. And while there is still a long way to go to achieve equal pay, the situation for women has significantly improved since my grandma was in the labor market.

Her average salary as a non-trained assistant nurse in the early 1940s was $18 a month if she worked 7 days a week. So it was a big jump when in the spring of 1943, grandpa finally landed a job as a teacher in a small provincial town, a job which paid $40 a month. They packed up, left liberal Copenhagen and moved into a small apartment in Svendborg.

They really wanted kids, two kids, and now they could finally afford it. So within a couple of months grandma got pregnant. However, in the provincial town and in their new social setting, it was still largely expected that a teacher's wife would stay at home, raise the kids and take care of her husband. Grandma had her children and did as was expected, though going from being an active, outgoing breadwinner to being a wife and a mother was not at all easy. She felt tied down and under-utilized. But she accepted the situation, as she had always done, and made the best of it.

The Family Takes Many Forms

The world has changed a great deal in the area of family constellations, at least in some places of the world. For women in similar situations to my grandma, with two children and no formal education, there were not many alternatives. Yes, divorce was in principle possible, and yes there were laws for child support on the books, but the social stigma and logistic challenge of being a single mother in a society that was not yet structurally or culturally shaped for it made most women stay in their marriage.

The economic conditions and opportunities changed significantly in Denmark in the 1950s and 60s, not least because of an economic upswing and a law that made affordable childcare mandatory. This was also accompanied by major reforms in pensions, education, health and social security.

Today, Nordic women in general are economically independent, divorce does not bring social shame and it is no longer socially stigmatizing to be a single parent, remarry or have children with different partners.

The concept of family has been redefined over the years, and families now take many forms. Denmark was the first country in the world to legally recognize same sex partnerships, and the latest Danish statistics show that the number of single women with children is growing, as are the number of people with children living together without being married, and the numbers of same sex families with children.

The Danish language has also changed. Words like bastards, illegitimate and step-kids are almost gone from the vocabulary and replaced with bonus children, plus children and rainbow children.

Many of Myrdal's thoughts from the 30s have been implemented. Leunbach's ideas are also ingrained in the public, like a free healthcare system. And while there are significant cutbacks in the welfare system, the women's movement fight for equality and society's investment in it has paid off in terms of building healthier and happier populations, and prosperous societies.

This societal progress is not to be taken for granted. It should be treasured, upheld and improved. We are not there yet, and things are sliding backwards on some fronts. While the Nordics top all measures of gender equality, Denmark is trailing behind. If we take a broader look, there is still a lot of work ahead.

Fortunately, we know what needs to be done: investment in girls' and women's health and rights; expand women's education and political participation; grow women's economic opportunities and access to resources; combat violence against women; fight discrimination and social exclusion; and do all of this both at home in the Nordic countries and throughout the world. This is everybody's business, and it can't succeed without large civic participation.

Grandma and grandpa had a long and loving marriage. They built a warm and open home where the world was welcome. She took care of the house and the children, managed the family's economy, and made sure they were never indebted or poor again. She also saved my life when I was born almost five weeks too early as the first grandchild. The day grandpa retired she got herself a job. The day I had my first menstruation, she told me about contraception. The day I graduated college, she cried tears of joy. And on her death bed she made me promise that I would go out and change the world for girls and women.

She was a remarkable woman: Quiet, fierce, smart, hardworking and loving. I can only imagine how far she would have gone if she were born two generations later and been able to live life to her full potential. She is my yard stick when people say that change is impossible. It is not! It just takes time and people who will fight for the right thing.

Minority Women and Nordic Values

Deeyah Khan   Joanne Payton

"Ultimately, we need to transcend the idea of separate standards for separate cultures and separate groups, and instead work towards a society which is not splintered into different communities sharing the same space."

As a "third culture" woman, I've always had shifting understandings of what it meant to be Nordic. I was not always clear about how this intersected with my own ancestry, with parents from Afghanistan and Pakistan. It often felt like two very different states of life—Nordic and South Asian that could not coexist—different states that I switched between every day. I was born and educated in Oslo, and my parents made no attempt to separate me from children of other backgrounds, yet I still had a sense that Norway only really existed outside the home, and that inside it, I was in a different world —one where the air was filled with spices and the smell of onions, discussions in Punjabi, Urdu and English between exiled South Asian intelligentsia over endless tea, cigarettes and food, late into the night—and of course, within a house which echoed with my own training exercises in the North Indian and Pakistani classical Khayal music. There was no question that we were different from the blue-eyed, brown-cheese eating Norwegians that surrounded us.

Although the chasms between my life at home and in school sometimes felt unbridgeable, I did feel welcome in Norway. However I was not free from the racism of various men in the streets, who called me a "black bitch" amongst other insults—words designed to make me scurry towards the comforts of home, away from the Norway that existed on the other side of my front door. But the real source of my misery came not from the racist Norwegians, but from within my parents' own community—from traditionalists who opposed the idea of women singing, and from the growing extremist tendency of radical Islam that was spreading across Muslim communities around Europe from the 80s onward. As I would discover in my documentary *Jihad*, these young men's commitment to radical Islam often came, in its own way, from the same sense of disconnection I felt between the home and the outside world.

This opposition to my singing—expressed in violence and harassment—led to my decision to leave Norway at the age of 17, and take refuge outside the country. At that time, I felt betrayed and alone; all the people who had lauded me as an ambassador for Norwegian multiculturalism fell silent when the contradictions between my individual freedoms and their respect for what they perceived to be "my community" came into conflict. Norway has a well-deserved reputation for human rights, yet it was as if my rights to equality, freedom of expression, to a life free from the threat of violence, existed in a different universe from those of the rest of the population. My rights as a Norwegian citizen didn't appear to coexist with my unchosen membership within a supposed community: they disappeared on the other side of my front door.

Norway has not been alone in facing this conundrum: many other Northern and European countries have been forced to face the challenges in negotiating "respect" for minority cultures, and providing human rights protection to those who live within them. To some extent, these shortfalls have resulted from a failed appreciation of the diversity within minority cultures. Often, this comes from the acceptance of self-appointed "community leaders," who create a false impression of a unitary community, erasing the differences of opinion and experience within each group. There has also been a discomfort with challenging abuse occurring within minority cultures which are justified in the name of "culture."

However, our parents' communities are neither homogeneous nor static: they are riven with conflicts, from rivalries that predate immigration, to intergenerational and sectarian conflicts. Importantly, there are varying attitudes to such key issues as women's rights and the role of religion. Yet it often seemed that the most conservative members of these communities, those with the most repressive attitudes, were taken as the most authentic spokesmen for minority communities which were erroneously viewed as isolated and homogenous blocs. This tendency works towards respect for presumed "group rights" of cultural identity over the individual human rights of those who live within those groups. While the Nordic states have been front-runners in acknowledging the patriarchal roots of gender discrimination, there is a need to understand that challenging gender pay gap and getting women into the workforce is a very different project, requiring a very different set of tools than those used to address the subordination of young women in minority households. This is why we need to deal seriously with issues such as forced marriage, and to reinforce our support for the rights of the individual regardless of which "community" they were born into.

One particular issue in Nordic countries is the comparative lack of civil society organizations within minority communities which would provide an important "feminism from below," able to both inform and challenge the state's positions. When I filmed my documentary *Banaz: A Love Story*, an exploration of the circumstances surrounding a so called "honor killing" in the UK, I was able to make contact with many activists from minority communities in Britain who were working to ensure that women had places to go when they needed help—and to ensure that the "community" was also represented through women's, feminist and pro-secular voices defending the universality of human rights over repressions justified in the name of "culture" or "faith"—voices which came from within those very communities within which those abuses occurred. These voices were able to counter the dangerous myth of an undifferentiated "minority community" implacably bound to a "culture" that denies women agency. Instead they demonstrated the creative dissent and agency of feminist women within minority communities. A broad civil society brings the diversity of internal debates into the public sphere, showing that just as there is no unified "voice of the community," that there are important differences of opinion, even amongst feminists of minority origin.

It is not to disparage the Nordic approach to say that there is still a ways to go before we can claim to have addressed the issues of women within minority communities. Certainly, I hope we are beyond the point where a teenage girl can be threatened into exile simply because she wanted to sing or to choose how she wants to live her life. The balance we need to achieve is in recognizing the specific problems which affect minority women without stigmatizing their communities; and that the so-called "cultures" which produce such abuses as forced marriage, "honor"-based violence and female genital mutilation also produce the most vehement and effective critics of these practices. The mission to confront patriarchy, in all its manifestations, needs to involve those people with a proven commitment to developing women's agency, and working towards gender equality within the communities in which they live.

Some developments are less encouraging. The traditional five-party set-up of Nordic politics has been disrupted by a convergent populist hard right movement, which espouses the values of patriotism and social conservatism as authentically "Nordic." Their positions embrace scepticism towards immigration, gender equality and gay rights, and support of "traditional" families, the military, law-and-order policies and assimilationist policies. Here, such expressions of violence against women in minority communities may be categorized as "cultural" in order to denigrate minority communities. It also tends to disguise the Right's own, often lukewarm commitment to gender equality, distracting from the shared issues which affect women whether they are part of an ethnic or faith minority.

The right wing also tends to promote a kind of "welfare chauvinism" depicting minority communities as burdens upon the famously generous Nordic public purse. It is questionable how far violence against women in minority communities can be challenged if resources directed towards them are subject to suspicion. We need to be aware that framing violence against women as a problem of immigration, rather than of sexism, is a distortion which does not help vulnerable women. This tendency to "culturalize" violence within minority communities is not always limited to the political right-wing. Gender equality policies must be able to address the specific problems facing minority women in concrete ways, but without making wholescale assumptions about the "cultures" in which they occur.

Ultimately, we need to transcend the idea of separate standards for separate cultures and separate groups, and instead work towards a society which is not splintered into different communities sharing the same space, but one in which people from a variety of different heritages are accepted as participants in the Nordic way of life. This does not imply cultural relativism, but a greater commitment to the values which we share. This means confronting the implicit division between "Nordic values" imagined as gender egalitarian, against those of "minority cultures" imagined as intrinsically patriarchal.

While we can celebrate the values of democracy, equality, children's rights and a strong welfare state, we should recognize that this can be more than a specifically Nordic attribute, like fish for breakfast or saunas, but one which speaks to a set of values which can inspire us all, regardless of such identifiers as ethnicity or faith. Values can just as much be defended by brown women as they can be undermined by white men. Nordic values, inasmuch as they are based in the principles of universal human rights, must belong to us all.

Prospects for the Future

We have focused on solutions the Nordic countries have sought domestically, but with an acute awareness that these are challenges without borders. Solutions need to be found internationally to the loss of hope and opportunity among migrant populations and the failure to address climate change, population growth and those economic realities that place production where costs are lowest. This "Tsunami" of change of everything from technology that progresses at light speed, to growing vulnerable, heterogeneous populations heading "north," who have not had the good fortune to live in liberal democratic societies before now, present challenges the likes of which we have never experienced on such a grand scale. The Nordic model, a virtual billboard for sustainable growth, economic prosperity, a stunning lack of corruption, innovation on an enormous scale, and equality for all as part of the fabric of these societies, is at a crossroads. How we in the Nordic countries and in the United States respond will be testament to our ability to take on challenges before and not after they overwhelm us, to show compassion to those less fortunate, and perhaps most importantly, ensure that we never compromise our hard won identities as free and democratic societies built on equality, rights, and freedoms for all. It is a tall order, but one, we believe that the dynamic democracies in the Nordic countries and the United States can handle.

Nordic Ways is instructive on so many levels, not only because it provides insight into and wisdom about history, language, environment, sustainability, business, art, music, design, architecture, education and the struggles for equality, but because it also offers a sort of suggested blueprint for how to proceed in this uncertain cauldron we call the future.

Maintaining the Nordic welfare state in the midst of a growing globalized economy, substantial increases in migration, in combination with an aging population presents an enormous political challenge, but by and large the Nordic people still have strong support for these societal structures. How the Nordics and the United States cope, and still flourish as open liberal democracies capable of competing globally is a challenge we both share. Together we can find ways to temper some of these effects on society and create a prosperous future for the next generation. Social networks and the sheer speed of information sharing means that the political debates on both sides of the Atlantic are often more similar these days than not. So why not share solutions.

While Nordic free market capitalism paired with universal social policies might not work perfectly for the United States, it may offer some solutions for creating less adversarial relationships between management and labor and a softer landing for those disenfranchised by increasingly unpredictable market forces. And because the Nordic model has also served to stimulate substantial innovation and growth, and has led to greater competitiveness and rising profits on a global level, this may well appeal to corporate America.

Sustainable and livable cities, creating space for people to interact, protecting people and resources from natural disasters and the effects of climate change and doing so in ways that enhance the quality of life, should all appeal to American urban planners seeking answers to growing urban populations and their sustainable future. Similarly, educators in the U.S. could learn a great deal from the hugely successful Nordic education systems that are inclusive, that value play time and culture and the arts as part of education, and allow parents to envision a future for their children filled with possibilities.

Finally, we chose to focus on what is arguably the one thing we, the Nordic countries and the United States have most in common; the safeguarding of our democracies. Our unwavering commitment to these shared democratic values defines us and often prescribes how we engage with each other and the rest of the world. We cannot risk losing sight of what makes us who we are as we deal with the uncertainties of the future.

Debra L. Cagan and Madeleine Lyrvall
August 2016

Debra L. Cagan is the Senior State Department Fellow at Center for Transatlantic Relations, Johns Hopkins, SAIS. The views expressed by Debra Cagan are hers alone and not necessarily those of the U.S. Government.

We Thank Our Authors

Ahlin, Urban

Allarp, Anne-Sofie

Árnadóttir, Ragna

Arnason, Ragnar

Åström, Gertrud

Bergman, Nicklas

Bildt, Carl

Börestam, Ulla

Brochmann, Grete

Dybvad, Karsten

Finnbogadóttir, Vigdís

Gardell, Jonas

Gislason, Ingolfur

Haarder, Bertel

Hannesson, Rögnvaldur

Haraldsson, Gunnar

Hauksdóttir, Auður

Hedegaard, Connie

Helander, Karin

Holter, Øystein

Itäranta, Emmi

Iversen, Katja

Jutterström, Christina

Khader, Naser

Khan, Deeyah

Kleist, Mininnguaq

Lagercrantz, Hugo

Lammi-Taskula, Johanna

Lund, Jørn

Meyer, Claus

Møller, Per Stig

Nerjordet, Arne and Zachrison, Carlos

Paananen, Ilkka

Palme, Mårten

Payton, Joanne

Razmyar, Nasima

Rockström, Johan

Risom, Jeff

Ronaldsdóttir, Elísabet

Sahlberg, Pasi

Salto, Kasper and Sigsgaard, Thomas

Sauri, Pekka

Sigfusson, Thor

Sigsgaard, Thomas and Salto, Kasper

Signmark

Skogen Lund, Kristin

Støre, Jonas Gahr

Suhonen, Paola Ivana

Sverdrup, Ulf

Syse, Henrik

Stordalen, Petter

Thomsen, Steen

Trägårdh, Lars

Zachrison, Carlos and Nerjordet, Arne

Authors

Urban Ahlin is a Swedish Social Democratic Party politician since 1994 and Speaker of the Parliament of Sweden after 2014 Parliamentary elections. For the past twenty years, Urban has worked in the field of foreign policy in various capacities, such as Foreign Policy Spokesperson, and Chair of the Committee on Foreign Affairs. He is a founding member of the European Council on Foreign Relations ECFR, and member of the Trilateral Commission. In 2007, Urban Ahlin received the Cross of Commander from the President of Lithuania.

Urban Ahlin

Anne Sofie Allarp is an Author, Writer and Radio Presenter. She holds a Master's degree in International Law from the University of Copenhagen, and has among other been posted by the European Commission in Africa and South Asia. She published her first novel, a political thriller that was nominated for best literary newcomer award the same year. Her second novel, the critically acclaimed horror story *The Occurrence,* is available in English. In 2014 her non-fiction book *The Scandinavian Dream* was published. She is a frequent op-ed writer in the Danish press and now works as foreign affairs editor and presenter at a Danish public service talk radio station.

Anne-Sofie Allarp

Ragna Árnadóttir was the Minister of Justice from February 2009 to September 2010. Her previous positions include serving as the Director of Legal Affairs in the Ministry of Justice in Iceland and Senior Adviser in the Nordic Council's Secretariat in Stockholm and Copenhagen. She is currently the Deputy CEO of Landsvirkjun, Renewable Energy Company, and the Vice Chairman of the Red Cross in Iceland. Ragna completed her Candidata Juris law degree from the University of Iceland and holds a Master's degree in European Affairs, LL.M, from the University of Lund in Sweden.

Ragna Árnadóttir

Ragnar Árnason

Ragnar Árnason is a Professor of Economics at the University of Iceland and member of the board of the Central Bank of Iceland. He has a publication record of over 170 scientific articles and several books. He has written extensively on issues of social welfare, income distribution and social policy in Iceland.

Gertrud Åström

Gertrud Åström is an expert on gender equality and runs her own business HelaHUT AB. She is the former Executive Director at Ordfront, a member of Academy for Gender Equality at Swedish Farmers Association and the Swedish UN Association, as well as former President of the Swedish Women's Lobby 2009–2015. She is a noted author and expert on the gender pay gap. She formally headed the Swedish Government Committees on Leisure and Sport, and Gender Equality Policy.

Nicklas Bergman

Nicklas Bergman has worked as an entrepreneur and technology investor for more than 25 years. He is mostly focusing on investments and business development in emerging markets, web services, nanotechnology, computing, new materials, and new media art, currently through close to 15 direct and indirect technology investments. Nicklas is also Scandinavian representative of the TechCast Technology Think Tank in Washington D.C. and recently published a new book on how to deal with new technologies from a business perspective: ***Surviving the Techstorm - Strategy in Times of Technological Uncertainty,*** Lid Publishing (London, 2016).

Carl Bildt is the former Prime Minister and Foreign Minister of Sweden. He served as EU Special Envoy to the Former Yugoslavia, High Representative for Bosnia and Herzegovina, UN Special Envoy to the Balkans, and Co-Chairman of the Dayton Peace Conference. He is Chair of the Global Commission on Internet Governance and a member of the World Economic Forum's Global Agenda Council on Europe.

Carl Bildt

Ulla Börestam is a Professor in the Department of Scandinavian languages at Uppsala University. Her main field of study is inter-comprehension between the related languages of Scandinavia. She has for example studied communicative strategies, language choices and the formation of a Scandinavian speech community abroad.

Ulla Börestam

Grete Brochmann is Professor of Sociology, Department of Sociology and Human Geography at the University of Oslo. She has published several books and articles on international migration; sending and receiving country perspectives, EU policies, welfare state dilemmas as well as historical studies on immigration. She has served as a visiting scholar in Brussels, Berkeley, and Boston. In 2002 she held the Willy Brandt Visiting Professorship in Malmö, Sweden. She is currently head of a governmental commission in Norway on long term consequences of comprehensive immigration.

Grete Brochmann

Karsten Dybvad

Karsten Dybvad is Director General and Chief Executive Officer of the Confederation of Danish Industry (DI) - Denmark's largest employers- and business organization. Before Karsten Dybvad came to DI in November 2010, he was the Permanent Secretary of State (Chief of Staff) in the Danish Prime Minister's Office for five years and before that Permanent Secretary of State in the Ministry of Finance. Karsten Dybvad is a member of the boards of the Novo Foundation, PensionDanmark, PFA Pension, PFA Holding and the Executive Board of BUSINESSEUROPE and he is Chairman of Copenhagen Business School. He holds a Master's degree in Economics from the University of Copenhagen (1985).

Vigdís Finnbogadóttir

Vigdís Finnbogadóttir became the world's first democratically elected female head of state when she was elected President of Iceland in 1980. In addition to serving as President until 1996, she has been a UNESCO Goodwill Ambassador for Languages for almost two decades, and held numerous other official positions both in Iceland and internationally. She was a founding chair of the Council of Women World Leaders and chair of COMEST, the World Commission on the Ethics of Scientific Knowledge and Technology, within UNESCO. As well as numerous orders and distinctions she has received from countries throughout the world, Vigdís was awarded 21 honorary doctorates from universities in the Americas, Asia and Europe. See www.vigdis.is for details.

Jonas Gardell

Jonas Gardell was born in 1963 and made his highly praised literary debut in 1985 with the novel *Passionsspelet/The Passion Play,* a novel about homosexual love. Since then he has published several books, plays and other texts. He is one of Scandinavia's most popular stand-up comedians and a highly appreciated playwright. In his books he portrays all kinds of human beings, the humor is natural and obvious as is also pain and sorrow. In Jonas Gardell's writings there are no taboos, he moves with preciseness between the big and the small, between dreams and stern reality. Jonas Gardell's books have been translated into 13 languages.

Ingólfur Gíslason was born in Reykjavík in 1956 and has lived there apart from 9 years in Sweden. He has a BA-degree in Political Science from the University of Iceland and a PhD in Sociology from the University of Lund. For many years he worked at the Centre for Gender Equality. Currently he is an Associate Professor in Sociology at the University of Iceland. He has three children and four grandchildren and considers himself a very lucky and privileged man.

Ingólfur Gíslason

Bertel Geismar Haarder has had an extensive career in Danish politics. Currently he is the Minister for Culture and Church in the Danish Parliament. He was appointed by Prime Minister Lars Lykke Rasmussen in 2015. Prior to this, he served as Minister for Nordic Cooperation from 2007 to 2010. In February of 2010, he was appointed Interior and Health Minister under Anders Fogh Rasmussen. He has published a number of coveted socio-critical publications on the the state of Danish society and the political system. In 2011, Haarder celebrated his 20-year anniversary as a minister in Danish Parliament. The anniversary made him the second-longest serving minister in Parliament since the system change in 1901.

Bertel Haarder

Rögnvaldur Hannesson was born and raised in Iceland. He has a PhD in economics from University of Lund, Sweden. His academic career has been in Norway; from 1983 to retirement in 2013 he was professor at the Norwegian School of Economics. His research has mainly been on the economics of fisheries and petroleum. He is the author of several books, the most recent of which are *Ecofundamentalism* and *Debt, Democracy and the Welfare State.*

Rögnvaldur Hannesson

Gunnar Haraldsson

Gunnar Haraldsson is an Economist with wide ranging experience from working in academia, for the public and private sector as well as for international organizations. Among other responsibilities he is currently the Chairman of the Icelandic Fiscal Council. He is the founder of Intellecon, an economic consultancy.

Auður Hauksdóttir

Auður Hauksdóttir is a Professor of Danish and Managing Director of The Vigdís Finnbogadóttir Institute of Foreign Language at the University of Iceland since its establishment in 2001. Her field of research includes Danish as a foreign language in Iceland, Danish language and culture in Iceland past and present, and comparative studies of lexical phrases in Danish and Icelandic.

Connie Hedegaard

With two decades of experience in international and domestic executive policy making *Connie Hedegaard* holds several key positions in support of a low-carbon and green economy. She is the former European Commissioner for Climate Action from 2010 to 2014. Prior to her position as Commissioner, she was the Danish Minister of Climate and Energy from 2007 to 2009, and Danish Minister for Environment from 2004 to 2007. Hedegaard accepted the position as Director at Danfoss A/S in 2016. She is also Chairman of the OECD's Round Table on Sustainable Development and the Chairman of the Board of the sustainability foundation, the KR Foundation, and the green think tank CONCITO.

Karin Helander is Vice-Chancellor and Professor of Performance Studies at the Department of Musicology and Performance Studies and former Director of the Centre for the Studies of Children's Culture at the Department of Child and Youth Studies, Stockholm University. She has been a long time member of the Board of the Swedish Arts Council. She has published numerous books and articles stemming from her areas of research – mostly on the art of acting, contemporary theatre, opera as well as youth and children's theatre.

Karin Helander

Øystein Holter was born in Oslo in 1952 and is married, and father of four children. Having worked with gender research over many years, he feels privileged, as a researcher (and as a man), to witness major social change. He participated in studies of work democracy and work life reconciliation at the Work Research Institute in Oslo in the 1980s and 90s, and in Nordic and European projects later, and became a professor at the Centre for Gender Research, University of Oslo, in 2007. Recently, he has worked in survey research, creating a model for a detailed gender equality survey that has been adapted in other countries, including Poland (2015). His books in English include *Can Men Do It* (2003), and *Gender Equality and Quality of Life* (with Helge Svare and Cathrine Egeland, 2009).

Øystein Holter

Emmi Itäranta is a Finnish author whose award-winning debut novel *Memory of Water* has been translated to over 20 languages. She resides in Canterbury, United Kingdom.

Emmi Itäranta

Katja Iversen

Katja Iversen is the President/CEO of Women Deliver, a leading global advocate for investment in the health, rights and wellbeing of girls and women. Iversen, an internationally recognized speaker and expert on gender equality and advocacy for girls and women, has more than 25 years of experience working in NGOs, corporates and the United Nations. She has counseled and trained multiple Fortune 500 executives on cross cultural management, and is currently an advisor to the Clinton Global Initiative, to the World Bank and to the UN Secretary General's Every Woman Every Child initiative. In May 2016 she hosted the Women Deliver conference – the world's largest conference on gender equality and the health, rights and wellbeing for more than a decade, convening almost 6000 world leaders, influencers, activists and journalists from 169 countries.

Christina Jutterström

Christina Jutterström was a political reporter from 1966–1975 and Swedish public service radio and TV personality. Permanent Africa Correspondent 1975–77, Managing Editor Swedish Radio 1977–81, Editor in Chief Dagens Nyheter and Expressen 1982–1995, CEO Swedish Public Service Television 2001–2006.

Naser Khader

Naser Khader is a member of the Danish Parliament for The Conservative Party, a columnist/contributor to several Danish and international media outlets, radio host and an acclaimed author on books about Islam, *The Arab an Islamic World and Democratic Integration.* Naser Khader is co-founder of The Muslim Reform Movement—an international initiative that aims to fight violent Islamist ideologies and political Islam and promote a peaceful modern Islam, human rights and secular governance. Naser Khader was a Hudson Institute Fellow in Washington, D.C. and has been awarded several prizes in recognition of his fight for freedom of speech, secularity, and integration of immigrants into Danish society.

Deeyah Khan is an award winning documentary filmmaker and is the founder of Norwegian media and arts production company Fuuse. Fuuse explores the issues of diverse societies through enabling women and minorities to share their experiences and stories.

Deeyah Khan

Mininnguaq Kleist is currently Head of the Greenland Representation to the EU in Brussels, Belgium. Kleist was born in Nuuk, Greenland in 1973, and married to Mari in 2014. He holds a Master's degree in Philosophy from the University of Århus, Denmark. Kleist has been deeply involved in the work of the joint Greenlandic-Danish Self-Government Commission and was Head of Department for the Self-Government Office and later in the Department of Foreign Affairs of Government to Greenland. Kleist was previously director in The Premier's Office of the Government of Greenland.

Mininnguaq Kleist

Hugo Lagercrantz, MD, PhD, was appointed Professor of Pediatrics at the Karolinska Institute 1989. He was director of the Neonatal Programme at the Astrid Lindgren Children´s Hospital until 2004. He has been a member of the Nobel Assembly, Chairman of the Swedish Pediatric Society and European Society for Pediatric Research. He is presently Senior Professor and Editor-in-chief for Acta Paediatrica. He is also a honorary member of the American Pediatric Society.

Hugo Lagercrantz

**Johanna
Lammi-Taskula**

Johanna Lammi-Taskula is a Research Manager with a PhD in Sociology, mother of two and employed at the National Institute for Health and Welfare in Helsinki, Finland. Her research interests include work and family policies and gender equality. She is a long-standing member of the Subsection on Men at the Council for Gender Equality, and an expert member of the Working Group on Gender Equality Statistics at Statistics Finland. She was one of the founding members of SUMS (Finnish association of research on men and masculinities).

Jørn Lund

Jørn Lund was born 1946. He was an Assistant Professor at the University of Copenhagen from 1968 to 1980, and a Professor at the Royal Danish Academy of Educational Studies, and member of the board at the University of Copenhagen from 2005 to 2011. He has been a member of the Danish and Norwegian Academy of Language and Literature since 1979, Leader of The Danish Society of Language and Literature 2002–2011, Head of the Board of the Danish Language Council since 2012 and member of The group of Nordic Language Experts since 2005.

Claus Meyer

Claus Meyer is the co-founder of the renowned restaurant, Noma, which has been voted the best restaurant across the globe in 2010, 2011, 2012 and 2014. In addition to being a chef, Meyer is a professor, has authored 14 cookbooks, and was the host of Meyer's Kitchen from 1991 to 1998, and most recently, host of season 5 of New Scandinavian Cooking. Meyer also has a number of businesses, including the Melting Pot, which was started in 2013 to help establish food schools in South America, and chocolate and fruit supply companies. He is an affiliated Professor, Lecturer and Culinary Advisor at the Department of Food Science and Food Chemistry at the Royal Veterinary and Agricultural University.

Per Stig Møller has been a Conservative People's Party Member of the Danish National Parliament from 1984 to 2015. In 1990 he was the Minister of Environment, Foreign Minister in 2001, and the Minister of Culture and Church until 2011. Before his political campaign he was a radio talkshow host on Danmarks Radio and has taught at universities in both Copenhagen and France.

Per Stig Møller

Scandinavians *Arne Nerjordet* and *Carlos Zachrison* are highly regarded designers, textile artists and best-selling authors. They are best known for their craft books and their original, colorful and visually striking designs. Their work is highly influenced by their Scandinavian background and their everyday life in rural Norway. They work under their artist name ARNE & CARLOS, which they established in 2002.

Arne Nerjordet and Carlos Zachrison

Ilkka Paananen is the CEO and Co-founder of Supercell, the Helsinki-based mobile games developer behind Clash of Clans, Hay Day, Boom Beach and Clash Royale. Since its founding in 2010, Supercell's four games have amassed 100m daily players and have remained in the global top 10 years after their launch. In June 2016, Supercell became the first European technology start-up to reach a valuation of $10 billion. In addition to his role at Supercell, Ilkka helps other entrepreneurs as both an investor and as an active member of the Helsinki-based startup community where he mentors and coaches other founders. Alongside his Co-founder Mikko Kodisoja, he has established the We Foundation to fight social inequality and help marginalized children and families in Finland.

Ilkka Paananen

Mårten Palme

Mårten Palme is Professor of Economics at Stockholm University and previously at the Stockholm School of Economy. He is the son of Swedish Prime Minister Olof Palme. He has done research on income inequality, earnings mobility, returns to education as well as the effect of income taxes and income security systems on labor market behavior. Publications include papers in Journal of Public Economics, Economica, Journal of Human Resources and Labour Economics.

Joanne Payton

Joanne Payton is an expert on issues of violence against women and multiculturalism. She has a PhD in criminology from Cardiff University.

Nasima Razmyar

Nasima Razmyar is a Member of Parliament and City Council of Helsinki. She is also involved in many non-governmental organizations such as MONIKA—Multicultural Women's Association and Finnish Settlement Movement that works for multicultural Finland. Razmyar was born in Afghanistan but due to regime change in 1992 her whole family had to seek refuge in Finland. Razmyar has worked for years with refugees and immigrants. In spring 2015 Razmyar was elected into Parliament as the first refugee woman.

Johan Rockström is the Director of the Stockholm Resilience Centre (SRC) and a Professor in Environmental Science with emphasis on water resources and global sustainability at Stockholm University. He is an internationally recognized scientist on global sustainability issues. He is one of the leading scientists within the science on planetary boundaries. Professor Rockström has more than 15 years of experience of research on agriculture, water resources and ecosystem services. He has served as advisor to several governments, international policy processes and business networks, and has published several books and over 100 scientific articles. He chaired the design phase for Future Earth and currently chairs the Earth League, the EAT initiative, and the CGIAR program on Water, Land and Ecosystems.

Johan Rockström

Passionate about the relationship between social science and design, *Jeff Risom* works at the intersection of urban design, governance, business and culture to deliver projects that are economically viable and socially equitable while efficiently using energy, land and time. Building on global best-practice experience Jeff strives toward processes that catalyze local engagement and design solutions that remove barriers to diverse and equitable urban environments. An American, with degrees in Architectural Engineering from the U.S. and City Design and Social Science from the London School of Economics, Jeff lives in Copenhagen with his wife and two children.

Jeff Risom

Elísabet Ronaldsdóttir was born on July 6, 1965 in Iceland. As a film editor she is known for, among other works, *Trapped* (2015), *John Wick* (2014), *Contraband* (2012) and *Jar City* (2006). She has won 3 Edda awards and in 2016 she was invested with the Order of the Falcon for her contribution to Icelandic and international film.

Elísabet Ronaldsdóttir

Pasi Sahlberg

Pasi Sahlberg is a Finnish educator, author and scholar who has worked as a schoolteacher and teacher-educator in Finland and researched education systems around the world. He has worked with the Finnish Government, World Bank, European Commission and Harvard University and advised governments and international organisations about education policy and change. He is author of *Finnish Lessons 2.0: What can the world learn from educational change in Finland* and winner of the 2013 Grawemeyer Award, the 2014 Robert Owen Award, and the 2016 Lego Prize. He is currently Professor of Practice at the University of Helsinki and at Arizona State University. Twitter: @pasi_sahlberg

Kasper Salto and Thomas Sigsgaard

Since 2001, *Kasper Salto and Thomas Sigsgaard* have worked side-by-side in their design studio in Copenhagen. They are known for their ability to look at projects from all ends of the creative spectrum. Sigsgaard is an educated furniture craftsman and industrial designer, and Salto is an architect. Together they use a design method, unique for considering all facets that can affect a project, before beginning to mold it into something. Their motto is: "Design is to take something and make it better."

Pekka Sauri

Pekka Sauri is Deputy Mayor of the City of Helsinki since 2003. In his previous life, he was a psychologist. He is author of a number of books on psychology, politics and the psychology of politics, and the novel *Better Than Sex* (2014).

Thor Sigfusson is an entrepreneur and business network nerd. He is the founder of the Iceland Ocean Cluster and several other startups in seafood related industries. Thor received his PhD in International Business from the University of Iceland in 2012. He has written several books on subjects as different as business and salmon. His main interest (and frankly obsession) is better utilization of global seafood resources.

Thor Sigfusson

Finnish musician **Signmark** (Marko Vuoriheimo) was born deaf into a world where music is for the hearing. Passionate about fulfilling his dreams, in 2010 Marko made one of his impossibles possible and signed a record deal with Warner Music. Signmark continues his determination to help everyone find their own voice.

Signmark

Kristin Skogen Lund is Director-General of the Confederation of Norwegian Enterprise. She is a former media and telecom executive and a current board member of Ericsson. Since 2015, she is a member of the Global Commission on the Economy and Climate, also known as the Calderón Commission. Kristin Skogen Lund holds an MBA from INSEAD and a Bachelor's degree in International Studies and Business Administration from the University of Oregon.

Kristin Skogen Lund

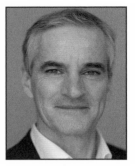

Jonas Gahr Støre

Jonas Gahr Støre is the leader of the Norwegian Labour Party. He served as Minister of Foreign Affairs 2005–2012 and as Minister of Health and Care Services 2012–2013. Mr. Støre has held various positions at the Prime Minister's Office from 1989 to 1997, including as Special Advisor to Prime Minister Gro Harlem Brundtland, for whom he also served as Chief of Staff (1998–2000) during her time as Director-General of the WHO. Among other positions, Mr. Støre served as Secretary General of the Norwegian Red Cross. He has a degree in Political Science from Institut d'Études Politiques de Paris.

Paola Ivana Suhonen

Paola Ivana Suhonen is the multi-talented designer behind the independent Fashion/Art brand Ivana Helsinki from Finland; leading the rapidly growing brand of exciting new design talent from the Finnish capital that has been named as 'World Design Capital' for 2012. Highlighted by uniquely feminine, Finnish hand knits and original print designs – the Ivana Helsinki women's label is now regularly seen within the pages of all the international fashion magazines, as well as gaining celebrity fans including Helena Christensen, Juliette Lewis, Peaches Geldof, Beth Ditto and Maja Ivarsson. Suhonen's signature style melds Slavic rough melancholy and pure Scandinavian moods with stories from her own experiences in life. She is also the newly appointed Creative Director for the U.S.-based magazine, *Love Contemporary.* Having recently moved from New York, Paola now lives and works in Los Angeles where she also studies cinematography at the famous AFI.

Ulf Sverdrup

Ulf Sverdrup is the Director of the Norwegian Institute of International Affairs (NUPI). He holds a doctoral degree in Political Science from the University of Oslo. Before taking up the position at NUPI, he was a professor at the Norwegian Business School BI, and a research professor at ARENA, Centre for European Studies, at the University of Oslo. He earned his Master's degree at the University of Bergen. Sverdrup has published extensively on various topics in international politics, with a particular emphasis on European politics, European integration and Norwegian foreign policy. He has been a Jean Monnet fellow at the European University Institute, a Visiting scholar at the Mannheimer Zentrum für Europäische Sozialforschung, and he was a senior advisor in the Norwegian Ministry of Foreign Affairs. He is a regular contributor to Dagens Næringsliv.

Henrik Syse (b. 1966) holds a Master's degree in Political Theory from Boston College and a Doctorate in Philosophy from the University of Oslo. He is a senior researcher at PRIO (Peace Research Institute Oslo) and a Professor of Peace and Conflict Studies at Björknes University College. Henrik is a much-used lecturer in Norway and internationally, and he has published widely within the fields of ethics, political philosophy, business, and religion. His main area of academic concentration has been the ethics of armed conflict. He is currently a member of the Norwegian Nobel Committee.

Henrik Syse

Petter Stordalen is a Norwegian investor, hotel magnate and property developer. Stordalen has sole proprietorship of Nordic Choice Hotels, one of the largest hotel companies in the Nordic region. Nordic Choice Hotels consists of 3 chains, 184 hotels and employs 13,000 people. He is also Co-founder and board member of Stordalen Foundation, owner of Home Invest, Chairman of the Board of Home Capital, Home Properties and Nordic Choice Hotels.

Petter Stordalen

*Steen Thomsen i*s Professor of Corporate Governance at Copenhagen Business School (CBS) and Chairman of the Center for Corporate Governance. His academic publications include 35 international journal articles and several books on the subject including the McGraw-Hill textbook *Corporate Governance: Mechanisms and Systems* (with Martin Conyon). His research is currently focused on industrial foundations – foundations that own business firms.

Steen Thomsen

Lars Trägårdh

Lars Trägårdh received his PhD in history from UC Berkeley and is currently a Professor of History and Civil Society Studies at Ersta Sköndal University College in Stockholm, Sweden. He has written extensively on Sweden and the Nordic Model, including the acclaimed book, ***Är svensken människa? Gemenskap och oberoende i det moderna Sverige,*** written with Henrik Berggren (Norstedts 2006, revised and enlarged 2015). Between 2011 and 2013 he served as a member of the Swedish Prime Minister's Commission on the Future of Sweden. Currently he is writing a book on children's rights in Sweden, the United States and France.